Genetics and Learning Disabilities

Genetics and Learning Disabilities

Edited by
Shelley D. Smith, Ph.D.

Boys Town National Institute for
Communication Disorders in Children
Omaha, Nebraska

 College-Hill Press, San Diego, California

College-Hill Press, Inc.
4284 41st Street
San Diego, California 92105

©1986 College-Hill Press, Inc.

Library of Congress Cataloging-in-Publication Data
Main entry under title:

Genetics and learning disabilities.

    Includes indexes.
    1. Learning disabilities — Genetic aspects.
I. Smith, Shelley D., 1949–
RJ496.L4G46   1985   618.92'89   85-19532
ISBN 0-88744-141-6

Printed in the United States of America

Contents

Contributors

Bruce G. Bender, Ph.D.
National Jewish Hospital and Research Center / National Asthma Center and University of Colorado School of Medicine, Denver, Colorado 80206

Pamela R. Fain, Ph.D.
Boys Town National Institute for Communication Disorders in Children, Omaha, Nebraska 68131

Joan M. Finucci, Ph.D.
The Johns Hopkins School of Medicine, Baltimore, Maryland 21205

Rosalie B. Goldberg, M.S.
Montefiore Medical Center, Albert Einstein College of Medicine, Bronx, New York 10467

David E. Goldgar, Ph.D.
University of Mississippi Medical Center, Jackson, Mississippi 39216

Emily L. Harris, Ph.D., M.P.H.
Present address: Environmental Epidemiology Branch, National Cancer Institute, Bethesda, Maryland 20205

William J. Kimberling, Ph.D.
Boys Town National Institute for Communication Disorders in Children, Omaha, Nebraska 68131

Richard S. Nowakowski, Ph.D.
University of Mississippi Medical Center, Jackson, Mississippi; Rutgers University, New Brunswick, New Jersey 39216

Bruce F. Pennington, Ph.D.
University of Colorado School of Medicine, Denver, Colorado 80262

Mary H. Puck, M.A.
National Jewish Hospital and Research Center / National Asthma Center and University of Colorado School of Medicine, Denver, Colorado 80206

Arthur Robinson, M.D.
National Jewish Hospital and Research Center / National Asthma Center and University of Colorado School of Medicine, Denver, Colorado 80206

James A. Salbenblatt, M.D.
National Jewish Hospital and Research Center / National Asthma Center and University of Colorado School of Medicine, Denver, Colorado 80206

Robert J. Shprintzen, Ph.D.
Montefiore Medical Center, Albert Einstein College of Medicine, Bronx, New York 10467

Shelley D. Smith, Ph.D.
Boys Town National Institute for Communication Disorders in Children, Omaha, Nebraska 68131

Karen P. Spuhler, Ph.D.
University of Colorado Health Sciences Center, Denver, Colorado 80262

PREFACE

Learning disabilities are a collection of disorders that challenge educators, psychologists, physicians, learning disability specialists, researchers, and families. There is controversy around the issues of definition, diagnosis, remediation, and underlying causes of learning disabilities. A genetic approach to the analysis of learning disabilities does not provide all of the answers, but it is the purpose of this book to demonstrate that consideration of genetic factors is essential to the understanding of these problems. The recognition that a learning disability may be genetically influenced in some children does not mean that such children are doomed to failure because they are slaves to their genes or that efforts of remediation are futile; rather, knowledge of a genetic basis can help the family and educators plan appropriate intervention and can lead to research into the most effective diagnostic procedures and therapy. Ultimately, more can be discovered about all learning disabilities through an understanding of the learning processes involved in genetically mediated disabilities.

Research in learning disabilities has suggested that they are heterogeneous and that many are based on variations in the central nervous system. The evidence for genetic influences on learning disabilities is substantial, and the combination of sophisticated techniques for studying the biologic and neurologic characteristics of learning disabilities and new developments in geneticists' abilities to examine the genetic contributions to complex, heterogeneous disorders makes this a particularly fruitful area for study. It is imperative, then, that the strengths and limitations of genetic approaches be recognized by professionals involved in studies of learning disabled children and, conversely, that geneticists understand the appropriate measures and the most profitable methods of genetic analysis.

This book is divided into three sections; studies aimed at defining the genetic influences; studies directed toward the characteristics of learning disabilities that potentially could result from gene action; and the characteristics of learning disorders found in known genetic syndromes. Each author has endeavored to provide ample background into his or her topic and an explanation of the methodology, so that the reader can understand the contributions of each approach and critically analyze the literature on these topics. The implications of each author's research and guidelines for future investigations are discussed with an eye to an expansion of knowledge in each area. Finally, the summary integrates ideas from each of the authors into recommendations for future research into the genotypes and phenotypes of learning disabilities.

Although the most significant contribution of genetic knowledge to the field of learning disabilities probably will be from future research, there are applications of this knowledge that are important to children and their families now. Recognition that certain children are at high risk for genetically influenced learning disabilities, whether it is because of family history or genetic syndome, can ensure that diagnosis and appropriate remediation are not delayed. Thus, genetics should be an important aspect in the multidisciplinary attack on learning disabilities.

PART I

THE GENETICS OF LEARNING DISABILITIES: GENOTYPIC STUDIES

Chapter 1

The Contribution of Twin Research to the Study of the Etiology of Reading Disability

Emily L. Harris

Reading disability is a diagnosis of exclusion (i.e., underachievement in reading that is not due to mental retardation, a sensory deficit, emotional problems, or cultural disadvantage) and as such is likely to include a variety of more subtle deficits from many causes. Studies of etiologic factors usually are undertaken with phenotypically similar disabilities (i.e., subtypes), although little is known about the etiologic homogeneity of such classifications. This problem is not unique to behavioral or psychologic variables; for example, diabetes mellitus may be classified as insulin-dependent or non-insulin-dependent based on phenotype, but etiologic heterogeneity within these two groups is likely (Rotter, 1981). The researcher or clinician also needs to consider whether the trait or disease under study is truly an abnormal state or whether it represents the lower end of a normal distribution curve where an arbitrary limit or threshold has been imposed. Turning to another medical example, consider a person with atherosclerosis that results in cardiac arrest. The arrest is clearly a disease state; however, if disease is measured by the degree of blockage of the coronary arteries by atherosclerotic lesions, a disease state per se would not be so clear but could be defined by an arbitrary threshold. Is reading disability an abnormal state or the lower end of a reading ability distribution (taking general learning ability as defined by IQ into account) with an arbitrary threshold imposed? Turning to a psychologic example,

3

recognized etiologic factors for severe intellectual deficit mainly include single gene defects, chromosomal abnormalities, and early environmental insults (e.g., brain injury or infectious diseases such as meningitis); however, the cause of less severe deficits seems multifactorial in nature and more often includes cultural influences and lower than average intellectual ability of the parents (Vogel and Motulsky, 1979). Definition of "disease" is much more difficult when an abnormal state is not apparent and the point along the distribution curve at which the threshold is imposed may greatly affect results of etiologic research.

The cause of disability may be approached in two ways: (1) by studying determinants of individual differences within the normal range with the hope of gaining insight into possible defects resulting in disability; and (2) by studying disability determinants, which in turn may provide information about sources of normal variation. Twin research can make important contributions to research on causation through both of these approaches.

DESCRIPTIVE EPIDEMIOLOGY

Epidemiologic studies of reading disability are difficult to conduct and evaluate because of the arbitrary nature of definitions of reading disability. What standards are appropriate to define "underachievement" in reading? Should the standards reflect local expectations or should they reflect more countrywide or worldwide expectations? What instruments are used to assess reading achievement? How are the expectations adjusted for general learning ability? Can educational experience be taken into account? These difficulties are evidenced in the wide range of prevalence estimates for reading disability (0.5 to 16 percent) (Badian, 1984). For example, Berger, Yule, and Rutter (1975) conducted an epidemiologic study of specific reading retardation in 10 year old children in Britain. They investigated the entire school-age population of 10 year olds in two circumscribed areas, an inner London borough and the Isle of Wight. The definition of disability took into account general learning ability (as assessed by the Wechsler Intelligence Scale for Children). A child was classified as having specific reading retardation if his or her reading achievement test score fell two standard errors of prediction or more below the predicted value. On the Isle of Wight, an area of small towns, the prevalence of reading disability was estimated to be 3.9 percent. This contrasts with the prevalence estimate of 9.9 percent in the inner London borough, a metropolitan area. Badian (1984), in a study conducted in the Boston area, found a prevalence of reading disability (reading underachievement in children with IQs greater than or equal to 85) of 4 percent in 8 to 12 year old children.

Reading disability is a recognized problem in Western nations, but is perhaps not so well appreciated or not so prevalent in Asian countries (Stevenson et al., 1982). Stevenson and colleagues (1982), after comparing children in China, Japan, and the United States, suggested that it is perhaps a matter of a lack of recognition of the problem rather than a deficit. Mittal and associates (1977), in a study of communication disabilities in New Delhi, India, also provided evidence that reading disability is prevalent in Indian children; however, their definition seems to be based solely on letter reversals.

The increased prevalence of reading disability in males is well recognized; the male-female ratio is about 3.5:1 (Satz and Zaide, 1983). Are there differences in the causes of reading disability between males and females? Are males more likely to be exposed to certain risk factors? Are females better able to protect themselves against the adverse effects of certain risk factors? The importance of this finding in etiologic studies is that causal pathways may be different in males and females. Genetic constitution may be more important in one sex than in the other; environmental factors and their interaction with the genotype may differ. (Satz and Zaide, 1983, present a more detailed discussion on the implications of sex differences.)

ADVANTAGES AND DISADVANTAGES OF TWIN RESEARCH

Twin research depends on two major assumptions: one about the nature of co-twins' genetic similarity and one regarding the nature of their environmental similarities. Since monozygotic twins (MZ), by definition, arise from the splitting of one fertilized egg or zygote, we assume that their genetic constitution is the same. Dizygotic twins (DZ), on the other hand, are generally assumed to be the result of the uniting of two ova with two sperm; therefore, they have on the average one half of their genes in common, the same as other full siblings. What differentiates fraternal twins from sibling pairs is the more common environment of the twins (in utero, birth order, and other temporally associated environmental factors). When comparing the similarities of MZ co-twins (i.e., to each other) with that of DZ co-twins, the major assumption is that of equal environmental covariance (i.e., the degree to which MZ co-twins share environments is equal to that of DZ co-twins).

The major advantages and disadvantages of twin research relate to the uniqueness of twins. In studying twins we have a natural experiment in which the degree of environmental similarity is equal and the degree of genetic similarity for the two types of co-twins can be reasonably estimated. This permits assessment of the relative contributions of heritable factors to the observed variation in phenotype. Because of the uniqueness of the twinning situation, however, it is not always reasonable to generalize the findings of twin research to the general population. Are twins representative of the general population for the particular trait or disease being studied? Are there etiologic factors that could be unique to the twinning situation for that particular variable? Twinning is not an uncommon event, having an incidence of about 1 in 80 births, but when the object of the study is an uncommon disease, obtaining a sufficient sample is difficult. Also, because twin registries in the United States represent a volunteer sample, it is difficult to define an acceptable ascertainment scheme. Studies of individual variation of a trait still suffer from the volunteer sample problem, but the difficulty of obtaining a sufficient sample should be lessened.

TWIN RESEARCH DESIGNS

Various designs may be used in twin research to gain information about the causes of variation in a population. The traditional design for detection of a genetic contribution to individual differences compares the similarity of monozygotic (identical) co-twins with the similarity of dizygotic (fraternal) co-twins. With a continuously measured trait such as reading achievement, the degree of similarity may be measured through an intraclass correlation coefficient, which is the proportion of the total phenotypic variation due to between-pair differences. Since this correlation is a proportion, its value should range from zero to one. An intraclass correlation (r_I) equal to zero indicates that individuals within the groups (here, each twin pair represents a group) are no more alike on that characteristic than are two persons chosen at random from the sample. At the other extreme, an r_I equal to one indicates that individuals within each group are the same on that characteristic and the variation in the sample is due to between-group differences. If there were a genetic contribution to the variation, it would be expected that the r_I for the MZ pairs would be greater than that for the DZ pairs, and the DZ co-twins should be more alike than two persons chosen at random (i.e., r_I greater than 0). Detection of genetic variance may be accomplished in a more formal way using a nested analysis of variance approach (Christian, Kang, and Norton, 1974).

An assumption is made that there is no effect of zygosity type on the trait being measured (i.e., the mean for the MZ twins is equal to the mean for the DZ twins), which can be tested in a twin sample using a t'-statistic (Christian and Norton, 1977). Given that this assumption is valid, the analysis for the detection of genetic variance can proceed. The preferred statistical test is a ratio of the within-pair mean squares (WMS) for the DZ and the MZ twins ($F = WMS_{DZ} / WMS_{MZ}$); the validity of this test relies on the assumption that the total variation in the MZ sample is not different from the total variation in the DZ sample. This assumption can be tested using an F'-statistic, and an alternative statistic may be calculated if the total variation in the two zygosity groups is found to differ (Christian et al., 1974). To aid interpretation of a statistically significant finding indicating the presence of genetic variance, the degree of similarity of the DZ co-twins must be examined (i.e., are they more alike than two individuals chosen at random?). For many reports in the literature, however, only one of two statistics is reported: the significance of the F test comparing the within-pair mean squares of the MZ and DZ twins, as described above; or the significance of the difference between the intraclass correlation coefficients for the MZ and the DZ twin pairs. The major problem in these instances is that no information is provided about the assumptions that were tested (or not tested) and were found (or assumed) to be valid.

For categorical variables, such as disease state, probandwise or pairwise concordance rates may be calculated as measures of similarity. (Calculation of concordance rates requires the ascertainment of a series of affected twins and assessment of the disease status of their co-twins.) Once again, it is assumed that there is no effect of zygosity on the prevalence of the disorder or disability (i.e., the prevalence of the disorder is not different in MZ twins and DZ twins). In the presence of genetic variance, it would be expected that the MZ co-twins would more often be concordant than DZ co-twins and that the DZ co-twins would more often be concordant than expected by chance given the prevalence of the disorder in the overall twin population. A test for the difference between proportions can then be used to detect genetic variance. A crucial assumption of the traditional twin model, as previously mentioned, is the equality of environmental covariance for the MZ and the DZ pairs. If the MZ twin pairs are more often concordant than the DZ pairs because the environments of MZ co-twins are more alike than the environments of the DZ co-twins, the test for genetic variance may be positive even in the absence of genetic effects. If the similarity of the MZ co-twins is due entirely to greater environmental covariance, it would be expected that the DZ concordance rate would be no different from that expected by chance. Therefore, it is important to test whether the DZ concordance rate is greater than that expected by chance on the basis of the twin population prevalence.

In addition to the detection of genetic variance, it may also be of interest to estimate the proportion of individual variation in a population resulting from such genetic variation, which is termed heritability (or broad heritability). A heritability estimate is specific for the trait being measured, the population under study, and the point in time at which it is estimated; it is not an unchanging parameter in a population. Changes in environment, genetic diversity, or even measurement error may affect heritability. Consider two broad categories into which total phenotypic variance may be divided: genetic and environmental.

Genetic variance includes additive genetic variance (small, equal effects of alleles at multiple loci) plus dominance variance and variance due to epistasis (which represent interaction between alleles at a locus and interaction between loci, respectively). It is additive genetic variance that may be estimated through twin studies; the proportion of the total variation due to additive genetic variance is termed narrow heritability.

Environmental variance includes shared as well as nonshared (or random) environmental effects plus variation due to measurement error. The genetic and environmental effects may covary; that is, certain genotypes may be more likely to be exposed to certain environments. For example, children who show an aptitude for music or for sports may be more strongly encouraged to participate in those activities than other children. In addition, there may be an interaction between genetic and environmental effects; different genotypes may react in different ways to the same environmental factor. As a hypothetical situation, return to the sports and music example. Individuals who do well in sports or music without training may improve at a different rate or to a different extent with training than those who are not "naturally gifted." Estimation of heritability from twin studies requires the assumption that genetic-environmental covariance and genetic-environmental interaction contribute negligibly to the total variation. It is also assumed that the genetic variance is composed primarily of additive genetic variance, with negligible contributions from dominance and epistasis. The estimates of heritability from twin studies, therefore, are very approximate, with the biases affecting heritability estimates in an unpredictable manner. (Vogel and Motulsky, 1979, discuss the concept of heritability in more detail.)

The MZ correlation or concordance rate provides a measure of the familiality of the trait or disease (i.e., variation due to genetic or common environmental sources, or both). The deviation of this value from unity represents nonshared environmental factors or measurement error, or both. Therefore, MZ co-twins provide information about the contribution of nonshared environmental factors to individual variation. Through the comparision of MZ co-twins by placental type, in utero environmental effects may be detected. In addition, MZ co-twins discordant for disease may be studied in a retrospective manner to identify possible risk factors, or MZ co-twins discordant for exposure (e.g., anoxia at birth) may be studied prospectively with regard to adverse outcomes. Studies of adult MZ co-twins, their spouses, and their children can also provide a unique set of information; this includes the evaluation of maternal influences on individual variation through the comparison of the similarity of offspring of female co-twins (i.e., genetic maternal half-siblings) with the offspring of male co-twins (i.e., genetic paternal half-siblings).

Twin studies may also provide information about the etiologic relationship between several diagnoses or subtypes. For example, if twin pairs that are concordant for reading disability are used, concordance and discordance for specific subtypes can be examined. Do twin pairs tend to have the same subtype of reading disability? If so, this may be an indication of independent causal factors for the subtypes. If, on the other hand, the distribution of subtypes seems random among the twin pairs, this strongly indicates an overlap of etiologic factors for the subtypes.

An essential part of any twin research design is determination of zygosity of the same-sex twin pairs. (Opposite-sex twin pairs are necessarily dizygotic twins.) The most reliable and practical method is the typing of polymorphic genetic markers (e.g., blood group antigens). Any pair that differs at any marker(s) can be categorized as DZ. For the remaining pairs whose markers are the same, the probability of that pair being dizygotic can be calculated given that they are alike on given markers (i.e., the probability of misclassifying a DZ pair as MZ) (see Vogel and Motulsky, 1979, for details). As more markers are studied, the probability of misclassification will decrease. A median probability of misclassification of less than 2 percent for a twin sample can easily be attained. Other methods that may be used for zygosity determination or for supplementation of the previous method include dermatoglyphics, anthropometric measurements, and questionnaire data regarding similiarity and "confusibility." ("Confusibility" is assessed by how often parents, friends, teachers, and others cannot identify the co-twins correctly.) In large twin samples, such as those often used in epidemiologic research, typing of genetic markers for the entire sample may not be feasible. Multivariate techniques (multiple discriminant analysis and multiple logistic regression) have been used to produce maximum discrimination between monozygotic and dizygotic twin pairs based on questionnaire data. Using blood markers as the standard, Sarna and colleagues (1978) and Sarna and Kaprio (1980), reported that fewer than 2 percent of twin pairs were misclassified when a combination of deterministic classification and logistic analysis was used; each method, when used alone, misclassified 6 to 8 percent of that sample. Magnus, Berg, and Nance (1983) developed a discriminant function for the situation in which only one co-twin response was available as well as a function for the usual situation of complete pair responses. They reported a misclassification frequency of less than 3 percent when data were available from both twins and of 4 percent if only the responses from one co-twin were used. They point out that discriminant analysis will provide a probability of a particular zygosity for each twin pair. Therefore, it would be feasible to choose for genetic marker typing those pairs whose scores on the discriminant function are close to the cutoff point. These techniques were developed for use with adult twins, in situations in which study variables would normally be collected through records or through additional questionnaires. It is not clear how or at what age these techniques may be generalized to children. When the twins will be seen personally during the study, it is still desirable to collect biologic data that can be used to determine zygosity. A technique less invasive than blood drawing — analysis of dermatoglyphic patterns — has also been studied for zygosity diagnosis using discriminant analysis; Reed, Norton, and Christian (1977) were able to classify correctly up to 89 percent of twin pairs. As with the discriminant functions developed from questionnaire data, twin pairs can be chosen for genetic marker typing on the basis of their probability of having a particular zygosity. Once again, genetic marker typing is the most reliable method of zygosity determination and should be used to the fullest extent possible in twin research.

TWIN RESEARCH IN READING DISABILITY

Prior to 1950, published information about specific reading disability in twins consisted primarily of case reports of concordant MZ twins. Hallgren (1950) identified five twin pairs in a systematic way through a larger family study of dyslexia; probands were identified through a child guidance clinic and schools, without regard to whether other affected family members existed. Information about reading and other school problems was obtained on an individual basis through testing and interviews. Zygosity determination was accomplished in an objective manner using blood typing and physical similarity for the same-sex twin pairs. Of the five pairs, two were concordant MZ pairs (one male, one female), one was a concordant opposite-sex DZ pair, and two were discordant opposite-sex DZ pairs (male affected, female unaffected; female affected, male unaffected). In addition, a concordant female MZ pair was referred to Hallgren by a colleague during the study period.

Later in the 1950s, two other investigators reported concordance for specific reading disability in twins. Norrie's twin series was reported by Hermann and Norrie (1958), but no details about ascertainment, testing, or zygosity determination were included. All nine MZ pairs were concordant. Of the 19 same-sex DZ pairs, four were concordant, and of the 11 opposite-sex twin pairs, six were concordant. Hermann (1956) also reported the ascertainment of four twin pairs; one was a concordant MZ pair, two were concordant DZ pairs, and one was a discordant DZ pair.

Bakwin (1973) surveyed several mothers-of-twins clubs and identified 97 children between the ages of 8 and 18 years with a history of reading disability. Zygosity was determined by physical similarity and blood group typing. Of the 31 MZ twin pairs (19 male and 12 female pairs), 26 (16 male and 10 female) were concordant; this resulted in a pairwise concordance rate of 84 percent (84 percent and 83 percent for males and females, respectively). Of the 31 same-sex DZ twin pairs, nine (eight male pairs and one female pair) were concordant, producing a pair-wise concordance rate of 29 percent for the overall DZ sample (42 percent for males and 8 percent for females). These concordance rates differed significantly for the MZ and DZ twin pairs. The prevalence of a history of reading disability was 14.5 percent in his sample of 676 twin children. The prevalence was similar in the identical (14.0 percent) and the fraternal pairs (14.9 percent) but was more frequent in boys (17.7 percent) than in girls (10.8 percent). In addition, this investigator examined the possible relationship of birth weight and birth order with subsequent reading disability. No difference was found between the mean birth weight of the normal reading twins and the twins with reading disability; children below and above the mean birth weight were equally likely to develop reading disability (13.0 percent and 13.8 percent, respectively). Data regarding birth order were available for a limited number (42) of the reading-disabled twins; 20 were firstborn and 22 were second-born twins.

Matheny, Dolan, and Wilson (1976) examined a group of twins from the Louisville Twin Study who were identified by their school authorities as showing poor academic performance; these 46 twins included 31 pairs. When compared with a group of control twins, the index twins' average reading level was 1.9 grade-equivalents below matched controls; the median age at testing was 10 years. Prior testing at age 6 years with the Wechsler Preschool and Primary Scale of Intelligence (WPPSI) revealed a significant difference for the Full Scale IQ score (102 versus 94 for the controls and cases, respectively). However, the authors point out that it is clearly the measure of achievement rather than the ability measures that differentiate the two groups (i.e., reading achievement rather than WPPSI scores). Of the 17 MZ pairs, 13 (76 percent) were concordant for poor academic performance; the same-sex DZ twins showed a pairwise concordance rate of 20 percent (2 in 10), which was significantly different from the MZ rate. None of the four opposite-sex DZ twin pairs were concordant. Developmental histories of the children with academic problems were compared with their matched control group. Several preschool characteristics distinguished the children with problems from the controls. These behaviors included sleeping and feeding problems, being temperamental, being overly active, and being distractible.

One bias to keep in mind in the study of disease concordance in twins is preferential ascertainment of concordant pairs, which will inflate the true concordance rate. Rates calculated from combining published reports may be especially susceptible to this bias because details about ascertainment are not always available and often include "interesting cases" (i.e., concordant pairs) who were not selected blindly with respect to whether or not the co-twin was affected. Also, the affected child of a discordant pair may not be identified as a twin to the referral center, but twinship status of a concordant pair will most likely be known.

In summary, twin studies of reading disability have revealed a higher concordance rate in MZ twin pairs than in DZ pairs. However not all co-twins of affected MZ twin children are affected, revealing the existence of important nonfamilial environmental factors in addition to genetic factors in the causation of specific reading disability.

TWIN RESEARCH IN READING ABILITY

Traditional twin studies provide strong evidence of a substantial genetic component to individual variation in reading achievement in school-age children. Specifically, Newman, Freeman, and Holzinger (1937) collected data concerning mental ability, achievement, and temperament from a group of 100 same-sex twin pairs from ages 8 through 18 years in the United States. Zygosity was determined through careful comparison of physical characteristics. Intraclass correlation coefficients were calculated with the effect of age removed because of the wide range of ages of the twin pairs. Subtests relevant to reading achievement from the Stanford Achievement Test (Word Meaning, Spelling, and Educational Age) showed substantial familiality ($r_I = 0.86$, 0.87, and 0.89, respectively, for each subtest for the MZ pairs); evidence of genetic contributions to individual differences ($r_I = 0.56$, 0.73, and 0.70, respectively, for each subtest for the DZ pairs) was demonstrated through significantly different intraclass correlation coefficients for the MZ and DZ pairs.

Wictorin (1952) and Husén (1959, 1960) studied twins in Sweden and found similar results. Husén (1959) reported briefly the findings of Wictorin's dissertation research in relation to school achievement for a group of 9 to 14 year old twin pairs (N = 247). For grades in reading, the similarity of the MZ pairs ($r_I = 0.92$) was substantial and was significantly different from the similarity of the same-sex DZ pairs ($r_I = 0.61$); however, the possible effect of age on these correlations was not examined. Husén (1959) examined a group of male twins who appeared for induction into the armed services from 1948 through 1952, as required by the Military Service Act in Sweden. Zygosity was determined by similarity of physical characteristics; in addition, blood typing (mainly ABO) was available for some of the twins. Information gathered at that time included school marks and level of schooling. Examining the grades in reading during primary school of over 1000 male twin pairs, Husén found slightly lower similarity for the MZ pairs ($r_I = 0.72$) than Wictorin, but the difference between MZ and DZ ($r_I = 0.57$) intraclass correlation coefficients was nonetheless significant. Through the school system, Husén (1960) was able to identify a group of 689 twin pairs in which both co-twins were completing the sixth form in school (usually 12 to 13 years old). Achievement test scores were available for 314 same-sex pairs and 180 opposite-sex pairs in addition to the scores for singleton children. For each of the achievement tests, the distribution of scores for the twin children tended to be similar to that for the singleton children, but with a shift toward lower scores. Zygosity for the same-sex twin pairs was determined through physical similarity and questions regarding "confusibility." Again, for reading achievement, the MZ pairs were quite similar ($r_I = 0.89$); the same-sex DZ pairs showed significantly less similarity ($r_I = 0.62$), and opposite-sex DZ pairs were even less similar ($r_I = 0.45$).

Vandenberg (1962) studied the causes of individual differences in a large battery of psychological tests, including reading achievement as measured through the Gray Oral Reading Paragraphs, in high school age twins (81 pairs) in Michigan. Blood typing was used for zygosity determination. Vandenberg reported a significantly greater amount of within-pair variation in DZ twin pairs than in MZ twin pairs, indicating the presence of an important contribution of genetic variation to differences in reading achievement.

Matheny and Dolan (1971) reported results for 70 same-sex twin pairs, aged 9 to 12 years, from the Louisville Twin Study (a longitudinal study), who were individually administered the California Achievement Test. Zygosity was determined through blood typing. The reading subtests (Reading Vocabulary, Reading Comprehension, and Total Reading) revealed substantial familiality ($r_I = 0.84$, 0.85, and 0.89, respectively, for the MZ pairs) and a significant contribution of genetic variation to individual differences ($r_I = 0.65$, 0.52, and 0.61 for each subtest for the DZ pairs plus significantly greater within-pair variation for the DZ pairs).

Harris (1982) studied the causes of individual differences in reading achievement and related skills in first and second grade twin children from Indiana and neighboring states (108 pairs). The test battery included the Woodcock Reading Mastery Tests, a highly reliable, individually administered set of tests. The primary method of zygosity determination was through blood typing. Harris also reported a high degree of familiality for reading achievement ($r_I = 0.93$ for the composite test score for the MZ pairs) and a significant contribution of genetic factors to individual variation ($r_I = 0.59$ for the composite test score for the DZ pairs, and the DZ pairs showed greater within-pair variation than the MZ pairs).

The most remarkable aspect of these studies is their consistent results of a high degree of familiality, with genetic factors making important contributions to this familiality. These findings occur despite the varying age groups (with and without adjustment for age effects), two different languages (English and Swedish), temporal range (1930s through 1970s), and the variety of measures of reading achievement.

Since reading is a complex of skills, research into the genesis of its component skills is warranted, under the hypothesis that it is the aggregation of the development of these skills that produces the individual variation in reading achievement. Two types of approaches have been used to determine what skills are related to reading ability: (1) comparison of normal or adequate readers with poor or retarded readers; and (2) studies of the development of normal reading ability. These studies have implicated a number of factors in the development of reading ability or a reading deficit, including auditory and visual memory, auditory and visual perception, auditory-visual and spatial-temporal integration, visual perceptual speed, vigilance, learning ability, and impulsivity (Badian, 1977; Barker, 1976; Birch and Belmont, 1964, 1965; Blackman and Burger, 1972; Blank and Bridger, 1966; Block, 1968; Bryant, 1975; Bryden, 1972; Calfee, 1975; Doehring, 1968; Hare, 1977; Harris, 1982; Kahn and Birch, 1968; Margolis, 1977; Muehl and Kremenak, 1966; Pelham and Ross, 1977; Pezzullo, Thorsen, and Madaus, 1972; Reilly, 1971; Samuels and Turnure, 1974; Strandskov, 1955; Torgensen, 1975; Vandenberg, 1962; VandeVoort and Senf, 1973; VandeVoort, Senf, and Benton, 1972; Vernon, 1971; Warren, Anooshian, and Widawski, 1975; Whiton, Singer, and Cook, 1975).

Several twin studies have included measures of auditory short-term memory (Block, 1968; Harris, 1982; Pezzullo et al., 1972; Strandskov, 1955; Vandenberg, 1962), with conflicting results about the contribution of genetic variation to individual differences. Investigators using the Digit Span of the Wechsler Intelligence Scale for Children (WISC) (Block, 1968; Pezzullo et al., 1972; Vandenberg, 1962) and the Auditory Sequential Memory subtest of the Illinois Test of Psycholinguistic Abilities (ITPA) (Harris, 1982) found evidence of a genetic contribution to individual variation in these tasks. Children in first grade through adolescence were included in these studies. In contrast, investigators using the Primary Mental Abilities Test, which includes memory as a primary ability, found no evidence of a genetic contribution to the variation among a group of adolescent-aged children (Strandskov, 1955; Vandenberg, 1962).

In addition to auditory memory, Harris (1982) included visual-spatial and auditory-temporal comparison tasks plus an auditory-visual (temporal-spatial) integration task in her study of first and second grade twin children. The auditory comparison task was not a reliable measure in that sample, probably because of its difficulty for young children. The visual comparison and auditory-visual integration tasks were reasonably reliable and both showed a modest degree of familiality ($r_I = 0.42$ and 0.55, respectively for the MZ twin pairs). The within-pair variation for the DZ pairs was significantly greater than that for the MZ pairs, but the correlation coefficient for the DZ pairs for the integration task was only marginally significant ($r_I = 0.19$, $p < .10$). In contrast, the DZ correlation coefficient for the visual comparison task was significantly different from zero ($r_I = 0.32$), but there was no evidence for a genetic contribution to individual variation. These findings suggest that the lower level skills measured in this study are not as familial as reading achievement itself and that genetic factors may account for a portion of the familiality of the auditory-visual (temporal-spatial) integration task. Factor analysis including the reading achievement tests, the auditory-visual integration test battery, the auditory memory measure, and two subtests from the Wechsler Intelligence Scale for Children — Revised (WISC-R) yielded three interpretable factors, none of which corresponded to an auditory-visual or temporal-spatial integration factor. Instead, the variance of the auditory-visual integration task was split between the three factors (reading achievement, auditory memory, and visual-spatial ability).

In summary, twin studies comparing the similarity of MZ co-twins with the similarity of the DZ co-twins for reading achievement have demonstrated a substantial heritable component contributing to the genesis of individual differences. Research exploring the causes of individual differences in skills underlying reading have not proved so fruitful, however. There is still much work to be done in this area to determine what skills can explain the differences between individuals in reading achievement and what, in turn, determines individual variation in those factors contributing to the development of reading skills.

FUTURE RESEARCH

Traditional twin studies often represent the first effort to formally investigate the familial nature of a trait which, until that time, was only anecdotally described. Family studies are then undertaken to better describe transmission patterns. Twin studies can and should play a larger role in etiologic studies.

First, in reading disability, a large and well ascertained sample of affected twins and their co-twins, whose affection status is documented and zygosity is determined by highly reliable methods, has not to my knowledge been described and would be a welcomed addition to research in this area. Ascertainment schemes that assure that the probability of being identified as a reading-disabled twin individual is not related to the affection status of the co-twin are essential. A sample of sufficient size to permit evaluation separately by sex would be highly desirable because of documented sex differences in prevalence.

In addition to the comparison of the concordance rates of the MZ and DZ twins, separation of the sample by sex may provide information about the causes of sex differences in population prevalence. Given that an individual has a "vulnerable" genotype, as evidenced by an affected MZ co-twin, does the risk of being affected vary between males and females? Does the pattern of concordance for MZ and DZ same-sex twins differ by sex? Does the DZ concordance rate differ by sex? One interpretation of the findings of Bakwin (1973) regarding the sex differences in the DZ concordance rates with no differences in MZ concordance, for example, is the interaction of genetic and environmental influences. Further research in this area is warranted.

MZ twins discordant for reading disability may provide important information about specific environmental variables, although few variables explored thus far show promise. MZ co-twins discordant for certain environmental insults may be followed in a prospective manner concerning development of reading skills. These studies may simply reveal causative factors specific to MZ twins or to twins in general; but these designs may be used to generate hypotheses for larger studies of causation in singleton children.

Although twin studies of reading achievement have established the existence of an important heritable contribution to individual variation, little is known about the more basic skills that contribute to success in reading and the causes of individual differences in those skills. In relation to reading disability, it is hoped that such studies will be able to identify underlying skills whose variation is explained primarily by genetic variation and in which a deficit produces reading disability.

In summary, twin research designs can make important contributions to etiologic research. The interpretation of the results depends on the adequacy of the ascertainment schemes and the validity of the assumptions that must be made to analyze such data meaningfully. The greater problem is the generalization of the results from twin research to the general population. Twin studies, therefore, are important in generating hypotheses concerning etiology, which then may be tested in non-twin populations.

REFERENCES

Badian, N.A. (1977). Auditory-visual integration, auditory memory, and reading in retarded and adequate readers. *Journal of Learning Disabilities, 10,* 108–114.

Badian, N.A. (1984). Reading disability in an epidemiological context: Incidence and environmental correlates. *Journal of Learning Disabilities, 17,* 129–136.

Bakwin, H. (1973). Reading disability in twins. *Developmental Medicine and Child Neurology, 15,* 184–187.

Barker, B.M. (1976). Interrelationships of perceptual modality, short-term memory and reading achievement. *Perceptual and Motor Skills, 43,* 771–774.

Berger, M., Yule, W., and Rutter, M. (1975). Attainment and adjustment in two geographical areas. II. The prevalence of specific reading retardation. *British Journal of Psychiatry, 126,* 510–519.

Birch, H.G., and Belmont, L. (1964). Auditory-visual integration in normal and retarded readers. *American Journal of Orthopsychiatry, 34,* 852–861.

Birch, H.G., and Belmont, L. (1965). Auditory-visual integration, intelligence and reading ability in school children. *Perceptual and Motor Skills, 20,* 295–305.

Blackman, L.S., and Burger, A.L. (1972). Psychological factors related to early reading behavior of EMR and nonretarded children. *American Journal of Mental Deficiency, 77,* 212–229.

Blank, M., and Bridger, W.H. (1966). Perceptual abilities and conceptual deficiencies in retarded readers. *Proceedings of the American Psychopathological Association, 56,* 401–412.

Block, J.B. (1968). Hereditary components in the performance of twins on the WAIS. In S.G. Vandenberg (Ed.), *Progress in human behavior genetics* (pp. 221–228). Baltimore: John Hopkins Press.

Bryant, P.E. (1975). Cross-modal development and reading. In D.D. Duane and M.B. Rawson (Eds.), *Reading, perception and language* (pp. 195–213). Baltimore: York Press, Inc.

Bryden, M.P. (1972). Auditory-visual and sequential-spatial matching in relation to reading ability. *Child Development, 43,* 824–832.

Calfee, R.C. (1975). Memory and cognitive skills in reading acquisition. In D.D. Duane and M.B. Rawson (Eds.), *Reading, perception and language* (pp. 55–95). Baltimore: York Press, Inc.

Christian, J.C., Kang, K.W., and Norton, J.A., Jr. (1974). Choice of an estimate of genetic variance from twin data. *American Journal of Human Genetics, 26,* 154–161.

Christian, J.C., and Norton, J.A., Jr. (1977). A proposed test of the difference between the means of monozygotic and dizygotic twins. *Acta Geneticae Medicae et Gemellologiae, 26,* 49–53.

Doehring, D.G. (1968). Patterns of impairment in specific reading disability. Indiana University Publications: Science Series, No. 23. Bloomington: Indiana University Press.

Hallgren, B. (1950). Specific dyslexia ("congenital word blindness"): A clinical and genetic study. *Acta Psychiatrica et Neurologica Scandinavica* (Supplement), *65,* 1–287.

Hare, B.A. (1977). Perceptual deficits are not a cue to reading problems in 2nd grade. *Reading Teacher, 30,* 624–628.

Harris, E.L. (1982). Genetic and environmental influences on reading achievement: A study of first- and second-grade twin children. *Acta Geneticae Medicae et Gemellologiae, 31,* 64–116.

Hermann, K. (1956). Congenital word blindness. *Acta Psychiatrica et Neurologica Scandinavica* (Supplement), *108,* 177–184.

Hermann, K., and Norrie, E. (1958). Is congenital word blindness a hereditary type of Gerstmann's syndrome? *Psychiatria et Neurologia, 136,* 59–73.

Husén, T. (1959). *Psychological twin research: A methodological study.* Stockholm: Almqvist & Wiksell.

Husén, T. (1960). Abilities of twins. *Scandinavian Journal of Psychology, 1,* 125–135.

Kahn, D., and Birch, H.G. (1968). Development of auditory-visual integration and reading achievement. *Perceptual and Motor Skills, 27,* 459–468.

Magnus, P., Berg, K., and Nance, W.E. (1983). Predicting zygosity in Norwegian twin pairs born 1915–1960. *Clinical Genetics, 24,* 103–112.

Margolis, H. (1977). Auditory perceptual test performance and the reflection-impulsivity dimension. *Journal of Learning Disabilities, 10,* 164–172.

Matheny, A.P., Jr., and Dolan, A.B. (1971). A twin study of genetic influences in reading achievement. *Journal of Learning Disabilities, 7,* 99–102.

Matheny, A.P., Jr., Dolan, A.B., and Wilson, R.S. (1976). Twins with academic learning problems: Antecedent characteristics. *American Journal of Orthopsychiatry, 46,* 464–469.

Mittal, S.K., Zaidi, I., Puri, N., Duggal, S., Rath, B., and Bhargava, S.K. (1977). Communication disabilities: Emerging problems of childhood. *Indian Pediatrics, 14,* 811–815.

Muehl, S., and Kremenak, S. (1966). Ability to match information within and between modalities and subsequent reading achievement. *Journal of Educational Psychology, 57,* 230–239.

Newman, H., Freeman, F.N., and Holzinger, K.J. (1937). *Twins: A study of heredity and environment.* Chicago: University of Chicago Press.

Pelham, W.E., and Ross, A.O. (1977). Selective attention in children with reading problems: A developmental study of incidental learning. *Journal of Abnormal Child Psychology, 5,* 1–8.

Pezzullo, T.R., Thorsen, E.E., and Madaus, G.F. (1972). The heritability of Jensen's Level I and II and divergent thinking. *American Education Research Journal, 9,* 539–546.

Reed, T., Norton, J.A., and Christian, J.C. (1977). Source of information for discriminating MZ and DZ twins by dermatoglyphic patterns. *Acta Geneticae Medicae et Gemellologiae, 26,* 83–86.

Reilly, D.H. (1971). Auditory-visual integration, sex and reading achievement. *Journal of Educational Psychology, 62,* 482–486.

Rotter, J.I. (1981). The models of inheritance of insulin-dependent diabetes mellitus or the genetics of IDDM, no longer a nightmare but still a headache. *American Journal of Human Genetics, 33,* 835–851.

Samuels, S.J., and Turnure, J.E. (1974). Attention and reading achievement in first-grade boys and girls. *Journal of Educational Psychology, 66,* 29–32.

Sarna, S., and Kaprio, J. (1980). Use of logistic analysis in twin zygosity diagnosis. *Human Heredity, 30,* 71–80.

Sarna, S., Kaprio, J., Sistonen, P., and Koskenvuo, M. (1978). Diagnosis of twin zygosity by mailed questionnaire. *Human Heredity, 28,* 241–254.

Satz, P., and Zaide, J. (1983). Sex differences: Clues or myths on genetic aspects of speech and language disorders? In C.L. Ludlow and J.A. Cooper (Eds.), *Genetic aspects of speech and language disorders* (pp. 85–105). New York: Academic Press.

Stevenson, H.W., Stigler, J.W., Lucker, G.W., Lee, S., Hsu, C., and Kitamura, S. (1982). Reading disabilities: The case of Chinese, Japanese, and English. *Child Development, 53,* 1164–1181.

Strandskov, H. (1955). Some aspects of the genetics and evaluation of man's behavioral characteristics. *Eugenics Quarterly, 2,* 152–161.

Torgensen, J. (1975). *Problems and prospects in the study of learning disabilities.* Chicago: The University of Chicago Press.

Vandenberg, S.G. (1962). The hereditary abilities study: Hereditary components in a psychological test battery. *American Journal of Human Genetics, 14,* 220–237.

VandeVoort, L., and Senf, M. (1973). Audiovisual integration in retarded readers. *Journal of Learning Disabilities, 6,* 170–179.

VandeVoort, L., Senf, G.M., and Benton, A.L. (1972). Development of audio-visual integration in normal and retared readers. *Child Development, 43,* 1260–1272.

Vernon, M.D. (1971). *Reading and its difficulties: A psychological study.* London: Cambridge University Press.

Vogel, F., and Motulsky, A.G. (1979). *Human genetics: Problems and approaches.* New York: Springer-Verlag.

Warren, D.H., Anooshian, L.J., and Widawski, M.H. (1975). Measures of visual-auditory integration and their relations to reading achievement in early grades. *Perceptual and Motor Skills, 41,* 615–630.

Whiton, M.D., Singer, D.L., and Cook, H. (1975). Sensory integration skills as predictors of reading acquisition. *Journal of Reading Behavior, 7,* 79–89.

Wictorin, M. (1952). Bidrag till raknefardighetens psykolog: En tvilling undersokning. Goteborg: Ph.D. thesis. Cited in T. Husén (1959), *Psychological twin research: A methodological study.* Stockholm: Almqvist & Wiksell.

Chapter 2

Quantitative Genetics and Learning Disabilities

Pamela R. Fain,
Karen P. Spuhler, and
William J. Kimberling

Before the infinite can be thine
You must first break it down and then recombine
Goethe, quoted by Johanssen, 1903

The field of genetics is a center where converging lines of evidence from all the life sciences are focused into an integrated explanation of biologic variation and its sources. Historically, the application of mathematical models to this purpose has caused both confusion and controversy. The intense struggle that preceded the development of a unified theory of inheritance that could account for Darwinian concepts of evolutionary change, Galton's "law of regression," and the phenomenon of Mendelian segregation stemmed largely from disagreements regarding the significance of the mathematical approach to problems in biology. So, for example, Weinberg (1910) wrote that "the stumbling block in the dispute between Pearson and representatives of experimental research in inheritance . . . is due to . . . an overvaluation of biometrics." More recent attempts to force empirical data on complex phenotypes into mathematically imposed structures have provoked similar reactions, as voiced by Motulsky (1984), who advised that clinical research workers understand basic principles underlying genetic analyses lest they be "bedazzled by quantitative conclusions that sometimes depend on 'soft' data based on assumptions not necessarily applicable to the situation at hand" (p. 144).

The efforts of Pearson and the Biometrical School were inspired by Galton, who was the first to study human inheritance using quantitative techniques. Galton's work was significant at a time when the scientific terrain relating to intermediate steps in the observed resemblence of relatives was void of details. Quantitative genetics developed as a ramification of Galton's "black box" approach (Vogel and Motulsky, 1982) when Fisher (1918) provided a more general statistical framework consistent with the mechanical aspects of Mendelian inheritance. Perhaps more important, Fisher's work demonstrated that while genetic variability for multiple genes with cumulative effects leads to predictable correlations between relatives, results of the "black box" approach cannot be used to deduce the details of an underlying biologic system.

Given certain assumptions, quantitative genetic analyses provided a convenient method for summarizing evidence for genetic variability in a population. However, a knowledge of the extent of nonspecific genetic variation is of limited relevance to any given individual. A mere description of sources of variability is especially dissatisfying for clinical phenotypes, for which the primary concerns are prediction, prevention, diagnosis, and remediation. These ends require the investigation of more specific sources of genetic variation.

Principles relating to the mechanics of chromosomal inheritance form the basis for what has been termed "*static* genetics" (Goldschmidt, 1951). Studies of the consequences of specific gene differences in humans and other organisms became possible through the addition of principles of static genetics to the framework of biologic science and contributed to a better understanding of the more *dynamic* aspects of the relationship between genotype and phenotype. A description of observed characteristics associated with specific genotypes required new concepts and terms, including *variable expressivity*, to refer to individual differences in the phenotypic effects associated with a specific genotype; *pleiotropy*, to refer to the tendency for specific genotypes to influence a number of different characteristics; and *genetic heterogeneity*, to refer to the finding that similar phenotypic effects can be caused by genotypes at different loci.

Effects that complicate and obscure the relationship between single genes and phenotypic expression can be expected to occur on a grander scale for phenotypes that are developmentally complex. Evidence from all facets of genetics points to the need to view phenotype as an endpoint mediated by a highly variable and complexly integrated system. Not surprisingly, attempts to identify specific genotypes related to common diseases often lead to inconsistent and even contradictory results.

Genetic studies of learning disabilities and other complex behavioral phenotypes are most productive when evidence from genetics and the neurosciences are combined to build working models that relate phenotypic measures to underlying biologic processes and, eventually, to conceivable mechanisms of gene action. Models provide a logical structure that is essential for the design of effective research strategies and for the interpretation of empirical results (Murphy, 1978). This chapter covers basic principles of quantitative genetics as they apply to the study of genetic factors in learning disabilities, with reference to developmental dyslexia (RD) as a specific example.

BIOLOGIC MODELS

Since the etiology of RD is complex and as yet poorly understood, it is impossible to avoid the fact that investigation must begin at a level far removed from the action of specific genes. Complex problems in genetics are best approached using an iterative procedure (Murphy, 1978). Models of the relationship between phenotype and genotype can be built from mechanistic interpretations of measures that discriminate affected from normal individuals or subtypes within affected individuals. Family studies can be used to determine evidence for genetic variability in individual measures and genetic correlations between measures. Clinical characterization of distinct genetic subtypes provides an empirical description of the relationship between genotype and phenotype that can be used to refine the original model. Results may provide additional clues for identifying more specific pathways and related measures. As new measures are incorporated into the model, the research strategy is recycled. A durable model has the ability to provide a concise and logical explanation of existing evidence and the flexibility to incorporate new knowledge into its structure.

Information that relates to underlying mechanisms cannot be derived from genetic analysis but must be inherent in the specific measures selected for study. General evidence from studies of complex and heterogeneous phenotypes demonstrates the need to devise techniques that bring measurement progressively closer to the level of gene action (Motulsky, 1982; Murphy, 1978). Findings from neuroanatomical studies of dyslexic subjects encourage further pursuit of CNS measurement. These include case reports of dyslexic individuals by Galaburda and Kemper (1979) and Galaburda and Eidelberg (1982) who found evidence of cellular disorganization in the cortex of the left cerebral hemisphere, particularly aberrant in the posterior temporoparietal language area, and of lesions in nuclei of the thalamus, including the posterior lateral nucleus, which connects with the parietal speech area of the cortex. Cerebral asymmetries in cortical and thalamic areas of the human brain have been well documented (Damasio and Geschwind, 1984). Initial studies employing computerized cranial tomography have reported a higher frequency of either an increased width of the right occipital region compared with the left (reversed cerebral asymmetry; Hier, LeMay, and Rosenberger, 1978) or more symmetry of this region (Haslam, Dalby, Johns, and Rademaker, 1981) in dyslexic subjects compared with normal control subjects.

Practical considerations limit the use of brain scanning measurements in family studies. However, other noninvasive neurophysiologic measurements have also shown discriminatory powers for subtyping dyslexic individuals and could be obtained from family members. The possibilities include (1) the computerized classification of brain electrical activity (EEG and evoked potentials; Duffy, Denckla, Bartels, and Sandini, 1980; Duffy, Denckla, Bartels, Sandini, and Kiessling, 1980); (2) tests assessing CNS auditory deficits (e.g., dichotic listening tasks and auditory evoked potentials; Fried, Tanguay, Boder, Doubleday, and Greensite, 1981; Greenblatt, Bar, Zappulla, and Hughes, 1983; Johnson, Enfield, and Sherman, 1981; Welsh, Healy, Welsh, and Cooper, 1982); (3) tests of visual half-field asymmetries and evoked responses (Cohen and Breslin, 1984; Johnstone, Galin, Fein, Yingling, Herron, and Marcus, 1984; Ludlam, 1981; Obrzut and Hynd, 1983); and (4) visual fixation and eye dominance tasks (Bishop, Jancey, and Steel, 1979; Haddad, Isaacs, Onghena, and Mazor, 1984; Martin and Lovegrove, 1984; Stein and Fowler, 1982).

Neuropsychologic test batteries may provide a more practical means of measuring specific types of brain dysfunction in family studies. Rourke (1982) proposed a three-factor unified neuropsychologic model of learning disabilities initially focusing on the interaction of left and right hemispheric functions and deficits in these areas to account for the subtypes Reading and Spelling Disability and Arithmetic Disability. The potential of family studies in validating models and measures from neuropsychology has not been fully exploited.

Measures currently known to discriminate dyslexic from normal individuals represent levels of phenotype that are a considerable distance from specific gene effects. Research that has led to an extensive categorization of neurologic mutants in animal models (Rose and Behan, 1980) and a growing list of hereditary neurological disorders in man (Baraitser, 1982) indicates that genes influencing CNS development and function have many characteristics in common with genes influencing other functional systems.

At developmentally complex levels of phenotype, the expression of specific genetic defects is subject to continual modification by multiple genetic and environmental stimuli, leading to marked variability in observed neurologic and behavioral effects. In addition, owing to the complexity of the interdependent circuitry established by the genetic program during neuronal differentiation, single gene defects are often expressed as multiple neurologic aberrancies, and the extent of pleiotropy is not necessarily restricted to the behavioral realm. As a result, it is difficult to distinguish primary and secondary effects of particular genes even at the level of neurochemical-neurophysiologic measurement (Hall, Greenspan, and Harris, 1982; Mullen and Herrup, 1979).

Developmental plasticity also contributes to variability in the expression of specific gene defects. Alternate pathways may provide a needed redundancy to allow the development of adaptive functioning despite disturbances due to specific genetic and environmental conditions. The capacity of the mammalian brain for synaptic plasticity has been well documented. Anatomic and functional studies have indicated the capacity of certain brain regions to regenerate connections and concomitant partial recovery of function following specific experimentally induced lesions (e.g., of the spinal cord, hippocampus, olfactory bulb, cortex, locus coeruleus, retina, and red nucleus; Berry, 1983; Cotman, 1978; Lund, 1978). These studies emphasize the need to view phenotypic expression as a dynamic process and suggest developmental changes in the relationship between genotype and phenotype.

Figure 2–1 incorporates these concepts into a simple model. Because RD is developmentally complex, it is conceivable that several different genetic defects could lead to a single endpoint. As a working hypothesis for genetic analysis we suppose that the development of dyslexia can be

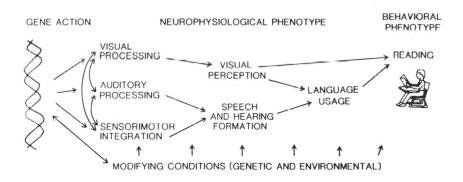

Figure 2–1. A hypothetical framework for genetic studies of RD.

a consequence of a defect in the functional product of any one of a number of specific genes that influence developmental programming in the visual, auditory, and speech formation systems and the coordinating activities involved in sensorimotor integration. The interaction of these systems is depicted in the model by bidirectional arrows. An individual mutation arrests the normal development or activity of a particular neural system by causing a specific defect in a required structural or regulatory product. The variability in phenotypic expression related to one gene is influenced by other genes that modify interacting systems or substitute functional products for the primary genetic lesion.

Plasticity may be envisioned in the model as the availability of alternate pathways to the phenotypic endpoint of reading when a genetic lesion has blocked a more primary path. The effectiveness of compensatory strategies is dependent upon the relative importance of different pathways and is likely to increase with continuous usage of alternate pathways. Compensatory mechanisms in the brain are genetically controlled but may be modified by environmental inputs (Goldman and Lewis, 1978). The degree of adjustment controlled by secondary genetic and environmental inputs has limits defined by the degree of aberrancy of the primary genetic lesion. These limits are a function of the stage of neuronal development at which the gene operates, the level within the hierarchical structure of the brain at which the gene product functions, and the centrality of gene action in the functional regulation of a neural system.

The model for reading in Figure 2-1 is a gross oversimplification of CNS control of language development and usage and its relationship to RD. A more realistic model would include greater emphasis on the multifaceted components of functional neural systems that relate to language-based deficits. The model serves only as a specific example that accentuates a general need to develop a logical framework for pursuing genetic analyses. In addition, it incorporates specific concepts from genetics, including (1) variability in the phenotypic expression of single genes as a result of modification by genetic background and the environment and (2) the fact that a variety of genetic defects could result in RD. These genetic events are the basis of the methodologic problem of genetic heterogeneity, which has been increasingly recognized as a variable to be reckoned with in family studies of traits showing a complex mode of inheritance.

STUDY DESIGN

The model in Figure 2-1 provides a scheme that, however deficient in form and in detail, demonstrates the manner in which genetic differences between individuals may lead to differences in their ability to learn to read given conventional educational stimuli. However, the measurable effect of specific genes is strictly dependent upon the level of observation. The level of observation becomes more complex as the number of links in the chain of events between the gene defect and the measured response increases. Abnormalities caused by specific genes will be less apparent for tests designed to assess reading than for measures of intermediate neurophysiologic events. An accumulation of minor genetic and environmental effects may be sufficient to cause RD, but it is probable that samples of RD probands also include a collection of different specific defects. Quantitative genetic analysis relies on the assumption that phenotypic correlations between relatives are homogeneous, which is not true in family studies of probands who are affected as a result of different causes.

Studies of normal reading in random samples of families are probably less sensitive to the assumption of homogeneity. Although genetic variation in normal reading may be of some general interest, it may not be the best guide to the problem of disability. In particular, it would be difficult to identify the effects of specific genotypes that are relatively rare but that cause severe disability in a limited number of individuals.

In the absence of a unified definition of dyslexia, the initial selection of cases for study is a major barrier to progress. Selection of probands is usually through liability (Falconer, 1965; 1967), which is defined in this case as the sum of effects of all variables that make an individual more or less prone to have recognizable deficiencies in reading. Liability for RD necessarily includes a complex network of genetic, neurologic, educational, and social events. Individual differences for these factors lead to differences in the risk that an individual in the population will be diagnosed as RD. The distinction of genetic and environmental sources of individual differences is the general subject of quantitative genetic analysis.

Liability is a nebulous concept that in most studies cannot be subjected to precise measurement. However, it becomes an important consideration in family studies because probands are often selected through a liability that reflects the investigator's perception of the nature of RD. In evaluating the results of different studies, it may be helpful to consider that each individual in the population has a score on a hypothetical scale of liability, and that probands represent a random sample of individuals above an arbitrary cutoff or threshold on the scale. Liability scores based on different definitions of the phenotype are not likely to be perfectly correlated with each other. In addition, the correlation of liability scores with scores that reflect an underlying genetic predisposition is likely to differ with different phenotype definitions, and results of quantitative genetic analyses will also differ.

A common trend is to be more restrictive in defining cases, with the implicit intention of restricting variation in liability. Perhaps the most common definition of RD is "reading difficulties in a child with normal IQ." Cases associated with mental deficits are eliminated by this definition, but the broader purpose of eliminating variation in liability associated with individual differences in (normal) IQ has not been achieved. A disproportionate number of cases selected for study are often in the lower range of IQ, while RD children with high IQs may be excluded from consideration as probands. Burns (1984) noted that this effect could account for the fact that mean IQ for samples of RD children, although in the normal range, is significantly lower than average.

Liability defined as a deviation from grade level in a child with normal IQ is different from liability defined when the diagnosis is based upon a deviation from IQ. When the phenotype is defined by standardizing for IQ, variation related to IQ is removed from liability. Combining these study designs, such as selecting probands through school referrals and subsequently analyzing test scores (which may be standardized for IQ) from probands and family members, causes special problems. The general problem of genetic analysis of measures imperfectly correlated with liability as it is defined through the ascertainment scheme is mathematically intractable (Dawson and Elston, 1984).

In view of the evidence for pleiotropic effects of genes, any restriction in the definition of phenotype rests on precarious assumptions. The exclusion of cases on the basis of IQ assumes that a reading deficit is secondary to a low IQ and not the reverse. Standardization through regression techniques also assumes a unidirectional relationship between IQ and reading and can be justified only if the variation in liability removed by "correcting" for IQ is irrelevant. Similar arguments apply to the practice of excluding cases on the basis of other variables, including emotional and neurologic impairment. In general, refinements in diagnosis based on ancillary variables rarely reduce the complexity of the genotype-phenotype relationship and may distort it in unpredictable ways. The exception is the exclusion of cases attributable to a specific genetic or environmental cause.

Genetic analysis of family data is further complicated by differences in the prevalence of RD in different subpopulations. Sex differences are of special interest because of consistent reports of higher prevalence in males. Males and females develop in somewhat different environmental realms, and an uneven distribution of social and educational factors related to the recognition and diagnosis of RD may contribute to observed sex differences. In addition, the response to similar environments may involve different sets of biologic pathways, leading to differences in the way in which particular genes relate to a given phenotype. Functional differences in brain development and the reliance upon different mechanisms to compensate for genetic errors in specific pathways are also factors that could contribute to sex differences in the observed prevalence of RD.

Differences in the validity of phenotypic measures in different age groups also complicate the analysis of family data. The opportunity for divergence in environmental factors increases with age, so that a greater proportion of phenotypic variation attributable to the environment is expected in adults compared with children. In addition, the adult brain has had more time to experiment with the efficiency of different biologic routes for accomplishing a given task, and the relationship between genotype and phenotype may be different and, in particular, more heterogeneous among adults compared with children.

Quantitative genetic analyses are poorly suited for the study of heterogeneity in the genotype-phenotype relationship as a function of variables such as age and sex. An understanding of developmental differences in the relationship between genotype and phenotype requires longitudinal family studies involving multiple measurements of a phenotype over time (Morton, 1982). However, some information can be obtained from cross-sectional data by examining, for example, differences in the correlation between relatives as a function of their differences in age, or differences in the correlation between same-sex and different-sex relatives.

The problems discussed in this section are not peculiar to RD, but seem to be characteristic of genetic studies of complex phenotypes in general. They should discourage indiscriminate applications of quantitative genetic analyses to complex phenotypes in a heterogeneous sample. Two complementary research strategies may be productive in attacking complex problems: (1) population and family studies of specific neurophysiologic, neuroanatomic, and neuropsychologic measures thought to be related to RD and (2) family studies of unrestricted (heterogeneous) samples of RD probands that focus on the genetic overlap of proposed subtypes. For both strategies, measures are chosen that provide information for evaluating a particular biologic model for reading deficits.

Population studies of measures thought to be related to RD are essential for understanding their contribution to the risk for RD. Genetic studies of these measures within families of RD probands selected through liability are difficult to interpret in the absence of information relating to appropriate scales of measurement, genetic variability and mechanisms of inheritance, and the prevalence of dyslexia-related abnormalities in the general population. The classical techniques of quantitative genetics are more appropriate for random samples of families and can be used to screen measures for genetic variation that is relevant to biologic models of RD.

The second approach deserves attention considering the literature that has accumulated with regard to possible subtypes of RD (Satz and Morris, 1980). Family studies can be used to examine evidence for the genetic overlap or distinction of subtypes. The results of these studies may suggest more objective criteria for defining the RD phenotype, leading progressively to the application of classical techniques in quantitative genetic analysis to a more homogeneous sample. Results of both types of study designs provide feedback to the reading model, and progress can be weighed by the internal consistency of the results.

MODELS FOR QUANTITATIVE VARIATION

An understanding of the nature of genetic variation is a prerequisite for successful attempts at statistical genetic modeling and analysis. Confounding effects that have been emphasized in previous sections imply that an analysis of genetic sources of variation in liability for RD is unlikely to be productive. Meaningful interpretations of genetic variability are dependent upon family studies of measures that bear a closer relationship to etiology. The importance of a particular risk factor or measure can be quantified by its contribution to the variance of, or by its correlation with, liability. The correlation between the measure and liability can be determined from mean differences between affected and unaffected individuals (Curnow and Smith, 1975).

Figure 2-2 gives two extreme models of quantitative variation relating to a specific measure in a particular population. Individuals above a certain threshold, T, are abnormal by some criteria. The threshold may be defined as an arbitrary cutoff for a quantitative measure, or it may represent a natural phenomenon. In Figure 2-2a, differences in effects of alleles at a single locus, A, cause discontinuity in the distribution, so that all individuals of genotype A_mA_n are abnormal and all other individuals are normal. Alleles at other loci and the environment also contribute to individual differences for the measure, but on a smaller scale. Discontinuity in the distribution of an observed phenotype does not by itself prove the existence of locus A, since similar effects could result from environmental accidents or from a natural threshold on an underlying continuous scale. In either case, individuals can be classified unambiguously, and little can be gained from an analysis of the quantitative measures. Segregation analysis is used to determine if family data so categorized are consistent with a particular Mendelian hypothesis.

In Figure 2-2b, the effect of any particular locus or environmental condition is dampened by other sources of variation, and the phenotypic distribution is continuous. Although most individuals who inherit A_mA_n are abnormal, most abnormal individuals have inherited other alleles at locus A. In relation to other sources of variation, the effects of alleles at locus A are small, despite "high penetrance." It should be noted that distributions of observed measures often deviate from normality, particularly at the

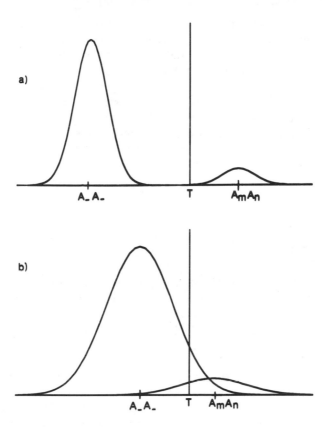

Figure 2-2. Two extreme models for quantitative variation: (a) discontinuous variation, (b) continuous variation.

extremes. Observed skewness may reflect rare alleles with large effects, increased variability of extreme genotypes, or a property of the scale. Segregation analysis is unable to make this distinction (MacLean, Morton, and Lew, 1975; Elston, 1984). The "mixed model" (Morton and MacLean, 1974) of segregation analysis allows for an overlap in the phenotypic distributions of different genotypes at a single locus, but is not sufficiently general to include the large number of equally plausible genetic hypotheses that could account for measures with continuous phenotypic distributions.

For some phenotypes the threshold represents a biologic phenomenon, as when a self-regulatory mechanism breaks down (Wright, 1968). Abnormality is defined by a clear-cut distinction rather than as an arbitrary cutoff on a measured scale. Mendelian hypotheses are rarely in dispute for rare phenotypes showing typical segregation in families, but single-locus hypotheses lose credibility if incomplete penetrance is required to explain atypical results. An underlying continuous scale is often assumed even though there is no perceptible gradation from normal to abnormal. Since there is usually insufficient information to infer whether the underlying scale is continuous or discontinuous, the genetic analysis of "quasi-continuous" variation is particularly problematic. The expectations of Mendelian and multiple-factor models are quite similar for a wide range of single-locus gene frequencies and penetrances, indicating that the significance of their distinction may be limited (Edwards, 1960; Smith, 1971; Wilson, 1971; 1974).

LINEAR MODELS

A description of variation in components of observed measures can be obtained by proposing a simple mathematical function to represent the relationship between genotype and phenotype for the measure. Most genetic analyses are based on a simple linear causal model of the general form

$$P = G + E + e \qquad (1)$$

where P refers to the measurable phenotype, G to the genotype, E to the environment, and e to random error in measurement. In theory, the model can be made more complicated by decomposing G to allow for one or more major genes and a large number of minor or secondary genes and to allow for additive, dominance, and epistatic interactions related to these genes. Environmental effects could be partitioned into components common to certain family members and a component specific to the individual. Nonlinear interactions between genotype and environment are not allowed in the model; however, a transformation of measurement scale may be sufficient to eliminate nonadditivity.

Assuming that "causes" are uncorrelated, the phenotypic variance of an observed measure in a population is given by

$$V_P = V_G + V_E + V_e \qquad (2)$$

Covariance terms could be appended to allow for correlated causes. In practice, the complexity of the model is restricted by the material available for study. The magnitude of V_G depends on frequences of relevant alleles in the population, additive effects of these alleles and their interactions between and within loci, and assortative mating, or, more generally, population structure. Most important, V_P, V_G, and V_E are a property of the population studied.

The approach to genetic analysis is dependent upon the model of quantitative variation that is considered to apply to the measure (Figure 2-2). Assuming that the distribution of measures from pairs of relatives is bivariate normal and that error terms are uncorrelated, the phenotypic covariance between pairs of relatives X and Y is given by

$$\text{Cov}_{P_{XY}} = u V_G + v V_E \tag{3}$$

where u is the genetic correlation and v the environmental correlation between relatives. The extent of familiality is measured by the ratio of the covariance between pairs of relatives to the phenotypic variance. If it can be assumed that relatives do not share environments ($v = 0$), an estimate of the variance of genetic effects (V_G) can be derived, since u is given by the genetic relationship of the pairs.

When the environment is not random, a solution for V_G requires a series of equations in the form of equation 3 in which covariances are derived from observations of sets of pairs that differ for u or v, or both. Classical designs call for the study of special populations, including adopted children, twins, half-sibs, or relatives reared together and apart. An analysis of variation in special populations results in a better distinction of genetic and environmental variation in those populations. Once accomplished, it must be established that the phenotype is not specifically associated with the family condition, such as being an adopted child, a foster parent, a child from a broken home, or a twin.

The linear model given in equation 1 can also be extended to include terms for indices of specific components of variability. The indices are constructed from one or more variables that can be observed directly. Depending on the phenotype, it may be difficult to conceptualize phenotype, genotype, and environment in their proper relationship. A child's exposure to books may reflect culturally based opportunities or a personal choice largely dependent upon genotype. The educational opportunities for a child may be a function of parental genotype. It is not possible to discern the underlying phenotype-environment-genotype relationship from a genetic analysis, but it is possible to obtain estimates of genetic or environmental parameters such as those given in equation 3 if it is assumed that the relationship is known.

Once a model is specified in terms of equations 2 and 3, statistical manipulation of data is straightforward. Estimates of unknown parameters can be generated for a series of linear equations of the form given in equation 3 provided that a sufficient number of known parameters can be obtained from the observed data (i.e., phenotypic variances and covariances between relatives).

An alternative to partitioning variance components involves partitioning of phenotypic correlations for standardized measures using path analysis. A simple path diagram of the model defined by equations 1, 2, and 3 is given in Figure 2–3. The phenotypes, P, of pairs of relatives X and Y are shown as completely determined by G, E, and e as specified in equation 1. The genetic and environmental correlations between pairs is given by u and v as in equation 3. From the basic equation of path analysis (Wright, 1921), the phenotypic correlation between pairs, r_{XY}, is simply the sum of the products of connecting paths, or

$$r_{XY} = \sqrt{V_G/V_P} \cdot u \cdot \sqrt{V_G/V_P} + \sqrt{V_E/V_P} \cdot v \cdot \sqrt{V_E/V_P}$$
$$= u(V_G/V_P) + v(V_E/V_P)$$
$$= uV_G + vV_E$$

since, for standardized measures, $V_P = 1$. A comparison of this result with equation 3 illustrates the similarities between path analysis and variance components analysis. Both analyses are applied to data that are assumed to conform to a model of causal relationships that the investigator must specify in advance.

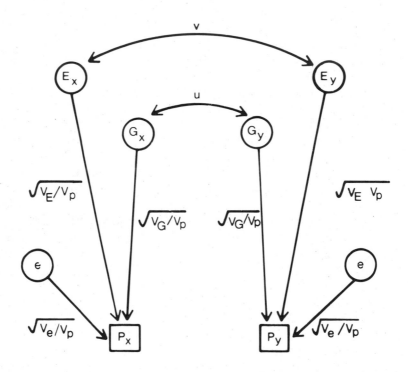

Figure 2–3. A simple path model for partitioning the phenotypic correlation between relatives.

The methods outlined are useful for determining evidence for genetic variability in quantitative measures known to be correlated with liability. Falconer (1965; 1967) derived methods for estimating the correlation between relatives when data are in the form of frequencies. The prevalence of a certain abnormality in the population pinpoints the position of a threshold on an underlying scale. If it can be assumed that the underlying distribution is normal, frequencies in the population and in relatives can be expressed in standard deviations from the mean by reference to tables of the normal distribution. The expression for the correlation between relatives is

$$r = (x_g - x_r) / a$$

where x_g is the normal deviate corresponding to the population frequency, x_r corresponds to the frequency in relatives of probands, and a is the mean of abnormal individuals. Tables of x_g, x_r, and a for different frequencies of abnormal relatives and population prevalences are given by Falconer (1965). A more precise estimate of the correlation between relatives for the threshold model trait was given by Reich, James, and Morris (1972). Threshold models have also been used for continuous measures when multivariate normality assumptions required by other methods are in doubt (Rice, Nichols, and Gottesman, 1981). However, the use of all of the information contained in a quantitative measure is generally preferable (Morton, 1982).

Since the advent of computer technology, statistical analyses based upon likelihood methods have gained popularity in human genetics. The likelihood approach is especially useful for pooling data from families with variable structure and in accounting for the scheme for ascertaining probands. In addition, estimates obtained from likelihood analysis have optimal properties from a statistical standpoint, and likelihood theory provides a means for testing the fit of the data to a particular hypothesis. However, it is important to emphasize that use of the likelihood method does not remove the basic limitations and assumptions inherent in any genetic model. Likelihood analysis merely provides the most precise estimates of parameters. Computer algorithms for handling computational requirements are available from a library of programs especially designed for genetic studies (Morton, Rao, and Lalouel, 1983). As noted previously, the problem of analysis of one measure in families selected on the basis of a different measure or criteria cannot be handled through likelihood analysis or any other approach, although approximate corrections for special cases have been suggested and applied successfully in practice (Dawson and Elston, 1984).

ANALYSIS OF GENETIC HETEROGENEITY

The purpose of an analysis of genetic heterogeneity is to delineate different genetic mechanisms independent of their effect on the phenotype. Results of the analysis may indicate that clinically similar phenotypes are associated with different genetic mechanisms in different individuals or, conversely, that individuals with clinically distinguishable phenotypes are similar genotypically. In the absence of family data there is no justification for infering that subtypes defined by either multivariate analysis or a more subjective grouping of clinical variables are etiologically distinct.

The analysis of genetic heterogeneity can be simple or elaborate. The minimum data required are (1) population frequencies for each subgroup and (2) numbers of normal relatives and affected relatives classified by subgroup for probands of each subgroup (Table 2-1). Population frequencies and frequencies in relatives must reflect the same criteria for classification as used for the proband. Few studies have reported these essential data.

Different liabilities are assumed for each subgroup of probands, and the interest is in their overlap. A simple test of identity of genetic components can be obtained from a 2×2 chi-square; a test for absence of association from a comparison of frequencies in relatives with population frequencies. For rare subtypes and small expected numbers, tables of the Poisson distribution (e.g., Rohlf and Sokal, 1969) are useful (Smith, 1976).

The primary interest is in extreme subgroups with little or no overlap; i.e., those in which the 2×2 chi square is significant and the cross-diagonal frequencies are nonsignificant. For intermediate cases, a more concise summary of the patterns in Table 2-1 can be obtained by computing correlations and cross-correlations. Falconer (1965; 1967) derived approximations for the genetic correlation between two traits as

$$r_g = h^2_{21} / h^2_{11} h^2_{22}$$

where h^2_{21}, h^2_{11}, h^2_{22} are estimates of the relative genetic variance obtained from correlations and cross-correlations as $h^2_{11} = u r_{11}$, where u is the degree of relationship for the pairs of relatives. Interpretation of the h^2s as the relative genetic variance and r_g as the genetic correlation requires the assumptions of additive effects of gene loci and absence of common environment.

Reich, Rice, Cloninger, Wette, and James (1979) have examined the problem from a different perspective by considering expected patterns for the values in Table 2-1 under the assumption that subgroups represent different levels of severity, as might be applicable for the analysis of sex and age differences in RD prevalence. Subgroups of RD children who differ in mean liability are viewed as representing multiple thresholds of a single underlying liability. Expected patterns for different models are

Table 2-1.   Data Needed to Evaluate Genetic Significance of RD Subtypes

Subtype of Proband	Subtype of Sibs	
	1	*2*
1	A	B
2	C	D
Population	X	Y

given in Table 2-2. Reich and colleagues (1979) also derived more precise estimates of the cross-correlations between probands of one subgroup and their relatives of another and an estimate for the familial component of the phenotypic correlation between subgroups.

The approach outlined is especially useful for testing the efficacy of subgroups that are based upon well-conceived biologic hypotheses. It is less likely to be productive as an analysis of subtypes derived solely from automated techniques (e.g., factor or cluster analysis), although the latter may contribute to validation of more subjective groupings based upon coherent biologic hypotheses.

GENE LINKAGE

Difficulties in interpretation of genetic analysis stem from the inability to obtain a concrete index of either genotype or environment. Until recently, the success rate of studies using genetic markers was very low, owing to an insufficient number of markers. Recent advances in DNA technology (Botstein, White, Skolnick, and Davis, 1980) promise to provide research tools in human genetics that are the observational equivalent of experimental animal studies using inbred strains. Rapid discoveries of new DNA polymorphisms to serve as genetic markers have replaced the frustration of previous attempts to identify gene linkage in humans with an optimism that extends to the possibility of constructing genotypic indices in humans (White and Skolnick, 1982).

Despite the once dismal prospects of identifying gene linkage even for clear Mendelian characters, efforts to establish a theoretical basis for linkage analysis of quantitative characters have not been lacking. Interest in this question has been stimulated by the importance of identifying chromosomal associations for complex associations of numerous diseases and HLA.

Penrose (1938) developed a sib-pair method for the detection of linkage between a quantitative character and a marker locus and was followed by others who approached the problem along similar lines (Haseman and Elston, 1972; Hill, 1975; Smith, 1975). The conceptual basis for these methods rests on the principle that sibs should be more or less similar for an

Table 2-2.   Interpretation of Within-family Patterns for Data in the form of Table 2-1 Assuming a Multiple-threshold Model to Account for RD Subtypes

Observed Results	Interpretation
$B = Y$, $C = X$; $r_{12} = r_{21} = 0$	Independent genetic components of liability
$A = C$; $B = D$; $r_{11} \neq r_{22}$	Correlated familial components of liability; subtype differences due to nonfamilial factors
$C > D > A > B$ $r_{11} = r_{12} = r_{21} = r_{22}$	Correlated familial components of liability; subtype differences due to level of severity

observed measure depending upon the number of alleles they share by descent for a linked marker locus. In most cases, the theoretical approach has focused on the consequences of a single marker locus and a single linked locus that contributes to genetic variation in the trait.

Goldgar (1981) dealt with the problem of linkage analysis for quantitative phenotype, making no assumptions with respect to the number or effects of loci contributing to the trait. In addition, the method incorporates information from several chromosome markers. Given a sufficient number of genetic markers that are suitably spaced along the length of a chromosome arm, it may be possible to partition genetic variation in a quantitative phenotype to specific chromosomes. The method relies on an estimate of the genetic correlation between sibs for a particular chromosome arm, which is obtained from observed marker phenotypes, the location of marker loci in relation to the centromere, and an assumed crossover distribution for the chromosome arm. Additional research is needed to determine chromosome specific crossover distributions and to select the most efficient battery of genetic markers for gene mapping studies.

DISCUSSION

Murphy (1978) defined a biological model as "a casting of a conjecture about biological mechanisms, in terms that may be manipulated mathematically, that may be tested and if false refuted, and that if substantiated will lead to insight and further profitable fields of empirical inquiry" (p. 8). Biologic models and mathematical models have in common a speculation about causal relationships, but little else (Murphy, 1982). The development of models necessarily involves a certain degree of subjective judgment. A mathematical model is one of many mathematically plausible structures, but in most cases, a relatively small subset of these represent biologically plausible hypotheses. Results of goodness-of-fit tests applied to empirical data may provide objective indications that an assumed model is wrong, but interpretations cannot extend to discounting untested structures that could also account for the observations. Since the value of a mathematical model is eventually judged in terms of biologic plausibility, it is more efficient to construct mathematical models from biologic ones rather than the reverse. Hence, we began with a biologic model for RD not to advocate any particular viewpoint in this regard, but to emphasize the importance of having one.

As experience with genetic analysis of complex phenotypes broadens, guidelines for improving the productivity of these studies have appeared (Cloninger, Rice, Reich, and McGuffin, 1982; Motulsky, 1982; Murphy, 1978; Sing, Hanis, and Moll, 1982). There is general agreement that extensions of classical mathematical models for genetic analysis are inadequate for handling the most common problem of genetic heterogeneity. Attempts to resolve this problem by restrictions in the phenotype definition are unlikely to be successful. In some cases, the definition may be so stringent as to eliminate relevant variation in liability, whereas in others there remains variation that the investigator had not intended. A direct confrontation of the problem of heterogeneity in family studies may provide a more productive alternative to quantitative genetic analysis of variation in liability.

Vogel and Motulsky (1982) describe the analysis of genetic heterogeneity as "carrying genetic analysis through different levels ever closer to gene action" (p. 107). The goal is to proceed systematically from the complex (Figure 2–2b) to the simple (Figure 2–2a). At the complex level, the "effect" of a particular allele on population variability is conceptually different from its effect on the individual who inherits it. A common allele that is relatively trivial for the individual has an effect on population variability similar to that of a rarer allele with more devastating consequences. Resolution of genetic heterogeneity involves dissection of a collection of risk factors to reveal genetic components that are highly relevant for one subgroup of affected individuals, but not for others. It requires systematic and rational study designs combined with an unrelenting search for measures that relate to intervening biologic pathways. The most productive approach is to begin with simple models, adding details and complications as they are indicated by results of statistical analyses. The least productive approach is to force data into stereotyped mathematical models (Wright, 1983).

The rationale for studying genetic factors in RD stems from the simple assumption that genes related to neurologic events associated with RD are unlikely to have escaped the enormous variation that seems characteristic of all other tissues and organs. Although the possibility that genetic variability may be important in determining individual differences in the risk for RD suggests that effective educational programs should be oriented to the individual, quantification of genetic variation cannot provide direction to this end. Information from genetic studies that has relevance to remedial programs can only come from the study of particular genotypes in particular environments.

Results of research that has focused on specific genetic risk factors related to other complex phenotypes have been promising. The identification of autosomal dominant forms of hypercholesterolemia exemplifies the genetic information that can be derived from family studies of intermediate phenotypes. Results of quantitative genetic analyses applied to serum cholesterol levels in samples of families from diverse populations are remarkably consistent (Cloninger, Rao, Rice, Reich, and Morton, 1983), whereas applications of similar analyses to the "heart disease" phenotype would undoubtedly be less informative. Application of the "mixed model" of segregation analysis also led to meaningful interpretations when applied to cholesterol levels, in marked contrast to the ambiguities apparent in results of similar analyses applied to more complex phenotypes, including reading disability (Lewitter, DeFries, and Elston, 1980). Interestingly, evidence for specific genotypes that are important in determining cholesterol levels was also apparent from analyses that, in comparison with the "mixed model," are relatively simple (Green, Owen, Namboodiri, Hewitt, Williams, and Elston, 1984).

Information that can be obtained from studies of specific genetic defects that influence pathways related to RD is often overlooked because of other aspects of the syndrome that are clinically more relevant. However, these disorders could provide clues for developing the biologic framework needed for more systematic genetic studies of RD. For example, further investigations of the associations between speech and language dysfunction and Fragile X syndrome (Howard-Peebles, Stoddard, and Mims, 1979; Lehrke, 1974; Newell, Sanborn, and Hagerman, 1984; Rosenberger, Wilson-Ciambrone, and Milunsky, 1982; Switzky, 1975) and other X-chromosome abnormalities (Chapter 8) could shed light on the relationship between speech and language deficits and reading disability. Additional research could also point to inferences with regard to the influence of specific X-linked genes on the reading phenotype.

In view of a possible linkage of an autosomal dominant form of RD to chromosome 15 (Smith, Kimberling, Pennington, and Lubs, 1983), it would be of interest to estimate the proportion of variation in measures related to reading deficits that can be attributed to genes on this chromosome. Although the gene linkage approach is becoming a promising addition to genetic analysis, the need to evaluate the plausibility of specific measures remains. The "shotgun" approach using random markers and complex liability is not recommended; i.e., the study of regional associations on a particular chromosome should be indicated on the basis of other evidence. Quantitative genetic analyses are useful in screening relevant measures for evidence of genetic variability sufficient to warrant the application of linkage analysis.

In this chapter we have emphasized the study of genetic factors in RD. Our neglect of the environment is not based on the view that environmental variables are unimportant to the etiology of RD, but does reflect our opinion that quantitative genetic analyses incorporating environmental measures cannot help to resolve the complexities that stem primarily from heterogeneous samples. Studies of environmental variables (e.g., Schmid et al., 1983) are of value in themselves, but the identification of environmental risk factors does not require a family study approach, nor are conclusions invalidated by results of family studies. So long as the etiology of RD is poorly understood, prevention and management are undoubtedly best approached through manipulation of environmental factors that are related to risk, and improvement of many cultural risk factors is likely to be justified on more general grounds. Attempts to study the complicated interrelationships of genotype, environment, and phenotype in the absence of studies that provide information on more specific neurologic components considered separately are likely to lie fallow.

REFERENCES

Baraitser, M. (1982). *The genetics of neurological disease.* London: Oxford University Press.

Berry, M. (Ed.). (1982). *Growth and regeneration of axons in the nervous system.* Bibliotheca Anatomica 23. New York: S. Karger.

Bishop, D.V.M., Jancey, C., and Steel, A.M. (1979). Orthoptic status and reading disability. *Cortex, 15,* 659–666.

Botstein, D., White, R.L., Skolnick, M., and Davis, R.W. (1980). Construction of a genetic linkage map in man using restriction fragment length polymorphisms. *American Journal of Human Genetics, 32,* 314–331.

Burns, E. (1984). The bivariate normal distribution and the IQ of learning disability samples. *Journal of Learning Disabilities, 17,* 294-295.

Cloninger, C.R., Rao, D.C., Rice, J., Reich, T., and Morton, N.E. (1983). A defense of path analysis in genetic epidemiology. *American Journal of Human Genetics, 35,* 733–756.

Cloninger, C.R., Rice, J., Reich, T., and McGuffin, P. (1982). Genetic analysis of seizure disorders as multidimensional threshold characters. In V.E. Anderson, W.A. Hauser, J.K. Penry, and C.F. Sing (Eds.), *Genetic basis of the epilepsies* (pp. 291–310). New York: Raven Press.

Cohen, J., and Breslin, P.W. (1984). Visual evoked responses in dyslexic children. *Annals of the New York Academy of Sciences, 425,* 338–343.

Cotman, C.W. (Ed.). (1978). *Neuronal plasticity.* New York: Raven Press.

Curnow, R.N., and Smith, C. (1975). Multifactorial models for familial diseases in man. *Journal of the Royal Statistical Society A, 138* (Part 2), 131–169.

Damasio, A.R., and Geschwind, N. (1984). The neural basis of language. *Annual Review of Neuroscience, 7,* 127–147.

Dawson, D.V., and Elston, R.C. (1984). A bivariate problem in human genetics: Ascertainment of families through a correlated trait. *American Journal of Medical Genetics, 18,* 435–448.

Duffy, F.H., Denckla, M.B., Bartels, P.H., and Sandini, G. (1980a). Dyslexia: Regional differences in brain electrical activity by topographic mapping. *Annals of Neurology, 7,* 412–420.

Duffy, F.H., Denckla, M.B., Bartels, P.H., Sandini, G., and Kiessling, L.S. (1980b). Dyslexia: Automated diagnosis by computerized classification of brain electrical activity. *Annals of Neurology, 7,* 421–428.

Edwards, J.H. (1960). The simulation of mendelism. *Acta Genetica, 10,* 63–70.

Elston, R.C. (1984a). Future trends in genetic analysis methodology. In D.C. Rao, R.C. Elston, L. Kuller, M. Feinleib, C. Carter, and R. Havlik (Eds.), *Genetic epidemiology of coronary heart disease: Past, present and future* (pp. 539–540). New York: Alan R. Liss.

Falconer, D.S. (1965). The inheritance to certain diseases, estimated from the incidence among relatives. *Annals of Human Genetics, 29,* 51–76.

Falconer, D.S. (1967). The inheritance of liability to diseases with variable age of onset with particular reference to diabetes mellitus. *Annals of Human Genetics, 31,* 1–20.

Fisher, R.A. (1918). The correlation between relatives on the supposition of mendelian inheritance. *Royal Society (Edinburgh) Transactions, 52,* 399–433.

Fried, I., Tanguay, P.E., Boder, E., Doubleday, C., and Greensite, M. (1981). Developmental dyslexia: Electrophysiological evidence of clinical subgroups. *Brain and Language, 12,* 14–22.

Galaburda, A.M., and Eidelberg, D. (1982). Symmetry and asymmetry in the human posterior thalamus. *Archives of Neurology, 39,* 333–336.

Galaburda, A.M., and Kemper, T.L. (1979). Cytoarchitectonic abnormalities in developmental dyslexia: A case study. *Annals of Neurology, 6,* 94–100.

Goldgar, D.E. (1981). *Partitioning the genetic variance of a quantitative trait to specific chromosomes: An alternative approach to quantitative linkage analysis.* Unpublished doctoral dissertation, University of Colorado, Boulder.

Goldman, P.S. and Lewis, M.E. (1978). Developmental biology of brain damage and experience. In C.W. Cotman (Ed.), *Neuronal plasticity* (pp. 291–310). New York: Raven Press.

Goldschmidt, R.B. (1951). The impact of genetics upon science. In L.C. Dunn (Ed.), *Genetics in the 20th century* (pp. 1–23). New York: Macmillan.

Green, P., Owen, A.R.G., Namboodiri, K., Hewitt, D., Williams, L.R., and Elston, R.C. (1984). The collaborative lipid research clinics program family study: Detection of major genes influencing lipid levels by examination of heterogeneity of familial variances. *Genetic Epidemiology, 1,* 123–141.

Greenblatt, E.R., Bar, A., Zappulla, R.A., and Hughes, D.A. (1983). Learning disability assessed through audiologic and physiologic measures. A case study. *Journal of Communication Disorders, 16,* 309–313.

Haddad, H.M., Isaacs, N.S., Onghena, K., and Mazor, A. (1984). The use of orthoptics in dyslexia. *Journal of Learning Disabilities, 17,* 142–144.

Hall, J.C., Greenspan, R.J., and Harris, W.A. (1982). *Genetic neurobiology* (pp. 153–164, 187–194). Cambridge: MIT Press.

Haseman, J.K., and Elston, R.C. (1972). The investigation of linkage between a quantitative trait and marker locus. *Behavior Genetics, 2,* 3–19.

Haslam, R.H.A., Dalby, J.T., Johns, R.D., and Rademaker, A.W. (1981). Cerebral asymmetry in developmental dyslexia. *Archives of Neurology, 38,* 679–682.

Hier, D.B., LeMay, M., and Rosenberger, P.B. (1978). Developmental dyslexia: Evidence for a subgroup with a reversal of cerebral asymmetry. *Archives of Neurology, 35,* 90–92.

Hill, A.P. (1975). Quantitative linkage: A statistical procedure for its detection and estimation. *Annals of Human Genetics, 38,* 439–449.

Howard-Peebles, P.N., Stoddard, G.R., and Mims, M.G. (1979). Familial X-linked mental retardation, verbal disability and marker-X chromosomes. *American Journal of Human Genetics, 31,* 214–222.

Johnson, D.W., Enfield, M.L., and Sherman, R.E. (1981). The use of the staggered spondiac word and the competing environmental sounds tests in the evaluation of central auditory function of learning disabled children. *Ear and Hearing, 2,* 70–77.

Johnstone, J., Galin, D., Fein, G., Yingling, C., Herron, J., and Marcus, M. (1984). Regional brain activity in dyslexic and control children during reading tasks: Visual probe event-related potentials. *Brain and Language, 21,* 233–254.

Lehrke, R.G. (1974). *X-linked mental retardation and verbal disability.* New York: Intercontinental Medical Book Corporation. BDOAS X / 1–100.

Lewitter, F.I., DeFries, J.C., and Elston, R.C. (1980). Genetic models of reading disability. *Behavior Genetics, 10,* 9–30.

Ludlum, W.M. (1981). Visual electrophysiology and reading / learning difficulties. *Journal of Learning Disabilities, 14,* 587–590.

Lund, R.D. (1978). *Development and plasticity of the brain.* New York: Oxford University Press.

MacLean, C.J., Morton, N.E., and Lew, R. (1975). Analysis of family resemblance. IV. Operational characteristics of segregation analysis. *American Journal of Human Genetics, 39,* 485–491.

Martin, F., and Lovegrove, W. (1984). The effects of field size and luminance on contrast sensitivity differences between specifically reading disabled and normal children. *Neuropsychologia, 22,* 73–77.

Morton, N.E. (1982). *Outline of genetic epidemiology.* Basel: Karger.

Morton, N.E., and MacLean, C.J. (1974). Analysis of family resemblance. III. Complex segregation analysis of quantitative traits. *American Journal of Human Genetics, 26,* 489–503.

Morton, N.E., Rao, D.C., and Lalouel, J.-M. (1983). Methods of genetic epidemiology. In M.A. Klingberg (Ed.), *Contributions to epidemiology and biostatistics,* Volume 4. Basel: S. Karger.

Motulsky, A.G. (1982). Genetic approaches to common diseases. In B. Bonne-Tamir, T. Cohen, and R.M. Goodman (Eds.), *Proceedings of the Sixth International Congress of Human Genetics* (pp. 89–96). New York: Alan R. Liss.

Motulsky, A.G. (1984). Genetic epidemiology (Editorial). *Genetic Epidemiology, 1,* 143–144.

Mullen, R.J., and Herrup, K. (1979). Chimeric analysis of mouse cerebellar mutants. In X.O. Breakefield (Ed.), *Neurogenetics: Genetic approaches to the nervous system* (pp. 173–196). New York: Elsevier.

Murphy, E.A. (1978). Epidemiological strategies and genetic factors. *International Journal of Epidemiology, 7,* 7–14.

Murphy, E.A. (1982). Muddling, meddling, and modeling. In V.E. Anderson, W.A. Hauser, J.K. Penry, and C.F. Sing (Eds.), *Genetic basis of the epilepsies* (pp. 333–348). New York: Raven Press.

Newell, K., Sanborn, B., and Hagerman, R. (1984). Speech and language dysfunction in the fragile-X syndrome. In R. Hagerman and P. McBogg (Eds.), *The fragile-X syndrome: Diagnosis, biochemistry and treatment*. Denver: Spectra Publications.

Obrzut, J.E., and Hynd, G.W. (1983). The neurobiological and neuropsychological foundations of learning disabilities. *Journal of Learning Disabilities, 16,* 515–520.

Penrose, L.S. (1983). Genetic linkage in graded human characters. *Annals of Eugenics, 18,* 120–124.

Reich, T., James, J.W., and Morris, C.A. (1972). The use of multiple thresholds in determining the mode of transmission of semi-continuous traits. *Annals of Human Genetics, 36,* 163–184.

Reich, T., Rice, J., Cloninger, C.R., Wette, R., and James, J. (1979). The use of multiple thresholds and segregation analysis in analyzing the phenotypic heterogeneity of multifactorial traits. *Annals of Human Genetics, 42,* 371–389.

Rice, J.P., Nichols, P.L., and Gottesman, I.I. (1981). Assessment of sex differences for multifactorial traits using path analysis: Application to learning difficulties. *Psychiatry Research, 4,* 301–312.

Rohlf, F.J., and Sokal, R.R. (1969). *Statistical tables.* San Francisco: W.H. Freeman.

Rose, F.C., and Behan, P.O. (1980). *Animal models in neurological disease.* Baltimore: University Park Press.

Rosenberger, P.B., Wilson-Ciambrone, S., and Milunsky, A. (1982). Speech and fluency disorder in the fragile-X syndrome. *Neurology, 32* (2), A190.

Rourke, B.P. (1982). Central processing deficiencies in children: Toward a developmental neuropsychological model. *Journal of Clinical Neuropsychology, 4,* 1–18.

Satz, P., and Morris, R. (1980). Learning disability subtypes: A review. In F.J. Pirozzolo and M.C. Wittrock (Eds.), *Neuropsychological and cognitive processes in reading*. New York: Academic Press.

Schmid, A.U., Bachler, A., Frey, D., Gerth, J-H., Prim, J., Hanseler, A., and Augsberger, T. (1983). Genetic, medical and psychological factors in learning disorders in a cohort of 11-year-old children (Winterthur study). *Acta Paedopsychiatry* (Basel), *49,* 9–45.

Sing, C.F., Hanis, C.L., and Moll, P.P. (1982). Questions, measures and analytical strategies in human genetics. In V.E. Anderson, W.A. Hauser, J.K. Penry, and C.F. Sing (Eds.), *Genetic basis of the epilepsies* (pp. 239–248). New York: Raven Press.

Smith, C. (1971). Discriminating between different modes of inheritance in genetic disease. *Clinical Genetics, 2,* 303–314.

Smith, C. (1976). Statistical resolution of genetic heterogeneity in familial disease. *Annals of Human Genetics, 39,* 281–291.

Smith, C.A.B. (1975). A nonparametric test for linkage with a quantitative character. *Annals of Human Genetics, 38, 451–*460.

Smith, S.D., Kimberling, W.J., Pennington, B.F., and Lubs, H.A. (1983). Specific reading disability: Identification of an inherited form through linkage analysis. *Science, 219,* 1345–1347.

Stein, J.F., and Fowler, S. (1982). Diagnosis of dyslexia by means of a new indicator of eye dominance. *British Journal of Ophthalmology, 66,* 332–336.

Switzky, H.N. (1975). Review of Lehrke, R.G.: X-linked mental retardation and verbal disability. *American Journal of Mental Deficiency, 79,* 615–616.

Vogel, F., and Motulsky, A.G. (1982). *Human genetics.* New York: Springer-Verlag.

Weinberg, W. (1910). Further contributions to the theory of inheritance. In W.G. Hill (Ed.), *Quantitative genetics: Part I. Explanation and analysis of continuous variation* (pp. 42–57). New York: Von Nostrand Reinhold. 1984.

Welsh, L.W., Healy, M., Welsh, J.J., and Cooper, B. (1982). Cortical, subcortical and brainstem dysfunction. A correlation with dyslexic children. *Annals of Otolaryngology, Rhinology, and Laryngology, 91,* 310–316.

White, R., and Skolnick, M. (1982). DNA sequence polymorphism and the genetics of epilepsy. In V.E. Anderson, W.A. Hauser, J.K. Penry, and C.F. Sing (Eds.), *Genetic basis of the epilepsies* (pp. 311–316). New York: Raven Press.

Wilson, S.R. (1971). Fitting of models of incomplete penetrance to family data. *Annals of Human Genetics, 35,* 99–108.

Wilson, S.R. (1974). Fitting of multifactor models to family data. *Annals of Human Genetics, 38,* 231–241.

Wright, S. (1921). Correlation and causation. *Journal of Agricultural Research, 20,* 557–585.

Wright, S. (1968). *Evolution and the genetics of populations, volume I.* Chicago: University of Chicago Press.

Wright, S. (1983). On "Path analysis in genetic epidemiology: A critique." *American Journal of Human Genetics, 35,* 757–768.

Chapter 3

Single Gene Analyses and Their Application to Learning Disabilities

Shelley D. Smith and
David E. Goldgar

In contrast to a quantitative genetics approach, which measures the relative contributions of genetic and environmental influences on the variation in a trait, the purpose of single gene (single major locus) analysis is to determine if that variation is largely due to the alleles at one genetic locus. There is good reason to believe that much of the genetic influence on complex behaviors such as learning ability is mediated by multifactorial inheritance, since many different components are involved, and phenotype is continuous rather than discontinuous, and both genetic and environmental factors are implicated (Herschel, 1978). However, since the turn of the century there has been the suspicion that at least one learning disability, reading disability or dyslexia, can be traced to a major gene. The confirmation of this would have certain heuristic advantages. As Kidd has noted, the multifactorial model "can provide little insight into the genetic system. The very nature of the model relegates genetic factors into an amorphous pool of small indistinguishable components" (Kidd, 1981). In contrast, the effects of a single gene can potentially be isolated and characterized. Identification of a single gene with a detectable effect on a learning disability would allow conclusions to be made on an individual rather than on a population level and would ultimately be advantageous in understanding the biologic mechanism of the genetic influence. In addition, estimation of parameters such as dominance and penetrance would be useful in genetic counseling.

A basic obstacle that has hindered genetic analyses of learning disabilities has been the lack of a good definition of the phenotype(s). Learning disabilities have traditionally been defined by exclusion of known causes; that is, academic difficulties without demonstrable physical, intellectual, or environmental handicap. Such definitions encompass a heterogeneous group of disorders. Some studies have dealt with the problem of heterogeneity by defining subtypes based on similarities on various parameters, but there has been no real evidence that the subtypes represented etiologically different disorders. Clearly, any studies that attempt to fit a particular model of inheritance to a heterogeneous population are likely to be fruitless. In any such population, there may be several single gene disorders as well as multifactorial types, and combinations of these may exist. In addition, there would be nongenetic disorders represented. It is only very recently that genetic techniques have been developed that can minimize the problem of heterogeneity or that can measure the relative contributions of these different influences in a population. However, these techniques will still require a rigorous definition of the phenotype(s) if they are to reach valid conclusions (see Chapter 4).

SEGREGATION ANALYSIS: METHODOLOGY

Some of the earliest reports of reading disability noted that it was often familial (e.g., Fisher, 1905; Hinshelwood, 1907; Stephenson, 1907; Thomas, 1905). Finucci (1978) has provided an excellent review of these and other studies that have addressed the familial nature of reading disability. Only a few researchers attempted to specify a mode of inheritance. Two descriptions of single families with several generations affected suggested that an autosomal dominant gene was responsible (Drew, 1956; Op't Hof and Guldenpfennig, 1972). Particularly in the latter study, however, individuals were cited as affected that could not be examined. Moreover, such select pedigrees may represent fortuitous clustering of individuals rather than a genetic effect.

The purpose of segregation analysis is to test whether the observed distribution of phenotypes among randomly ascertained families is consistent with a hypothesized mode of inheritance. In its simplest form, this is based on computing the segregation ratio — the proportion of affected offspring from parents of given phenotype — and testing whether the observed segregation fits the expectations of a genetic model. For example, in a mating of a person who has a given disorder with an unaffected person, 50 percent of the offspring would be expected to be affected if the disorder is due to an autosomal dominant gene (assuming that the affected parent heterozygous and the gene is completely penetrant). Obviously, such a study cannot reach statistical significance with a single small family; multiple pedigrees must be studied, and the way the families are ascertained is critical to the analysis. Ascertainment refers to how the family was selected for the study. "Complete selection" is the ideal, in which families are included without regard to the phenotypes of the children. This is rarely feasible, particularly for recessive disorders in which the heterozygotes cannot be detected and are only identified when a child is affected. Complete selection for a dominant disorder would involve studying the offspring of a random population of affected individuals; this is certainly easier than the situation with recessive disorders, but it has never been used in studies of reading disability, since attention has been focused on the diagnosis in children.

Thus, the usual mode of ascertainment through affected children is incomplete, and this automatically biases the data by guaranteeing that there is at least one affected child in each sibship. To correct for this bias, the Weinberg proband method (Weinberg, 1912) was developed in which the proband(s) (an individual through which the family is ascertained) is (are) subtracted from the sibship, and the proportion of affected and unaffected individuals remaining in the sibship is computed. Calculation of the variance of the estimated segregation ratio is dependent upon the mode of ascertainment. Other methods were also developed, but the Weinberg proband method was favored since it was simple and provided good agreement with the other procedures (Crow, 1959). However, it still had several flaws. Although affected by the ascertainment probability, it provided no way to test the assumptions made about this probability, so that precise estimates of the segregation ratio could not be made. It also could not provide any estimate of the proportion of sporadic cases (nongenetic phenocopies or new mutations) in the population. The maximum likelihood method, developed by Fisher (1934), could take these and other parameters into account and test them and was therefore much more desirable, but because of the complexity of the calculations and the iteration required, it was not extended to segregation analysis until computers became available (Morton, 1969).

The extension of these basic models to more complete and powerful methods of genetic analysis led to the development of what is now generally referred to as complex segregation analysis.

Complex segregation analysis refers to a broad class of methodologies used to determine the mode of inheritance of a particular phenotype from family data, especially with regard to elucidating single gene effects. Genetic models for complex traits serve as hypotheses relating genes and genotypes, their frequencies in the population, and other relevant variables to the phenotypes and their distribution within the family. Identification of an appropriate genetic model for a specific disorder can often provide considerable insight into the biology of that disorder and serve as impetus for further research.

With the advent of high-speed computers and sophisticated genetic analysis software, both qualitative (e.g., normal/affected) and quantitative (e.g., continuous variables such as cholesterol level) phenotypes may be analyzed under a variety of genetic models. These include the major locus model, the polygenic model, and the mixed model, which is composed of a major locus with background polygenic variation. All these models include a random environmental component, and some allow for a common sibling environmental effect. The pioneering work in the development of these models was done in the late 1960s and early 1970s by N.E. Morton (Morton, 1969; Morton and MacLean, 1974) and R.C. Elston (Elston and Stewart, 1971; Elston and Yelverton, 1975) and their collaborators. The models proposed by Morton were designed to be analyzed using nuclear family data, whereas Elston's made use of extended pedigrees but did not allow for common family environment and did not initially include the mixed model. Morton's method has since been extended to analyze extended pedigrees, and Elston's method now includes a mixed model. Recently, attempts have been made to reconcile these two approaches with a unified theory (Lalouel, Rao, Morton, and Elston, 1983).

In any model containing a major gene effect, the relationship between genotype and phenotype must be specified. For a qualitative phenotype, it is the probability that individuals of each genotype are "affected." This is the usual notion of penetrance, and it may be sex-specific or dependent upon age. For a quantitative phenotype, the relationship between genotype and phenotype is specified by the mean and standard deviation of the trait for each genotype. Thus, to return to a point made in the beginning of the chapter, any analysis is dependent upon the definition of the phenotype.

Some major gene models also incorporate transmission probabilities, τ_1, τ_2, and τ_3, which represent the probability of an individual with the respective genotypes AA, Aa, and aa transmitting allele A to their offspring. Under Mendelian segregation, $\tau_1 = 1.0$, $\tau_2 = 0.5$, and $\tau_3 = 0.0$, whereas if the offspring "genotypes" are independent of the parental types — that is, not under genetic influence — these transmission probabilities are equal.

Hypotheses regarding the mode of transmission of a given trait are tested by first finding the values of the unknown parameters (e.g., penetrance and τ values) in the model that best fit the pedigree data (unconstrained model). This is usually accomplished using numerical optimization techniques. Next, the likelihood of the pedigree(s) are recalculated with the parameters fixed at their values corresponding to the hypothesis of interest. The log of the ratio of the two likelihoods gives a measure that can be used to test whether the hypothesis should be rejected. A series of hypotheses or subhypotheses are each tested in this manner. Ideally, all but one of these hypotheses could be rejected; for example, in a simple case, a researcher would want to reject the "environmental" hypothesis while not rejecting a Mendelian hypothesis. In reality, more than one model with various combinations of single gene, multiple gene, and environmental influences may be compatible with the data, and other methods are necessary to decide between alternate hypotheses.

As in the case of simple segregation analysis, attention must be paid to the way a family was sampled or ascertained; in practice, however, it is often difficult to determine the precise method under which a family was ascertained. This is especially true for large, multigenerational pedigrees. Appropriate correction of the segregation analysis for ascertainment bias remains a controversial topic in the implementation of these methods.

Among the primary computer programs available to estimate parameters and test hypotheses of these models are GENPED (Kaplan and Elston, 1972), POINTER (Lalouel and Morton, 1981), and PAP (Hasstedt and Cartwright, 1981). Owing to the large amount of computer time involved in the simultaneous estimation of these parameters in a large data set, it is sometimes useful to employ some simple screening procedures to examine the data for evidence of a major gene before using the more complex type of analysis described previously. Several such methods are available and include the sibship variance test (Fain, 1976) and the various SEDA (Structured Exploratory Data Analysis) statistics proposed by Karlin and coworkers (Karlin, Williams, and Carmelli, 1981; Karlin and Williams, 1981). These methods all assume that the phenotype under study is a quantitative one, and all use the nuclear family as the basic sampling unit. Although they have the advantages of being easily computed and not dependent on a particular genetic model, these screening tests are generally not very powerful; that is, they may not identify a major gene unless its effect is quite large compared with background genetic and environmental effects. A comparison of several of these statistics and an examination of their sensitivity and specificity is provided by Kammerer, MacCluer, and Bridges (1984).

APPLICATION OF SEGREGATION ANALYSIS TO READING DISABILITY

Hallgren (1950) performed the first recognized study that attempted to test the hypothesis of dominant inheritance of reading disability using forms of segregation analysis that were available at the time. He studied

112 families having at least one child with reading disability ascertained through his clinical population. He used the Weinberg proband method and found fairly good agreement with an autosomal dominant mode of inheritance, in that the segregation ratios obtained were within two standard deviations of expectation. It was also noted that there were more boys and men affected than girls and women among the siblings and parents of probands, but since sex-linked forms of inheritance could be ruled out, the excess of affected boys and men was thought to be due to interaction with other independent factors, genetic and nongenetic, which would make them more susceptible to a "generalized dyslexia." Perhaps the greatest flaw in this study, which was acknowledged by Hallgren, is that the classification of siblings and parents was not done as carefully as it was for the probands. As Finucci (1978) pointed out, he also tended to discount other possible nongenetic causes of dyslexia if those factors were also found in families with multiple affected members.

Sladen (1970) pursued the finding of excess boys and men in Hallgren's data and suggested that this could result from a single gene that was dominant in boys but recessive in girls; that is, that heterozygous boys would be affected, but girls had to be homozygous to show the disorder. Using estimates of frequency of reading disability in the population and the frequency of affected girls and women, she generated expected frequencies and penetrances for the various genotypes. This was proposed as a model to be tested and was not applied to any actual data.

Zahalkova, Vrzal, and Kloboukova (1972) used segregation analysis techniques to test the hypothesis of autosomal dominant inheritance, but their methodology precludes any conclusions from their results. Twenty-nine families with a positive family history of reading disability were selected from their clinic population. If a parent was affected, he or she was also included as a proband, and his or her sibship was added, thus increasing their population to 49 families. This is an unorthodox procedure; since the ascertainment of the parent was not independent of the ascertainment of the child, the parent is not a true proband. They had few female probands, so 38 more families were added. The method of ascertainment of these families was not specified. The method of classification of probands and of relatives was not described, but it was noted that several individuals, mostly female, were unaffected but were "obligate carriers" in that they were in the line of descent of a putative gene. It is not clear whether these individuals were included as "affected" in the ensuing segregation analyses, but the authors stated that the analyses "started from the genotype" (which was inferred from an autosomal dominant model) so it is likely that they were. Not surprisingly, the segregation was consistent with an autosomal dominant mode of inheritance, with the conclusion that there was sex limitation, in that women did not always manifest the gene.

An alternate mode of inheritance was proposed by Symmes and Rapoport (1972). In their study of 54 carefully defined disabled readers, only one was female. They also noted that the affected children had very good spatial visualization abilities. At that time, spatial visualization was thought to be X-linked, so their finding, along with the paucity of affected girls, led them to postulate that specific reading disability was X-linked. Although they noted that this would produce very characteristic pedigrees (e.g., no male-to-male transmission), no family histories were examined.

Thus, the first studies that tried to determine a mode of inheritance for reading disability suffered from various problems of design or diagnosis. In addition, Finucci, Guthrie, Childs, Abbey, and Childs (1976) pointed out one other possible complication, that of genetic heterogeneity. They studied 20 families, testing all family members and using rigorous criteria for classification, and found that the pedigrees did not fit any one mode of single gene inheritance. Multifactorial inheritance also could not be ruled out, but the pattern of affected males and females did not support a multifactorial threshold model with males (the most frequently affected sex) having a lower threshold. In addition, it was noted that the siblings of the more severely affected probands were more likely to show wider variation in reading ability, whereas the siblings of mildly affected probands showed less variation, tending to be mildly affected or normal readers. This suggested a major gene effect to the authors (Childs and Finucci, 1979). Unfortunately, the population was not large enough to allow a segregation analysis that was sophisticated enough to distinguish between multifactorial or single gene inheritance or genetic heterogeneity. Only one study, that of Lewitter, DeFries, and Elston (1980), has incorporated testing of all family members, advanced methods of segregation analysis, and considerations of genetic heterogeneity.

The population in the study by Lewitter and associates was 133 families included in the Colorado Family Reading study. All family members were tested. Instead of designating individuals as "affected" and "unaffected" for the segregation analysis, a continuous discriminant score derived from the various tests was used as the phenotype. This represents another advancement in the development of segregation analysis that is particularly useful in behavior genetics. Behavioral phenotypes are rarely discontinuous, and use of the measure itself rather than an arbitrarily determined dichotomization of the variable may be a more accurate expression of the genotype. However, this assumes that the variable actually measures something that is closely related to the gene product; if the nature of the trait being studied is not well-defined, this may make the use of the variable less, rather than more, informative. The use of a composite score such as a discriminant score may compensate for this danger somewhat (Matthysse and Kidd, 1981), but there is still no way to test whether the measure actually relates to the genotype. In the study by Lewitter and coworkers, the use of a variable based on testing may have been particularly misleading for adults, who may have compensated for an earlier reading disability.

When segregation analysis was performed on the population as a whole, several different hypotheses were tested. No support was found for autosomal dominant inheritance, autosomal recessive inheritance, codominant inheritance, dominance at a locus without the segregation specified, or strictly environmental (nongenetic) transmission. However, one or all of these mechanisms could have been operating in different subsets of the population, so the population was subdivided into families with male probands, those with female probands, and those with severely affected probands. In addition, children alone were analysed, since the measures may not have been reliable for adults. None of the hypotheses tested were supported by the data from the families with male probands, but autosomal recessive inheritance could not be rejected in the families with female probands. In the families with severely affected probands, the only hypotheses rejected were autosomal dominant and autosomal recessive inheritance, and the analysis of the children alone suggested codominant inheritance. In addition, a multifactorial-threshold model was not supported by the data. The authors concluded that if there was a genetic component, it was either polygenic or more complex than the models that were tested, or it was genetically heterogeneous and their subdivision of the population was not sensitive to the genetic differences. They favored the latter interpretation.

The types of segregation analysis just described are not able to take heterogeneity into account unless the population is quite large. This is a major problem in the study of behavioral disorders that do not have a clearcut (e.g., biologic) means of diagnosis and thus may have both genetic and nongenetic causes. Goldin, Kidd, Matthysse, and Gershon (1981) have noted that in such cases, segregation analysis is "limited but useful." Other variations of segregation analysis have been suggested, including pedigree analysis, which has the advantage of increasing the chances of homogeneity by studying large pedigrees with multiple affected individuals who presumably share the same causation. (Kidd, 1981; Pauls, 1983). Anderson, Chern, and Schwanebeck (1981) have also presented a model for studying common heterogeneous disorders by examining affected pairs of siblings. Through simulation studies they were able to demonstrate that a high percentage of sib pairs will have the same cause for their disorder and thus may point out characteristics that can be useful in the diagnosis of genetically different entities. Matthysse (1978) has also discussed the importance of grouping families by characteristics of the probands that may relate to a gene defect and emphasized the consideration that "outliers" in a study may represent etiologically different entities.

Moll, Berry, Weidman, Ellefson, Gordon, and Kottke (1984) have discussed how complex segregation analysis can be used to detect genetic heterogeneity between pedigrees. Segregation analysis, however, cannot distinguish between two distinct major genes resulting in similar phenotypes. While complex segregation analysis is useful for the detection of major genes governing a particular phenotype, it suffers from being critically dependent on the adequacy of the underlying genetic and environmental model that is assumed. However, if an appreciable proportion of the phenotypic variability can be accounted for by demonstrating a linkage relationship with a well-defined genetic marker system, it is difficult to avoid the conclusion that there is a major locus directly influencing that phenotype.

LINKAGE ANALYSIS: METHODOLOGY

Linkage analysis represents a very different approach to the analysis of major genes. Whereas segregation analysis is based on the fit of the data to the predictions of genetic models, linkage analysis tests whether the trait in question is transmitted in nonrandom fashion with another trait that is known to be genetic. This nonrandom segregation, or linkage, results when two genes are located close together on the same chromosome. Under unlinked conditions, the transmission of an allele derived from a given parent has no effect on the transmission of alleles for another trait. That is, the transmission of a paternally derived allele at one locus has no influence on whether a maternally or paternally derived allele at another locus is transmitted. However, the alleles for genes that are close together on the same chromosome tend to be inherited together. Thus, if the paternally derived allele for one trait is transmitted to a given child, the paternally derived allele for a linked trait will also be transmitted. The exception to this is the result of recombination, the exchange of alleles between the paternally derived and maternally derived homologs. The farther apart the linked genes are on the chromosome, the more likely it is that recombination will occur between them; if they are far enough apart, they behave essentially as unlinked genes. The proportion of recombinant offspring, termed the recombination fraction, is related to the distance between the genes. This will range from 0.00 recombination, indicating complete linkage, to 0.50, indicating no linkage.

Linkage is detected by comparing the segregation patterns of pairs of traits in families, testing to see if there is deviation from the expectations of independent (unlinked) assortment. Evidence for linkage is assessed by taking the ratio of the likelihood of the observed pattern of phenotypes at the two loci under the hypothesis of independent assortment (recombination fraction of 0.50) with the likelihoods of the pedigree at recombination fractions of 0.00, 0.05, 0.10, 0.20, 0.30, and 0.40. Since the number of offspring in a single family is rarely enough to give a statistically significant result, the log of each of these ratios is taken so that results from different families can be summed. This *log* of the *od*ds of likelihood of linkage is termed the LOD score. The recombination fraction that gives the highest total LOD score over all of the families is determined. The hypothesis of linkage is accepted when the maximum LOD score is greater than 3.0 (1000:1 odds in favor of linkage). Conversely, a LOD score of -2.0 (100:1 odds against linkage) is considered evidence for rejection of the hypothesis of linkage. The most commonly used computer program for linkage analysis of family data is LIPED (Ott, 1974).

Ascertainment of families for linkage analysis is quite different from the ascertainment for segregation analysis. Particularly if heterogeneity is suspected, with an admixture of polygenic and nongenetic types as well as a single gene type, selection of families for linkage analysis is biased toward those most likely to manifest a single gene. This may mean that families showing several generations of affected individuals, or those consistent with Mendelian transmission, are selected for linkage analysis. Unlike segregation analysis, such biases do not invalidate the analysis and are likely to be necessary for there to be any chance of detecting a major gene.

The definition of the phenotype in behavioral disorders is often inconsistent between investigators and may not be well documented within a study. The early studies of schizophrenia are good examples of this. The genetic influences were not verified until the diagnostic criteria became uniformly specified and studies became more rigorous in their requirements that relatives be examined instead of relying on historical information. Unfortunately, studies of learning disabilities, dyslexia in particular, have not yet reached this stage of sophistication. Ideas about what constitutes dyslexia and how to detect it are very different between studies. As with segregation analysis, linkage analysis can also utilize a continuous variable as the measure of the trait in question, instead of a dichotomous "affected-unaffected" determination. If the continuous variable is an accurate reflection of the gene effect, it can be much more powerful than an arbitrary classification; on the other hand, if it encompasses unrelated abilities, it may not reflect the presence of the gene (cf. Smith, Kimberling, Goldgar, Pennington, and Lubs, 1985).

Inaccurate definition of the phenotype will very likely be fatal to the detection of linkage; however, it is very unlikely that inaccurate diagnosis will lead to a spurious linkage (Morton, 1956; Spence, 1981). Thus, if a linkage is found, even with a rather vague definition of the trait, it can still be presumed that a major gene is present that influences the trait. Further studies can then be done with appropriate family members to refine the definition of the trait. If genetic heterogeneity is detected, studies can be directed toward clinical delineation of the genetically different disorders.

The necessity of being able to trace the transmission of alleles in a family leads to the requirement that at least one parent be heterozygous for both the genes being tested, so it may be determined if there is preferential transmission of alleles by that parent. Otherwise, no matter how large the family, the offspring are not informative and the data cannot be used. This is one of the hazards of linkage analysis. Another problem is that of expense; since the researcher usually has no idea of which genes may be linked, the strategy has been to compare the segregation of a given gene against that of a battery of other "marker" genes. This battery is made up of traits that are polymorphic; that is, that have at least two alleles, the rarest having a frequency of at least 2 percent in the population. This increases the chance that the parent who is heterozygous at the test locus is also heterozygous at the marker locus. For efficiency, the traits should also be easily determined. Generally, blood groups and enzyme markers have been used; more recently, restriction fragment length polymorphisms (RFLPs) have been developed. RFLPs are based upon variations in the genetic code itself and are quite numerous, and more are being developed each year. This has provided a tremendous impetus to linkage analysis, since the more genes that are available, spaced uniformly throughout the genome, the greater the likelihood that one of them will be linked to the gene in question (Botstein, White, Skolnick, and David, 1980).

USES OF LINKAGE INFORMATION

The traditional purpose of linkage analysis has been gene mapping, the determination of the location and order of the genes on the various chromosomes. More recently, it has been recognized that linkage can be used to demonstrate that a trait is influenced by a single gene. If the transmission of a known genetic trait and a trait that is suspected of having a single gene influence fulfill the requirements of linkage, it is assumed that the unknown trait is influenced by a gene located near the known gene.

One of the major advantages of linkage analysis is its ability to detect genetic heterogeneity. This can be seen when some families show linkage of the trait in question to a given marker and may even give evidence for linkage to a different marker. The ability to detect heterogeneity is dependent upon the number of families of each type available and upon the tightness of the linkage, so that discrepancies between groups of families can be seen. Genetic heterogeneity is detected by comparison of the LOD scores from individual families or predefined groups of families with the overall set of LOD scores obtained from the entire sample. Specific methods for detecting this type of heterogeneity can be found in Morton (1956), Smith (1963), Ott (1977, 1983), and Hodge, Anderson, Neiswanger, Sparkes, and Rimoin (1983).

The presence of a linked marker gene can be very useful in research and in genetic counseling, particularly in disorders with a late age of onset or with reduced penetrance, where an individual's genotype at the trait in question cannot be determined. Nei (1977) and Chakravarti and Nei (1982) have discussed how this information can be used under various circumstances of inheritance and family structure, and Price and Kidd (1984) have developed a method using the computer program LIPED to figure the likelihood of a pedigree given the data on the linked marker(s) so that the most accurate recurrance risks can be figured. The program PAP will also assess the risk to an individual in the pedigree of being a given genotype at the disease locus given the pedigree and marker data. The recent finding of a restriction fragment length polymorphism linked to Huntington's disease (Gusella et al., 1983) is dramatic example of the application of linkage analysis to genetic counseling. With this marker, family studies can indicate which individuals at risk for inheriting the gene have actually received it, before any of the symptoms appear (Conneally, Wallace, Gusella, and Wexler, 1984). Although this obviously is an emotionally loaded proposition, some at-risk individuals do want to know their status before they decide to have children. A less volatile situation would be the early detection of children at risk for a particular learning disability, allowing for early intervention rather than waiting for the child to fail in school.

A separate phenomenon that should be distinguished from linkage is association. Association occurs when specific phenotypes are found together in a population more frequently than would be expected by chance. This differs from linkage, in which certain phenotypes segregate nonrandomly within a family, but the population as a whole shows random assortment between phenotypes. Association may be due to epistasis; that is, the genotype may actually function to produce a susceptibility to a particular disorder. It could also result from linkage disequilibrium, in which two genes are so tightly linked that recombination between them is very rare and balance between the different alleles has not been reached. Association can suggest a genetic influence on susceptibility to a disorder, but it does not prove that a single gene is present.

Nevertheless, knowledge of the association between a disorder and a given allele can be useful in genetic counseling, in much the same way that a linked marker gene is used. The presence of disequilibrium between linked genes increases the utility of marker genes in genetic counseling, since the alleles for the trait and the marker are much more likely to be inherited together (Chakravarti and Nei, 1982). Conte and Rotter (1984) have also shown how the combination of information from linkage within the family and association in the population at large can be used to predict an individual's genotype. For example, if an individual is shown through linkage analysis to have inherited a major gene with an influence on diabetes and also has the HLA haplotype associated with diabetes in the population as a whole, that person's susceptibility to diabetes may be higher than that of a person who has just the major gene or the susceptible haplotype. This could be particularly useful in disorders that are influenced by more than one locus, as one would anticipate with complex behavioral disorders.

APPLICATIONS OF LINKAGE ANALYSIS TO BEHAVIORAL DISORDERS

Linkage analysis with specific reading disability tentatively localized a major gene to chromosome 15. A LOD score of 3.241 was obtained between reading disability and chromosome 15 heteromorphisms at a recombination fraction of 0.13 (Smith, Kimberling, Pennington, and Lubs, 1983). Within the eight families for which linkage data was available, one family had markedly negative LOD scores, which could suggest heterogeneity; however, a test for heterogeneity (Morton, 1956) was not significant. Since then, eight more families have been ascertained by Pennington. Four of these also showed recombination between the chromosome 15 heteromorphisms and reading disability. Again, Morton's (1956) test for heterogeneity of LOD scores over all 16 families was not quite significant ($X^2_{15} = 23.73$, $p < 0.10$). Further studies with larger families will be needed to detect heterogeneity of linkage. Replication of the linkage with an RFLP localized to chromosome 15 would be especially valuable. Not only would it confirm the existence of a major gene on chromosome 15, but it would be a much easier marker to type and could be used to find probe sequences even closer to the gene. Linkage studies have been done with the eight families in the replication study using two probes from chromosome 15, but close linkage with reading disability was excluded for both. However, close linkage with the centromeric markers was also excluded, so the probe sequences may be too distant from the putative gene.

Studies investigating the phenotype in the families in the initial study have noted particular characteristics in spelling and neuropsychologic variables suggestive of problems in auditory processing of linguistic information (Pennington, McCabe, Smith, Kimberling, and Lubs, 1985; Smith, Pennington, McCabe, Kimberling, and Lubs, 1985). These studies are being continued and expanded, and it will be particularly interesting if genetic heterogeneity is confirmed and is reflected phenotypically. This illustrates the "bottom-up" approach of going from the genetic information to more precise definition of the phenotype, leading then to exposition of the gene effect.

In some families, affective disorder has appeared to be inherited as an X-linked trait, and linkage analysis with X-linked markers would confirm the existence of a gene on the X chromosome for affective disorder. The results of these studies have been inconclusive, with some studies indicating linkage with markers on the X-chromosome and with others showing nonlinkage (see Spence, 1981, or Risch and Baron, 1982, for reviews). Genetic heterogeneity may be a factor, as well as problems of reduced penetrance, assortative mating, association, or a combination of these, rather than linkage (Spence, 1981).

Examples of the application of linkage analysis to the search for major genes in behavioral disorders are limited. This is partly a result of problems in the definition of phenotype, but it is also because of the expense and unsure outcome of linkage analysis in the past. This situation may be altered by the development of restriction fragment length polymorphisms. The establishment of linkage between Huntington's disease and an RFLP on chromosome 4 (Gusella et al., 1983) is a good example of this. Although it had been clear that Huntington's disease was due to an autosomal dominant gene, attempts to find a linkage had been negative with the traditional genotyping markers. This was merely because there were no genotyping markers in the correct region of chromosome 4. The potential for development of a battery of RFLPs that cover the entire genome will make it virtually certain that, if a dominant gene exists for a trait, there will be a marker within detectable distance to it.

An example of behavioral disorder for which linkage analysis is appropriate is Gilles de la Tourette syndrome, which is a syndrome of multiple vocal or muscle tics, or both. The results of complex segregation analysis using the program POINTER were consistent with a major gene (Comings, Comings, Devor, and Cloninger, 1984; Devor, 1984), and, as Devor (1984) noted, linkage analysis in segregating families would serve to prove the existence of the gene. This disorder is particularly relevant to the study of learning disabilities, since reading disability and other neuropsychologic deficits have been reported in affected persons (Eldridge, Sweet, Lake, Ziegler, and Shapiro, 1977; Incagnoli and Kane, 1981; Nee, Caine, Polinsky, Eldridge, and Ebert, 1980; O'Quinn and Thompson, 1980). In addition, Comings and Comings (1984) have reported an association between Attention Deficit Disorder (ADD) and Tourette syndrome and have suggested that they both may be caused by the same gene in some families; however, studies by Pauls, Hurst, Kruger, Leckman, Cohen, and Kidd (1984) did not indicate that the two disorders cosegregated. The use of a linked marker to verify who actually carries the Tourette gene would make it possible to document whether or not ADD is present in Tourette gene carriers.

SUMMARY

The parallel development of complex segregation analysis methodology and restriction fragment length polymorphisms for linkage analysis has made detection of major genes in heterogeneous behavioral disorders much more feasible. Segregation analysis can be used to establish the possibility that a major gene effect exists and to estimate its influence in the population of affected individuals, and linkage analysis can confirm the existence of a specific gene, localize it in the genome, and detect genetic heterogeneity. In addition, the two techniques may be combined in one analysis. With the rapid advancement in computer capabilities, models can be developed that incorporate parameters relating to segregation analysis (e.g., penetrance and gene frequencies) along with linkage marker data and association data (Risch, 1984). The incorporation of disequilibrium (association) and recombination fraction (linkage) parameters into the complex segregation analysis allows for more precise determination of the mode of inheritance of a particular trait and permits more accurate estimation of all parameters in the model. This approach may be especially fruitful for analyzing complex disorders such as learning disabilities.

Ultimately, the confirmation that a single gene exists and its localization can be the first steps toward identifying the gene's function, its regulation, and its interaction with other genes.

REFERENCES

Anderson, V.E., Chern, M.M., and Schwanebeck, E. (1981). Multiplex families and the problem of heterogeneity. In E.S. Gershon, S. Matthysse, X.O. Breakefield, and R.D. Ciaranello (Eds.), *Genetic research strategies for psychobiology and psychiatry* (pp. 341–351). Pacific Grove, CA: Boxwood Press.

Botstein, D., White, R.L., Skolnick, M., and David, R.W. (1980). Construction of a genetic linkage map using restriction fragment length polymorphisms. *American Journal of Human Genetics, 32,* 314–331.

Chakravarti, A., and Nei, M. (1982). Utility and efficiency of linked marker genes for genetic counseling. II. Identification of linkage phase by offspring phenotypes. *American Journal of Human Genetics, 34,* 531–551.

Childs, B., and Finucci, J.M. (1979). The genetics of learning disabilities. *Ciba Foundation Symposium, 66,* 359–376.

Comings, D.E., and Comings, B.G. (1984). Tourette's syndrome and Attention Deficit Disorder with hyperactivity: Are they genetically related? *Journal of the American Academy of Child Psychiatry, 23,* 138–146.

Comings, D.E., Comings, B.G., Devor, E.J., and Cloninger, C.R. (1984). Detection of major gene for Gilles de la Tourette syndrome. *American Journal of Human Genetics, 36,* 586–600.

Conneally, P.M., Wallace, M.R., Gusella, J.F., and Wexler, N.S. (1984). Huntington disease: Estimation of heterozygote status using linked genetic markers. *Genetic Epidemiology, 1,* 81–88.

Conte, W.J., and Rotter, J.I. (1984). The use of association data to identify family members at high risk for marker-linked diseases. *American Journal of Human Genetics, 36,* 152–166.

Crow, J.F. (1959). Problems of ascertainment in the analysis of family data. In J.V. Neel, M. Shaw, and W.J. Schull (Eds.), *Genetics and epidemiology of diseases* (pp. 23–44). Washington, DC: Department of Health, Education and Welfare.

Devor, E.J. (1984). Complex segregation analysis of Gilles de la Tourette syndrome: Further evidence for a major locus mode of transmission. *American Journal of Human Genetics, 36,* 704–709.

Drew, A.L. (1956). A neurological appraisal of familial congenital word-blindness. *Brain, 79,* 440–460.

Eldridge, R., Sweet, R., Lake, C.R., Ziegler, M., and Shapiro, A. (1977). Gilles de la Tourette syndrome: Clinical, genetic, psychologic and biochemical aspects in 21 selected families. *Neurology, 27,* 115–124.

Elston, R.C., and Stewart, J. (1971). A general model for the genetic analysis of pedigree data. *Human Heredity, 21,* 523–542.

Elston, R.C., and Yelverton, K.C. (1975). General models for segregation analysis. *American Journal of Human Genetics, 27, 31*–45.

Fain, P.R. (1976). *Major gene analysis: An alternative approach to the study of the genetics of human behavior.* Unpublished doctoral dissertation, University of Colorado, Boulder, Colorado.

Finucci, J.M. (1978). Genetic considerations in dyslexia. In H.R. Myklebust (Ed.), *Progress in learning disabilities, Vol. IV* (pp. 41–63). New York: Grune and Stratton.

Finucci, J.M., Guthrie, J.T., Childs, A.L., Abbey, H., and Childs, B. (1976). The genetics of specific reading disability. *Annals of Human Genetics (London), 40,* 1–23.

Fisher, J. (1905). Case of congenital word-blindness (inability to read). *Ophthalmic Review, 24,* 315–318.

Fisher, R.A. (1934). The effects of methods of ascertainment upon the estimation of frequencies. *Annals of Eugenics, 8,* 255–262.

Goldin, L.R., Kidd, K.K., Matthysse, S., and Gershon, E.S. (1981). The power of pedigree segregation analysis for traits with incomplete penetrance. In E.S. Gershon, S. Matthysse, X.O. Breakefield and R.D. Ciaranello (Eds.), *Genetic research strategies for psychobiology and psychiatry* (pp. 305–317). Pacific Grove, CA: Boxwood Press.

Gusella, J.F., Wexler, N.S., Conneally, P.M., Naylor, S.L., Anderson, M.A., Tanzi, R.E., Watkins, P.C., Ottina, K., Wallace, M.R., Sakaguchi, A.Y., Young, A.B., Shoulson, I., Bonilla, E., and Martin, J.B. (1983). A polymorphic DNA marker genetically linked to Huntington's disease. *Nature, 306,* 234–238.

Hallgren, B. (1950). Specific dyslexia ("congenital word-blindness"): A clinical and genetic study. *Acta Psychiatrica et Neurologica Scandinavia, Supplement 65.*

Hasstedt, S.J., and Cartwright, P.E. (1981). *PAP: Pedigree analysis package* (Tech. Rep. No. 13). Salt Lake City: University of Utah, Department of Medical Biophysics and Computing.

Herschel, M. (1978). Dyslexia revisited: A review. *Human Genetics, 40,* 115–134.

Hinshelwood, J. (1907). Four cases of congenital word-blindness occurring in the same family. *British Medical Journal, 1,* 608–609.

Hodge, S.E., Anderson, C.E., Neiswanger, K., Sparkes, R.S., and Rimoin, D.L. (1983). The search for heterogeneity in insulin-dependent diabetes mellitus (IDDM): Linkage studies, two-locus models, and genetic heterogeneity. *American Journal of Human Genetics, 35,* 1139–1155.

Incagnoli, T., and Kane, R. (1981). Neuropsychological functioning in Gilles de la Tourette syndrome. *Journal of Clinical Neuropsychology, 3,* 165–169.

Kammerer, C.M., MacCluer, J.W., and Bridges, J.M. (1984). An evaluation of three statistics of Structured Exploratory Data Analysis. *American Journal of Human Genetics, 36,* 187–196.

Kaplan, E.B., and Elston, R.C. (1972). *A subroutine package of maximum likelihood estimation (MAX-LIK)* (Mimeo Series, No. 823). Chapel Hill: University of North Carolina, Institute of Statistics.

Karlin, S., and Williams, P.T. (1981). Structured exploratory data analysis (SEDA) for determining mode of inheritance of quantitative traits. II. Simulation studies on the effect of ascertaining families through high-valued probands. *American Journal of Human Genetics, 33,* 282–292.

Karlin, S., Williams, P.T., and Carmelli, D. (1981). Structured exploratory data analysis (SEDA) for determining mode of inheritance of quantitative traits. I. Simulation studies on the effect of background distributions. *American Journal of Human Genetics, 33,* 262–281.

Kidd, K. (1981). Genetic models for psychiatric disorders. In E.S. Gershon, S. Matthysse, X.O. Breakefield, and R.D. Ciaranello (Eds.), *Genetic research strategies for psychobiology and psychiatry* (pp. 369–382). Pacific Grove, CA: Boxwood Press.

Lalouel, J.M., and Morton, N.E. (1981). Complex segregation analysis with pointers. *Human Heredity, 31,* 312–321.

Lalouel, J.M., Rao, D.C., Morton, N.E., and Elston, R.C. (1983). A unified model for complex segregation analysis. *American Journal of Human Genetics, 35,* 816–826.

Lewitter, F.I., DeFries, J.C., and Elston, R.C. (1980). Genetic models of reading disability. *Behavior Genetics, 10,* 9–30.

Matthysse, S. (1978). Etiological diversity in the psychoses. In N.E. Morton and C.S. Chung (Eds.), *Genetic epidemiology* (pp. 311–328). New York: Academic Press.

Matthysse, S., and Kidd, K.K. (1981). Pattern recognition in genetic analysis. In E.S. Gershon, S. Matthysse, X.O. Breakefield, and R.D. Ciaranello (Eds.), *Genetic research strategies for psychobiology and psychiatry* (pp. 333–339). Pacific Grove, CA: Boxwood Press.

Moll, P.P., Berry, T.D., Weidman, W.H., Ellefson, T., Gordon, H., and Kottke, B. (1984). Detection of genetic heterogeneity among pedigrees through complex segregation analysis: An application to hypercholesterolemia. *American Journal of Human Genetics, 36,* 197–211.

Morton, N.E. (1956). The detection and estimation of linkage between the genes for elliptocytosis and the Rh blood type. *American Journal of Human Genetics, 8,* 80–96.

Morton, N.E. (1969). The detection of major genes under additive continuous variation. *American Journal of Human Genetics, 19,* 23–24.

Morton, N.E., and MacLean, C.J. (1974). Analysis of family resemblance. III: Complex segregation analysis of quantitative traits. *American Journal of Human Genetics, 26,* 489–503.

Nee, L.E., Caine, E.D., Polinsky, R.J., Eldridge, R., and Ebert, M.H. (1980). Gilles de la Tourette syndrome: Clinical and family study of 50 cases. *Annals of Neurology, 7,* 41–49.

Nei, M. (1977). Utility and efficiency of linked marker genes for genetic counseling. *Proceedings of the 41st Session of the International Statistical Institute* (pp. 698–711), New Delhi.

Op't Hof, J., and Guldenpfennig, W.M. (1972). Dominant inheritance of specific reading disability. *South African Medical Journal, 46,* 737–738.

O'Quinn, A.N., and Thompson, R.J. (1980). Tourette's syndrome: An expanded view. *Pediatrics, 66,* 420–424.

Ott, J. (1974). Estimation of the recombination fraction in human pedigrees: Efficient computation of the likelihood for human studies. *American Journal of Human Genetics, 26,* 588–597.

Ott, J. (1977). Counting methods (EM algorithn) in human pedigree analysis: Linkage and segregation analysis. *Annals of Human Genetics, 40,* 443–454.

Ott, J. (1983). Linkage analysis of family classification under heterogeneity. *Annals of Human Genetics, 47,* 311–320.

Pauls, D.L. (1983). Genetic analysis of family pedigree data: A review of methodology. In C.L. Ludlow and J.A. Cooper (Eds.), *Genetic aspects of speech and language disorders* (pp. 139–148). New York: Academic Press.

Pauls, D., Hurst, C., Kruger, S., Leckman, J., Cohen, D., and Kidd, K. (1984). Evidence against a genetic relationship between Tourette syndrome and attention deficit disorder. *American Journal of Human Genetics, 36,* 68S.

Pennington, B.F., McCabe, L.L., Smith, S.D., Kimberling, W.J., and Lubs, H.A. (1985). The spelling phenotype in a form of familial dyslexia. Manuscript submitted for publication.

Price, A.R., and Kidd, K.K. (1984). Utilizing automated methods to improve estimates of recurrence risk with linked genetic markers. *American Journal of Medical Genetics, 17,* 621–625.

Risch, N. (1984). Segregation analysis incorporating linkage markers. I. Single-locus models with an application to type I diabetes. *American Journal of Human Genetics, 36,* 363–386.

Risch, N., and Baron, M. (1982). X-linkage and genetic heterogeneity in bipolar-related major affective illness: Reanalysis of linkage data. *Annals of Human Genetics, 46,* 153–166.

Sladen, B. (1970). Inheritance of dyslexia. *Bulletin of the Orton Society, 20,* 30–40.

Smith, C.A.B. (1963). Testing for heterogeneity of recombination values in human genetics. *Annals of Human Genetics, 27,* 175–182.

Smith, S.D., Kimberling, W.J., Goldgar, D.E., Pennington, B.F., and Lubs, H.A. (in press). The use of linkage analysis in the study of behavioral and cognitive disorders. In D. Gray, R. Plomin, and J. Johnston (Eds.), *Developmental behavior genetics, behavior analysis, and learning.* Hillsdale, NJ: Lawrence Erlbaum Associates.

Smith, S.D., Kimberling, W.J., Pennington, B.F., and Lubs, H.A. (1983). Specific reading disability: Identification of an inherited form through linkage analysis. *Science, 219,* 1345–1347.

Smith, S.D., Pennington, B.F., McCabe, L.L., Kimberling, W.J., and Lubs, H.A. (1985). The cognitive phenotype in a form of familial reading disability. Manuscript submitted for publication.

Spence, M.A. (1981). Linkage methods in psychiatric disorders. In E.S. Gershon, S. Matthysse, X.O. Breakefield, and R.D. Ciaranello (Eds.), *Genetic research strategies for psychobiology and psychiatry* (pp. 295–304). Pacific Grove, CA: Boxwood Press.

Stephenson, S. (1907). Six cases of congenital word-blindness affecting three generations of one family. *Ophthalmoscope, 5,* 482–484.

Symmes, J.S., and Rapoport, J.L. (1972). Unexpected reading failure. *American Journal of Orthopsychiatry, 42,* 82–91.

Thomas, C. (1905). Congenital word-blindness and its treatment. *Ophthalmoscope, 3,* 380–385.

Weinberg, W. (1912). Methode und Fehlerquellen der Untersuchung auf Mendleschen Zahlen beim Menschen. *Archiv for Rassen- und Gesellschafts-Biologic, Einschliesslich Rassen- und Gesellschafts-Hygiene, 9,* 165–174.

Zahalkova, M., Vrzal, V., and Kloboukova, E. (1972). Genetical investigations in dyslexia. *Journal of Medical Genetics, 9,* 48–52.

PART II
THE CHARACTERISTICS OF LEARNING DISABILITIES: PHENOTYPIC STUDIES

Chapter 4

Issues in the Diagnosis and Phenotype Analysis of Dyslexia: Implications for Family Studies

Bruce F. Pennington

A number of chapters in this book describe the powerful genetic techniques that are becoming increasingly available for the study of inherited, complex behavior disorders, including learning disabilities. Yet the utility of these techniques is directly affected by how we define the behavioral phenotype in question. In this chapter are addressed the issues and problems that arise in phenotype definition in the study of dyslexia. Since some of these issues and problems are common to the study of any inherited behavioral disorder, these are discussed first and then the specific case of dyslexia is covered. Hence, the chapter is organized into three main sections: (1) general issues of diagnosis and phenotype analysis; (2) diagnostic issues in dyslexia; and (3) phenotype analysis in dyslexia. There is also a brief concluding section.

GENERAL ISSUES OF DIAGNOSIS AND PHENOTYPE ANALYSIS

We now have fairly convincing evidence that a number of complex behavioral disorders, including schizophrenia, major depression, and

This research was supported by a Research Scientist Development Award (MH00419-02) and a project grant (MH38820-01) from the National Institute of Mental Health, as well as by a grant from the March of Dimes (12-135). Helpful comments on an earlier version were provided by Susan Brady, Richard Olson, Marilyn Welsh, and Dianne Lefly.

dyslexia, among others, are genetically based. Some of these disorders have traditionally been considered in the province of psychiatry, whereas others have fallen in the province of neurology. What is important at this point is that all of them appear to be caused in part by an inherited brain defect, which eventually expresses itself in behavior and in some or all cases eventually results in a diagnosable case of the disorder in question.

However, the elucidation of the specific neurogenetics for any one of these disorders is much more difficult than accumulating indirect evidence that the disorder falls in the general neurogenetic category. Part of this difficulty has to do with issues in diagnosis and phenotype definition. In order to elucidate the genetics of a disorder, we must do family studies (i.e., either segregation analyses or linkage studies); in order to do family studies, we must have a clear and objective means of deciding which family members have the phenotype and which do not.

Whether the ideal definition of the phenotype for family studies will coincide with standard clinical criteria for the disorder in question depends on several things, including the possibility of reduced penetrance (i.e., not everyone with the genotype exhibits the phenotype), the age of onset of the disorder, and the possibility of developmental changes in the manifestation of the disorder. The ideal phenotype for family studies is one that is fully penetrant, manifests itself early in development, and persists in a similar form across development. Generally, the more complex the behavioral phenotype, the less likely it is to meet these conditions. For instance, schizophrenia appears to have reduced penetrance. What appears to be inherited is a susceptibility that eventually results in diagnosable schizophrenia in only a minority of family members. Depending on what behavioral marker is used for the diathesis, the number of affected family members may be as high as 50 percent, whereas the proportion who have or will develop schizophrenia is much smaller (Siegel, Waldo, Mizner, Adler, and Freedman, 1984). A family study that counted only the "true" schizophrenics" as affected would thus be unable to detect some forms of genetic transmission (e.g., dominant inheritance) and could obscure the genetic mechanisms involved. These problems have been discussed by Elston and Namboodiri (1980), who recommend that a multivariate definition of the phenotype be used in linkage studies of schizophrenia.

The problem of late onset is also true to some extent in schizophrenia and is much more acute in major depression, in which the usual age of onset is in mid-life. This considerably complicates family studies because many living family members cannot be categorized as affected or unaffected and are thus uniformative in genetic analyses. If a clear precursor of these disorders were known, it would greatly simplify genetic analyses.

Finally, developmental change or remission occurs in some complex behavioral disorders that appear to be genetic, most notably stuttering, dyslexia, and hyperactivity. Here we have the opposite problem of that found in schizophrenia and major depression. The disorder appears early in development, but adults who had the disorder in childhood no longer meet standard diagnostic criteria. This problem forces the investigator to rely on retrospective, historical information, which can be unreliable. Obviously, a behavioral marker that persists past the overt manifestation of the disorder would be very useful in these disorders.

So it can be seen that studies of genetic mechanisms force us to reconsider what is inherited in a complex behavioral disorder and to seek underlying phenotypes that persist across development. It is also clear that we have to be open to different diagnostic criteria in genetic studies than would be appropriate in clinical practice or other kinds of studies. If we focus too narrowly on individuals with standard diagnoses, we may impede progress in understanding causative mechanisms. An understanding of causative mechanisms may in turn cause standard diagnostic criteria to be reformulated. Eisenberg (1977), in a chapter on definitional issues in dyslexia, has discussed how the diagnostic criteria for the thalassemias (e.g., sickle cell anemia) were reformulated, as the underlying genetics became clearer. So it is important to remember that our standard diagnostic criteria for complex behavioral disorders, including dyslexia, are not absolutes; instead, they are likely to change as our understanding increases.

One may reasonably ask at this point how we arrive at phenotype definitions other than those provided by standard diagnostic criteria *before* having a complete understanding of the genetics and pathophysiology of the disorder in question. The answer is through careful phenotypic investigation of individuals who meet standard diagnostic criteria, followed by similar phenotypic investigations of their undiagnosed family members. In fact, in the case of many complex behavioral disorders, these kinds of studies need to be done before useful genetic analyses can be carried out.

We will call a phenotype definition that is ideal for family studies and that differs from standard diagnostic criteria a *marker* phenotype. In general, there are several criteria that a marker phenotype should satisfy. These are in addition to the criteria of complete penetrance, early onset, and developmental persistence discussed previously. The first concerns the distribution of the marker phenotype in the general population and in affected families. It is preferable that these distributions be bimodal, so that a clear assignment of most family members to the categories affected and unaffected can be made. Some genetic models permit continuous phenotypes, so this is not always an absolute criterion. Second, the marker phenotype must be present in all individuals who meet standard diagnostic criteria and in some but not all of their relatives who do not meet standard diagnostic criteria. Obviously, if the behavioral marker does not segregate within affected families, it cannot be useful in genetic analyses. Third, the marker phenotype must have a logical and potentially causal relationship to the full-blown syndrome. Ideally, it should be specific to the syndrome and not found in other complex behavioral disorders. So, for instance, there should be a double dissociation, as it were, between marker phenotypes for schizophrenia and major depression, or between those for dyslexia and hyperactivity. This last criterion is important because patients with most complex behavioral disorders differ from normal subjects on a host of behavioral dimensions, but many of these differences are not specific or intrinsic to the behavioral disorder in question. Finally, although it is ideal for a marker phenotype to involve a single test or trait, a marker phenotype can also be defined in a multivariate fashion (Elston and Namboodiri, 1980).

In what follows, we will see how these and other issues manifest themselves in the case of dyslexia; in particular, we will explore whether a potential marker phenotype exists for dyslexia.

DIAGNOSTIC ISSUES IN DYSLEXIA

This section is divided into three parts. The first is concerned with diagnostic criteria and the second with test procedures for identifying dyslexia. Most of this work has involved school-age children. Therefore, the third section concerns the special problems encountered in the diagnosis of adults, including the problem of compensation and the validity of diagnoses by history.

Diagnostic Criteria

There has been considerable discussion and controversy about what the appropriate diagnostic criteria are for diagnosing dyslexia in school-age children. Consequently, different criteria and measures have been used by various investigators, making comparison of results difficult.

Although there is broad agreement on most of the usual exclusionary criteria or negative aspects of the diagnosis (e.g., absence of socio-cultural deprivation, inadequate education, peripheral sensory disorders, neurologic disorders or serious psychiatric problems), there is less agreement on how to define the one positive symptom: a significant discrepancy between observed and expected reading level. There is also less agreement on how to define inadequate intellectual potential, which is another exclusionary criterion.

There are two fundamental reasons for the lack of consensus on how to define a significant discrepancy in reading achievement. The first is simply that, in the absence of a biologic understanding of dyslexia, we lack a definitive diagnostic test against which to validate commonly used diagnostic procedures. The second is that there is not clear evidence of a "hump" at the low end of the distribution of reading underachievement in school-age children.

Rutter and Yule (1975) reported such a hump in a epidemiologic survey of children in London and the Isle of Wight. In three of five samples, they found a significant increase (compared with the normal distribution) of 3 to about 6.5 times the number of children who were more than two standard errors of prediction below their predicted reading level; similar trends were found in the two other samples. They did not find a comparable hump at the high end of the distribution. However, their study has been criticized because there appears to have been a ceiling effect on the reading tests used in the three significant samples, causing a skew in the underachievement distributions (Olson, Kliegel, Davidson, and Foltz, 1985). Moreover, a large replication study, also performed in Great Britain, failed to find a similar hump (Rogers, 1983).

The presence or absence of a hump does not definitely confirm or disprove any particular etiologic hypothesis, though a continuous distribution is more consistent with a multifactorial or polygenic model, whereas a discontinuous distribution is more consistent with a single factor or major gene model. Causation aside, if there were clear evidence for a hump, then a nonarbitrary cutting point for the diagnosis of reading disability could be set. Without such evidence, any cutting point that is set is somewhat arbitrary. Given this problem, most investigators have preferred to be conservative in their criteria to insure that they identify children with severe reading problems who are thus likely to be "real" dyslexics.

The merits and limitations of various definitions of what constitutes a significant discrepancy between observed and expected reading level have been discussed elsewhere (Rutter, 1977; Siegel and Haven, in press) and they are only briefly reviewed here. The central issue is how to operationalize the concept of discrepancy so that it is statistically equivalent across ages, IQ levels, and possibly sexes.

Obviously, the commonly used, absolute standard of a two-year discrepancy between grade level and reading level has problems. What such a discrepancy means about a child's reading varies with his grade level and IQ: Both young and very bright dyslexics are likely to be diagnosed as normal using this definition of discrepancy, whereas both older and less bright normal children may be misdiagnosed as dyslexics.

Somewhat more sophisticated is the use of a relative discrepancy based on the difference (or ratio) between a child's standard score on a reading achievement test and his or her IQ. If the difference is significantly negative (Z score difference of -1.0 or -2.0) or the ratio is significantly below 1.00 (i.e., ratio $< .80$), the child is considered reading disabled. Interestingly, Finucci, Isaacs, Whitehouse, and Childs (1982) found very high correlations (.95 or greater) between absolute discrepancy scores (difference between observed and expected reading grade level) and relative discrepancy scores (a reading quotient) in samples of both normal children and children in reading disability classes. These high correlations suggest that for school-age children who are not at the extremes in terms of age or IQ, both absolute and IQ-related discrepancy criteria perform quite similarly.

However, both forms of discrepancy criteria commit an important statistical error, which has been mathematically described by Thorndike (1963) and empirically validated by Rutter and Yule (1975). This statistical error is a failure to correct for the regression effect. The relative discrepancy criterion assumes that a child's IQ is perfectly correlated with his expected reading achievement score, and therefore a discrepancy of a given size (e.g., -1 S.D.) means the same thing across children of various IQ and age levels. Since these two are not perfectly correlated ($r = .70$, depending on the measures used), the true expected reading score deviates increasingly from that predicted by a discrepancy approach, the further the IQ is from the mean. This is simply a regression effect; since reading and IQ are not perfectly correlated, a child's predicted reading score will be closer to the mean than his IQ. Therefore, the size of a significant discrepancy is relative to a child's IQ and must be computed from a regression equation that includes the child's IQ, age, and possibly sex. Hence, a relative discrepancy criterion, which does not correct for the regression effect, will overestimate the frequency of reading disability in children with high IQs and underestimate it in children with low IQs.

Interestingly, the absolute and relative discrepancy criteria have opposite intrinsic biases: The former overdiagnoses children with low IQs and underdiagnoses children with high IQs, whereas the latter does the reverse. If both criteria agree for a child wih extreme IQ, then an investigator could be quite confident about the diagnosis, without using a regression equation.

Even with the regression method, the choice of what constitutes a significant discrepancy (e.g., more than 1.0 or 1.5 or 2.0 standard errors of prediction) is arbitrary. But the regression approach ensures that whatever choice is made, the discrepancy will be equivalent statistically across children. Unfortunately, very few dyslexia investigators have used a regression approach, mainly because the regression equation must be derived from a large normal sample similar in age, education, sex, and SES to the potential dyslexics and must use the same IQ and reading tests that will be used for diagnosing reading disability. What would be most helpful is a validation study that compares the agreement of all three definitions of discrepancy — absolute, relative, and regression-based — in a large school-age population across ages and IQ levels. Then investigators who are unable to use a regression approach could more precisely estimate how serious the misdiagnosis problem will be in their population using either an absolute or relative discrepancy.

Regardless of which form of discrepancy an investigator uses, there are additional problems to be faced in the choice of IQ measures and the definition of "inadequate intellectual potential." Obviously, the IQ test utilized should not require reading, but there are other, less obvious problems with IQ. Chief among these is that many reading-disabled children have large Verbal-Performance IQ disparities, presumably for the same underlying reason that they are reading disabled. Thus, which IQ score (Verbal, Performance, or Full Scale) to use to calculate a score or decide whether the child had adequate intellectual potential becomes problematic (Siegel and Heaven, in press).

In addition to those more familiar diagnostic issues, there is the less discussed issue of *specificity*, which is particularly important in family studies of dyslexia. Reading and spelling problems are most salient to parents, teachers, and clinicians (and dyslexia researchers) than are other academic or cognitive problems. Therefore, many children identified as being dyslexic or reading-disabled by the criteria just discussed are likely to have other academic (mathematics or handwriting) or cognitive (visual-spatial skills, attention) problems that were not adequately diagnosed. Such unidentified problems introduce potential confounds, especially in any study that attempts to clarify the underlying cognitive deficits in reading disability.

This problem has not been widely recognized since most investigators, as discussed previously, have been mainly concerned that their diagnostic criteria identify only severe dyslexics. The preoccupation with severity arises both from the notion that severe dyslexics are more likely to represent a qualitatively distinct syndrome and from a concern with avoiding false-positive diagnoses. As we have seen, there is no strong evidence for a statistically distinct group of poor readers at the tail of the distribution. Moreover, Olson and coworkers (1985) have failed to find qualitative differences in reading-related skills between subjects below the usual cutting point for dyslexia and those above it who are below-average readers. In addition, some of the most informative studies of the underlying cognitive deficit (i.e., those of the Haskins group) have used poor readers in normal classrooms instead of severely dyslexic children as subjects. So it appears that the preoccupation with severity may be unnecessary. That is, dyslexic subjects with milder degrees of dyslexia who do not meet the usual discrepancy criteria but who do have a statistically significant discrepancy (e.g., one, instead of two, standard errors below prediction) are also useful to study. As discussed, this preoccupation may also be misleading, since there appears to be a trade-off between severity and specificity, such that more severely dyslexic children are less likely to be specific.

The relevance of the specificity issue for family studies is that some family members may have milder and more specific reading problems that do not meet the standard diagnostic criteria for dyslexia. In a genetic study, diagnosing such individuals as normal would be misleading. In our family studies of dyslexia, we have used a Specific Dyslexia Algorithm (Pennington, Smith, McCabe, Kimberling, and Lubs, 1984) in addition to a reading quotient to identify specific individuals with dyslexia (i.e., those who have normal math or general information scores, or both, with reading or spelling scores, or both, being significantly lower). Although many of the subjects who fit this Specific Dyslexia Algorithm (SDA) are also classified as dyslexic by reading quotient, some are not, even though they have a history of reading difficulty.

Clinically, the distinction between specific (i.e., fitting the SDA) and nonspecific (i.e., fitting the reading quotient but not the SDA) dyslexia also appears to be useful. Children in each group need to be identified and treated, but the prognosis for the specific group appears to be better, since they have more cognitive and academic strengths outside the area of reading and spelling.

In summary, the preceding review supports the following conclusions about diagnostic criteria for dyslexia in school-age children: (1) There is broad agreement on the usual exclusionary criteria, except for the tests and cutoffs to be used to determine inadequate intellectual potential, (2) The most statistically valid way to measure a discrepancy in reading achievement is through the use of a regression equation that includes age, IQ, and possibly sex, (3) The choice of what magnitude of discrepancy to use as a cutoff is arbitrary, (4) In making this choice, the investigator should be aware that there is a trade-off between severity and specificity. Investigators could handle the severity-specificity trade-off by identifying both a severe (two standard errors below prediction) and a mild (one standard error below prediction) group of dyslexic children and using the same experimental measures on both groups.

Diagnosis in Adults

Although more severely dyslexic adults meet the same criteria used with school-age children, many adults with milder cases do not, in spite of persisting deficits in reading or spelling. Moreover, some adults with clear histories of dyslexia as children have compensated so well that their performance on conventional reading and spelling tests is normal (Smith, Pennington, McCabe, Kimberling, and Lubs, in preparation). In such cases, the investigator must either rely on history or use an experimental measure of the phenotype. In this section, we discuss the validation research on diagnoses by history as well as measures of reading history that have been used with adults.

Two studies suggest there is some validity to self diagnosis of dyslexia in adults. Finucci, Whitehouse, Isaacs, and Childs (1984) found significant correlations in adults between a regression-based discrepancy score for reading and spelling achievement and scores on a self-report questionnaire of reading history, habits, and attitudes. The correlations were -0.43 in a sample of parents and other adult relatives of dyslexic children and -0.25 in a sample of adult controls. About a third of the dyslexic relatives had definite or borderline reading disability based on their scores on the regression measure. Of these, 72 percent had self-report scores above the median in the control group, as did 49 percent of the dyslexic relatives who were normal readers. Clearly, this self-report measure does not exhibit sufficient sensitivity and specificity to be used by itself in adult diagnosis, but it does provide helpful additional information in making such a diagnosis.

The second study is that of Decker, Vogler, and Defries (in preparation). Instead of a series of questions, they simply asked parents of dyslexic and control children whether they had had problems learning to read. In this way, they identified four groups of parents: RD family normal, RD family disabled, control family normal, and control family disabled. These groups were compared on a standardized reading composite score based on the PIAT, and significant main effects for both self-reported reading status and group membership were found. Both self-reported disabled parents and RD parents in general read worse. In addition, there was a significant interaction effect between group membership and self-reported reading status, such that the discrepancy in reading between disabled and normal parents in RD families was greater than in control families. There were no main or interaction effects of sex. These results validate self-report diagnoses in adults, especially in parents of dyslexic children. Decker and associates (in preparation) did not evaluate the sensitivity and specificity of their simple self-report measure for individual diagnosis, but it is unlikely that it would perform better than the more detailed questionnaire used by Finucci and colleagues (1984).

There are at least three logical reasons for the lack of closer agreement between adult test and self-report scores, as found by Finucci and coworkers (1984). One is partial compensation: the insensitivity of the measures to the phenotype in dyslexic adults. Another is genuine or complete compensation: The adult was affected as a child but currently exhibits no measureable phenotype. A third is erroneous reporting, whether under or over. Our continuing studies of familial dyslexia (Smith et al., 1983) provide evidence that both the first and third possibilities occur in fact. There has been insufficient experimental analysis of the adult phenotype to accept or reject the second possibility — complete compensation. Some adults in our studies, especially females, have shown at least partial compensation. In terms of underreporting, some adults' self-reports of normality in reading disagree with other family members' reports of their history as well as with test results. We have found this to occur mostly in elderly family members (i.e., grandparents), some of whom are more reluctant to admit academic problems. In our studies, underreporting appears to be more common than overreporting. Finally, our experience also indicates that partial compensation is a more frequent reason for nonagreement between test scores than is erroneous reporting.

Of course, validating that compensated dyslexic adults were dyslexic by test scores in childhood is difficult because such records are usually unavailable. However, it is preferable in genetic studies of dyslexic families to retain this diagnostic option than to obscure possible patterns of transmission. In our linkage studies of dyslexia (Smith et al., 1983), we have defined a compensated adult as an adult who is positive on our history measure but negative on both our achievement criteria: the Reading Quotient (RQ) (Finucci and colleagues, 1982) and the Specific Dyslexia Algorithm (SDA) (Pennington and associates, 1984). We have also included a third diagnostic option for adults, that of obligate carrier. An obligate carrier is negative on all three measures — history, RQ, and SDA — but has both an affected child and an affected sibling or parent. Such an individual's carrier status is obligatory under an autosomal dominant hypothesis, which is the hypothesis we have been testing in our linkage studies. Since marker coding for the linkage analysis is done blind with respect to diagnosis, the linkage analysis provides an independent test of the compensated adult and obligate carrier diagnoses. If these two diagnoses were not utilized in a linkage analysis, true autosomal dominant transmission might be falsely rejected, whereas including these diagnoses does not increase the likelihood of falsely accepting a dominant hypothesis.

We have found that the number of adults fitting either the compensated adult or obligate carrier category is small. In a sample of 107 adults from 20 extended families, 15 (14 percent) fell into the former category and one (1 percent) into the latter. If only acheivement test scores had been used, these 16 adults whould have been misdiagnosed as normal.

This example from our studies shows how standard diagnostic criteria must be modified for linkage studies, as was discussed at the beginning of this chapter. Naturally, in our phenotype analysis studies of these same samples we have excluded the compensated adults and obligate carriers from the main analysis and reserved them for post-hoc analysis. It is hoped that this example illustrates how the goals and, consequently, the diagnostic criteria utilized in genetic linkage studies and in phenotype analysis studies differ. A similar approach has been used to investigate the genetics of stuttering (Kidd, 1980). In those studies the diagnosis was based on having ever stuttered. In contrast, it is obvious that the phenotype analysis of stuttering should initially focus on individuals who are still stutterers.

Some of the problems posed by compensation will be resolved by a clearer analysis of the phenotype and, it is hoped, the identification of a marker phenotype. Progress in phenotype analysis in dyslexia is discussed in the next section.

PHENOTYPE ANALYSIS

This section is concerned with the experimental analysis of the cognitive phenotype(s) in dyslexia. Since most dyslexics appear to suffer from a deficit in linguistic processes (Vellutino, 1979) that disrupts the development of reading and spelling, this section restricts itself to such processes. A minority of dyslexic individuals may have a primary deficit in the visual processes important for reading and spelling, but there is considerably less work in this domain, and it is not discussed here. Most of the studies on the linguistic deficits in dyslexia have not been family studies, nor have they restricted themselves to familial dyslexia. However, since similar deficits are being found in familial samples (Olson et al., 1985) — even those restricted to one form of apparent transmission (Smith et al., in preparation) — studies of the general population of school-age dyslexics appear relevant to the familial case. This is fortunate because some of the methodologies discussed here would be much more difficult if restricted to familial samples.

There are three different reasons for studying the cognitive phenotype in dyslexia. The first is a practical one, which has already been suggested by the previous sections: a clearer understanding of the phenotype may help us to identify a marker phenotype that is present across a broad age span and that will make diagnosis easier in both adults and young children. As we will see, problems with phonemic awareness, lexical retrieval, and verbal short-term memory are each good potential candidates for such a marker phenotype. A second reason is that such studies may clarify the development and cognitive psychology of normal reading, just as the study of aphasic patients has yielded considerable information about normal language processes.

A third reason is an interdisciplinary one: the underlying cognitive phenotype will probably be easier to relate to the neurologic phenotype than will the surface symptoms themselves. Since reading and spelling are cultural inventions, which depend on instruction for their development, it is inappropriate to say that these skills themselves are genetically transmitted. Rather, the genetic influence on reading skill is better formulated as a genetic influence on linguistic skills necessary for normal reading development. We also know that many portions of the brain participate in the cognitive activity of reading (Duffy, Denckla, Bartels, and Sardini, 1980; Lassen, Ingvar, and Skinhoj, 1978), no one of which can appropriately be called a "reading center." So, for the goal of interdisciplinary integration in dyslexia, the task facing cognitive phenotype analysis is to identify a subset of linguistic skills that (1) are both necessary and fairly specific precursors of reading and spelling problems and (2) can eventually be related to the functional neuroanatomy of the brain. It is important to emphasize the specificity criterion because most patients with acquired aphasia have associated reading and spelling problems, and most patients with acquired alexias have associated aphasic problems. Therefore, the overlap between aphasia and alexia, at least in the acquired case, is fairly close. In contrast, in the developmental case, there are clearly dyslexic individuals who are not dysphasic (Tallal and Stark, 1982). Thus, the neuropsychologic puzzle posed by developmental dyslexia is that of finding an underlying linguistic deficit that does not also produce a developmental dysphasia.

Aphasiologic Context

These latter considerations place the phenotype analysis of dyslexia in an "aphasiologic context" (Critchley, 1970). It is worthwhile to discuss briefly the linguistic deficits that have been investigated in dyslexia in such a context before considering the experimental evidence for each of these possibly core deficits.

There are four areas of linguistic deficit that have been the focus of most research on the underlying cognitive phenotype in dyslexia. These are deficits in phoneme discrimination, phoneme awareness and transposition, verbal short-term memory, and lexical retrieval. Interestingly, nearly all of these are deficits that are also found in more marked forms in the acquired aphasias. The core symptoms that are used to classify the various subtypes of aphasia are deficits in fluency, naming (i.e., lexical retrieval), repetition, and verbal comprehension (both of the latter two require verbal short-term memory). It is worth discussing the nonoverlapping items on these two lists: deficits in fluency, phoneme discrimination, and phoneme awareness.

Dysfluency in spontaneous speech may occur in some dyslexic individuals, largely because of problems in verbal formation and word finding rather than because of problems in articulation. Dysfluency in oral reading is a key symptom in dyslexia. However, a primary fluency deficit, as is seen in Broca's aphasia and in children with expressive language disorders, is an unlikely candidate for the underlying phenotype in dyslexia for three reasons. First, many dyslexic individuals are not dysfluent in spontaneous speech and were not so as young children. Second, some children (Huttenlocher and Huttenlocher, 1973) with severe expressive speech problems are precocious at reading (i.e., hyperlexics). Third, dyslexsic individuals are deficient at some linquistic tasks that do not require expressive speech.

Deficits in phoneme discrimination, though not on the core list, are important symptoms in some types of aphasia (i.e., Wernicke's). A deficit in phoneme discrimination could also produce the other three deficits that are candidates for the underlying phenotype in dyslexia, as will be discussed further. However, if the underlying deficit in dyslexia is a problem in phoneme discrimination, it must be a relatively subtle one; otherwise, dyslexic individuals would have a receptive aphasia and more widespread problems with language development.

Possible deficits in phoneme awareness and transposition skills are not usually explored in aphasic patients, so it is not known for certain whether they would exhibit such deficits. It is reasonable to infer that patients with Wernicke's aphasia would probably have such deficits becasue their inability to monitor the phonemic accuracy of speech is so impaired. What is more important is that an individual could have a primary deficit in phoneme awareness and transposition skills and *not* be aphasic. That is because these skills are metalinguistic and require conscious awareness of the phonemic structure of speech (Mattingly, 1972), whereas the processes involved in normal expressive and receptive speech do not require this kind of awareness. Hence, a deficit in phoneme segmentation and transposition skills would solve the neuropsychologic puzzle posed by developmental dyslexia.

We will review the experimental evidence for each of the four candidate deficits and then discuss their possible interrelationships. We will focus on whether there have been several specific types of study: (1) studies of adults, (2) longitudinal studies of preschoolers, (3) studies employing reading age (RA) — matched controls, and (4) training studies. These types of studies address two of the criteria for a marker phenotype: developmental persistence and causal relationship. Adult and longitudinal studies address the issue of developmental persistence. Longitudinal, training, and reading age — matched control studies will all address the issue of whether the deficit causes dyslexia. Longitudinal studies and those employing RA matches address the possibility that reading problems cause the deficit in linguistic skill(s) rather than the reverse. It is always possible that lack of reading experience causes a child to be weak in a linguistic skill, rather than that a deficit in that skill causes reading problems. Training studies address the question of whether the linguistic skill in question, and not some correlated third factor, is causally tied to reading development. If reliable, positive results were found in all four types of study for a given linguistic skill, then the criteria of persistence and causal relationship would be satisfied. Other criteria for a marker phenotype would remain to be satisfied, including penetrance, segregation, and diagnostic utility.

Phoneme Discrimination

Before discussing the studies in this area, it is important to trace in a general way why a deficit in phoneme discrimination would be expected to disrupt reading development and how such a deficit might affect the other three linguistic skills to be discussed here. A deficit in phoneme discrimination would impair a child's phonologic development and make his phonologic categories less sharp. The central task in early reading development (and one most dyslexic individuals have difficulty with) is learning to map graphemes and grapheme clusters onto phonologic units. If these phonologic units are less precise, clearly this mapping will be more difficult. All the other linguistic skills to be discussed depend in different ways on an intact, underlying phonologic organization and thus would likewise be disrupted by a phoneme discrimination deficit. So such a deficit would parsimoniously explain much of the data, if it were characteristic of the large majority of dyslexic individuals and if it could occur without causing more generalized speech and language impairment.

This area has been investigated with three different sorts of paradigms, each of which addresses somewhat different levels of auditory processing.

At the most basic *acoustic-perceptual level*, Tallal (1976, 1980; Tallal and Piercy, 1973, 1974, 1975) has found that dysphasic adults and children and some dyslexic individuals have an inability to resolve auditory stimuli (whether linguistic or nonlinguistic) with brief interstimulus intervals (approximately 100 msecs or less). Such a deficit interferes with the perception of stop consonants because of the rapid formant transitions in their sound spectra. More generally, this basic acoustic-perceptual deficit would disrupt the various phonologic skills necessary for reading and spelling development. However, 12 of 20 of Tallal's (1980) dyslexic subjects performed normally on this task, so this cannot be the underlying deficit in all or most dyslexic individuals. Such a basic acoustic-perceptual deficit is also improbable for theoretical reasons because it would cause greater impairments in receptive and expressive language than many dyslexic subjects exhibit, as has been discussed and demonstrated by Tallal (1980; Tallal and Stark, 1982). To my knowledge, this paradigm has not been used in adult longitudinal or training studies with dyslexic subjects.

A second possible deficit is one at the *level of categorical phoneme perception*, which like the deficit discussed previously would, of necessity, be expected to affect not only reading and spelling, but also receptive and possibly expressive language. Godfrey, Syrdal-Lasky, Millay, and Knox (1981) and McIntyre and Dueckman-Krueger (1983) have each used a standard categorical phoneme perception paradigm (Liberman, Harris, Hoffman, and Griffith, 1957) with good and poor readers and found that poor readers showed less "sharp" phoneme boundary curves, suggestive of a subtle problem with phoneme perception. However, these studies did not employ reading-age (RA) controls. It is possible, for example, that good readers performed better because they have a better-structured phonologic lexicon (as a result of having more reading experience), and this could have generated a "top down" advantage in the categorical perception task. Godfrey and associates (1981) argue against a reading experience explanation of their results, since their analysis of covariance (with reading level as the covariate) also showed differences in phoneme perception between dyslexic and normal subjects. In the absence of studies with RA controls and longitudinal studies, however, the direction-of-effects question remains open. Moreover, Olson (personal communication) has used Godfrey and coworkers (1981) paradigm with 57 older dyslexic subjects and has failed to replicate their results. Although the dyslexic subjects make more errors overall, possibly for attentional reasons, the slope of their identification functions does not differ from that of normal subjects.

One study employed a categorical perception paradigm with adults (Lieberman, 1983). This study found that the majority of a sample of 19 dyslexic adults had deficits in categorical perception. This study did not employ RA controls.

Thus, at this point it is unclear whether a deficit in categorical perception is a reliable finding in dyslexic individuals and, if reliable, what the direction of effects is. If replicated in a study with RA controls or in a longitudinal study, the questions of whether this deficit is characteristic of most dyslexic individuals and whether it is intrinsic would still remain. A final concern about this proposed deficit is how slight shifts in category boundary would affect reading development in any case, since the stimuli that bracket the phoneme boundary are artificial ones that do not occur in everyday speech experience (Studdert-Kennedy, personal communnication).

The third level of analysis involves more *direct measures of speech perception*. Brady, Shankweiler, and Mann (1983) have shown that poor readers are less accurate than normal readers in identifying noise-masked words, but are equivalent in identifying noise-masked environmental sounds. Moreover, a word frequency manipulation did not differentially lower the poor readers' word perception scores, which argues against a lexical (as opposed to a perceptual) account of the group differences. In our own investigation of the cognitive phenotype in a form of familial dyslexia (Smith et al., in preparation), we found that dyslexic adults had significantly poorer results than their nondyslexic relatives on a noise-masked word perception task (Goldman-Fristoe-Woodcock Test of Auditory Discrimination: Noise subtest). Neither this study nor that of Brady and coworkers (1983) employed RA matches, and longitudinal and training studies have not been done.

Another issue is whether the deficiency on word perception tasks reflects an underlying deficit in single phoneme perception (as the results of Tallal, 1980, and Godfrey et al., 1981, suggest) or other problems in phonologic skills, including the efficiency or automaticity of using phonetic codes and memory for a sequence of several phonemes. A child could have normal phoneme boundaries but still have decreased efficiency in using phonetic codes to transfer items into verbal short-term memory. Such a child would perform normally on the categorical perception task, but possibly not on word perception tasks, especially on a task with noise-making (S. Brady, personal communication). Thus, efficiency in using phonetic or phonologic codes appears to be an important linguistic skill in understanding dyslexia, but it is difficult to neatly assign this skill to the domain of perception, short-term memory, or long-term memory. This is a basic theoretical problem that recurs in other sections of this chapter.

In summary, there is evidence for deficits in some but not all dyslexic individuals on tasks involving three different levels of phoneme discrimination. None of the studies have employed RA controls, and longitudinal and training studies have not been done. It is certainly possible that some dyslexic individuals have subtle deficits in phoneme discrimination, but such people are likely to have a more severe and less specific form of dyslexia, with more associated dysphasic symptoms, as has been discussed previously. Tallal and Stark (1982) have shown that the dyslexic population can be divided into those with and those without dysphasic symptoms. They studied a sample of dyslexic subjects who had been carefully screened to exclude receptive or expressive language delay and found they did not differ from control subjects on the aforementioned acoustic-perceptual tasks of Tallal, nor on other perceptual motor tasks in their battery. These nondysphasic dyslexic subjects did differ on serial memory tasks that involved verbal STM and on a concept task that involved phoneme awareness, which are two of the candidate deficits in our list. Thus, deficits in these higher linguistic skills that are intimately related to reading can occur in the absence of a more basic discrimination deficit. Therefore, it seems unlikely that having problems in phoneme discrimination will turn out to be a marker phenotype that is useful for studying most dyslexic subjects.

Phoneme Awareness and Transposition Skills

It is important to discuss briefly how such a deficit would impair reading and whether it could explain the other candidate deficits. The first task is simple. To learn the alphabetic code, children must become aware of the underlying phonologic code; otherwise, the mapping operations involved in early phonics instruction make no sense and cannot be learned (Wallach and Wallach, 1976). In contrast, it is difficult to argue that phoneme awareness per se is necessary for any of the other three linguistic skills, though phoneme awareness might increase the efficiency of the storage and retieval of phonologic name codes in long-term memory.

Before reviewing the evidence in this area, it is also important to describe briefly how these skills are measured. Basically, four techniques have been used: (1) phoneme vs. syllable counting (Liberman, Shankweiler, Fischer, and Carter, 1974), (2) an oddity task in which the child must identify which word in a string of three or four words does not share a common phoneme (Bradley and Bryant, 1978), (3) a choice task in which the child must pick which of two words begins with a pronounced phoneme (Wallach and Wallach, 1976), and (4) a pig Latin task in which the child must segment off the first phoneme, move it to the end of the word, and add -*ay* (Snyder, personal communication).

All of these tasks depend on metalinguistic awareness of the phonologic structure of language, not necessarily on underlying phonologic organization (Rozin and Gleitman, 1977). Therefore, an individual would not have to be deficient in phoneme discrimination or some other aspect of underlying phonologic organization to be deficient at phoneme awareness and transposition. However, decreased efficiency in using phonologic codes could lead to deficiencies in phoneme awareness and transportation skills.

It is also important to point out that not all of these tasks (e.g., the choice task) are difficult for older children, whether dyslexic or not. The pig Latin task is the only one that actually requires mental manipulation of phonemes in addition to awareness; it apparently remains difficult for dyslexic individuals into adulthood (Snyder, personal communication).

The experimental evidence on this possible deficit is the best of the four deficits considered. There have been several longitudinal studies, all of which have demonstrated a close relationship between phoneme awareness in preschool and kindergarten and later reading proficiency (Bradley and Bryant, 1983; Liberman et al., 1974; Mann, 1984; Wallach and Wallach, 1976). There has also been one study (Bradley and Bryant, 1978) in which reading-age (RA) matches were used; the poor readers performed worse on the oddity task than younger RA-matched controls.

Perhaps the most conclusive study in this area is one that combined a longitudinal study with a training study (Bradley and Bryant, 1983). As the authors note, this is a particularly powerful methodology, because both the direction and specificity of the causal relationship are evaluated in one overall study. This methodology has very rarely been used in dyslexia research. In their longitudinal study, Bradley and Bryant (1983) utilized partial correlations and demonstrated that performance on their oddity task of phoneme awareness at ages 4 and 5 accounted for significant proportions of the variance in reading and spelling at ages 7 and 8, even when the effects of IQ, final CA, and short-term memory for the oddity strings were partialled out. The last item is particularly important because their task, since it uses word strings, is confounded with possible problems in verbal short-term memory. Bradley and Bryant (1983) did not report how much of the later reading and spelling variance was accounted for by the short-term memory performance at ages 4 and 5; presumably, it was less than that accounted for by phoneme awareness.

Their training study involved a subgroup of the children in the longitudinal study, all of whom were markedly deficient (− 2 SD) in phoneme awareness. Children in this subgroup, matched on IQ, age, and phoneme awareness, were randomly assigned to one of four treatment groups: (1) sound categorization training, (2) sound categorization training plus training in sound-letter correspondences, (3) semantic categorization training, and (4) no training. On followup, there were no differences among the groups in math nor between groups 3 and 4 in reading and spelling. In contrast, group 1 was better than group 4 in reading, and group 2 was better than groups 3 and 4 in both reading and spelling. In summary, the results of Bradley and Bryant (1983) indicate a specific, causal relationship between phoneme awareness and reading skill.

It is important to point out that, although there is clear evidence for the expected direction of effects between phoneme awareness and reading, the causal relationship is not necessarily unidirectional. Morais, Cary, Algeria, and Bertelson (1979) found that adult illiterates who received literacy training were more proficient at adding or deleting phonemes in spoken nonwords than similar adults who received no training and remained illiterate. Since there were no obvious selection biases in terms of which illiterates received training, this study demonstrates that reading training and experience may increase phoneme awareness.

In conclusion, the existing evidence demonstrates that problems in phoneme awareness are intrinsically (i.e., causally) related to later reading problems and hence are an important aspect of the underlying cognitive phenotype in dyslexia. The evidence on the persistence of problems in phoneme awareness across development is less strong but suggestive (Bradley and Bryant, 1978; Snyder, personal communication). Clearly, a well-designed study of phoneme awareness and transposition skills in dyslexic adults and RA controls is needed to address the persistence issue. Such a study would need to employ a demanding task of phoneme transposition, such as the pig Latin task, to counter the possible compensation due to life-long training in reading (Morais et al., 1979).

Another important topic for future research in this area is the relationship between phoneme awareness and transposition skills and verbal short-term memory. Clearly, children with poor verbal short-term memories would have trouble attending to and manipulating the phonemic structure of words. Although Bradley and Bryant's (1983) results suggest that a deficit in phoneme awareness is not simply reducible to a verbal short-term memory deficit, more studies are needed on this point.

Verbal Short-Term Memory

We have mentioned how the deficits on the phoneme awareness tasks may be derivable from a more basic deficit in verbal short-term memory (STM). At the outset, it is important to trace these possible relationships more clearly, as well as the relationship of verbal short-term memory to lexical retrieval. As discussed by Baddeley (1978) and others, verbal STM interfaces with reading at two levels: word coding operations and sentence comprehension operations. Hence, a verbal STM deficit would be expected to interfere with learning and using the alphabetic code and with the later development of reading comprehension. Baddeley, Thompson, and Buchanan (1975) found a significant correlation between verbal short-term memory skills and single-word reading speed in normal adults. Phoneme awareness and especially phoneme transposition skills depend on working memory space, so a verbal STM deficit would disrupt these skills. Finally, new words to be stored in the lexicon must pass through verbal STM, so a verbal STM deficit could conceivably interfere with lexical storage and, hence, later retrieval efficiency. We now consider the evidence that dyslexic individuals have a basic deficit in verbal short-term memory.

It is well documented that many dyslexic subjects perform poorly on the Wechsler Digit Span subtest, which is a verbal short-term memory task (see Jorm, 1979, 1983; Rugel, 1974, and Stanovich, 1982, for reviews.) We found in our sample of familial dyslexic subjects many of whom were adults, that Digit Span was the only Wechsler subtest on which the dyslexic subjects performed more poorly than their non-dyslexic relatives (Smith et al., in preparation). The dyslexic subjects in the large Colorado Family Reading Study sample also performed worst on Digit Span (Olson, Kliegl, Davidson, and Davies, 1984). So there is fairly good evidence that a poor Digit Span performance is a consistent aspect of the cognitive phenotype in many school-age and adult dyslexic individuals.

Poor STM for digits does not appear to be a result of decreased reading experience in dyslexic individuals. Cohen, Netly, and Clarke (1984) found that disabled readers had a less pronounced recency effect in short-term memory for digits than did reading-age and IQ matched controls.

Recency effects are thought to be due to automatic, probably phonetic, encoding operations and not to strategic or metacognitive operations. Hence, this result suggests that decreased efficiency of phonetic coding may underlie the poor Digit Span performance of dyslexic subjects.

There are very few longitudinal studies on the relationship between verbal STM and reading development and no training studies. As discussed previously, the results of Bradley and Bryant's (1983) longitudinal study suggest that phoneme awareness skill is a more powerful predictor of later reading attainment than is verbal STM, but verbal STM does account for some of the variance in reading attainment. A similar finding has been reported by Mann (1984; Mann and Liberman, in press). In a longitudinal study employing separate measures of verbal STM and phoneme awareness, those authors found correlations of .56 and .75 between a verbal STM measure and a phoneme awareness measure, respectively, and later oral reading proficiency. Once again, both measures are predictive, but the association with phoneme awareness is stronger. These studies indicate that early problems in verbal STM predict later reading problems but leave unclear whether this effect is independent of the effects of phoneme awareness. Both phoneme awareness and verbal STM involve phonologic (or at least phonetic) coding efficiency, so that might be a common link between these two areas of deficit.

A number of studies have examined poor readers' use of phonetic coding on verbal STM tasks, mainly through the measurement of the decrement in memory span caused by rhyming items. A robust finding has been that young poor readers are less susceptible to rhyming confusion than young normal readers, suggesting that the poor readers rely less heavily on a phonetic code in STM (Mann, Liberman, and Shankweiler, 1980; Shankweiler, Liberman, Mark, Fowler, and Fischer, 1979). However, a fundamental problem in this literature is that decreased use or increased precision of phonetic codes may both lead to decreased rhyming confusion, and the rhyming paradigm cannot distinguish these two possibilities (Olson, personal communication). Therefore, maximal rhyming confusion would be expected to be found in younger normal subjects but to decrease with age as, presumably, phonetic codes become more precise. In contrast, maximal rhyming confusion might be found in older dyslexic subjects because of increased use of phonetic codes (Olson, personal communication). Essentially, these kinds of results have been found in a number of recent studies (Bisanz, Das, and Mancini, 1984; Hall, Ewing, Tinzmann, and Wilson, 1981; Johnston, 1982; Olson et al., 1984; Siegel and Linder, 1984). Hence, decreased reliance on phonetic coding in verbal STM, at least as measured by the rhyming confusion paradigm, is not a persistent part of the cognitive phenotype in disabled readers and cannot wholly account for their persistent deficits in verbal STM. In contrast, decreased precision or efficiency in phonetic coding may be a consistent aspect of the phenotype.

Other research has explored other possible explanations for the verbal STM deficit in poor readers, including deficient rehearsal and control strategies, deficient encoding, poor serial order memory, and a deficient ability to retrieve relevant phonologic codes from long-term memory (LTM). This research has been reviewed by Jorm (1983), Stanovich (1982), and Torgesen (1982; Torgesen and Houck, 1980). The general consensus appears to be that the cause of the verbal STM deficit is not metacognitive (i.e., due to deficient rehearsal and control strategies) and not entirely reducible to a deficient serial order memory. Instead, it appears more likely that there is a problem in phonologic or phonetic coding efficiency, probably because it is more difficult to retrieve the relevant codes from verbal LTM. It is also worth noting that in most studies, dyslexic individuals are not abnormal in either visual or motor STM. This result also argues against a general metacognitive or attentional deficit and instead restricts the deficit to specifically linguistic processes. What is still unclear is whether the primary deficit is in verbal short-term memory span itself or in other retrieval and coding processes on which verbal STM depends.

In summary, there is evidence to support deficits in verbal STM as a marker phenotype in dyslexia, in that such deficits are both predictive and persistent in dyslexia. However, the relevant training studies have not been done, and it is unclear whether the verbal STM deficits are primary or secondary to other deficits, such as those in phonetic coding, or the retrieval of phonologic information from LTM. This last possibility brings us to research on lexical retrieval deficits in dyslexia.

Lexical Retrieval

A number of studies have found deficits in speed and accuracy of name retrieval (i.e., a dysnomia) in dyslexic children (Denckla and Rudel, 1976a and b; Olson et al., 1984; Wolf, 1982). In adult alexia, dysnomia is a more frequently encountered associated deficit than are other aphasic symptoms (e.g., dysfluency, comprehension deficits, and repetition deficits). It makes sense on both neuroanatomic and cognitive grounds that reading and naming would be closely associated. Neuroanatomically, both processes would appear to require coordination between the visual association areas and the posterior speech areas. Cognitively, in both naming and reading, a visual stimulus evokes a phonologic name code from the portion of long-term memory called the lexicon. However, pictures, unlike words, depend on a semantic rather than a graphemic or phonemic access route to the lexicon. So, potentially, a comparison of reading and naming performance could help to specify more precisely what the cognitive deficit is in dyslexia. In addition, problems in the retrieval of phonologic name codes could reduce coding efficiency in verbal STM and make phonemic segments less available to awareness. A lexical retrieval deficit could not cause a phoneme discrimination deficit, but it could be a confound in some phoneme discrimination tasks.

The naming deficits in dyslexia hold up when reading-age matches are used (Wolf, 1984). More important, naming problems have been shown to be predictive of reading problems in two longitudinal studies (Jansky and de Hirsch, 1972; Wolf, 1984). In the former study, correlations of .54 were found between both letter and picture naming in kindergarten and second grade reading achievement. Moreover, these two tasks accounted for twice as much of the reading variance as other predictive tasks, including a sentence memory task, suggesting that naming may be more predictive of reading achievement than is verbal STM. In the second study (Wolf, 1984), similar correlations (ranging from .48 to .56) were found between kindergarten picture and letter naming tasks and second grade reading achievement.

Moreover, in this second study, somewhat larger correlations (ranging from .58 to .70) were found when the naming task required rapid alternation between letters, numbers and colors on the Rapid Automatized Naming tasks (RAN) devised by Denckla and Rudel (1976). Unlike a straight confrontation picture-naming task, on which the child names one picture at a time, the RAN more closely simulates reading because it presents the child with a text-like page of rows of things to be named as rapidly as possible. Perhaps lexical retrieval is most compromised in dyslexic subjects under conditions of rapid retrieval of a series of different names.

It is important to note that neither of these longitudinal studies used partial correlations to see how much unique variance was contributed by naming problems. Moreover, neither included measures of phoneme awareness or very good measures of verbal STM or phoneme discrimination, so it is impossible to evaluate the relative contributions of these different candidate deficits to later reading. These longitudinal studies do indicate that the naming deficits found in dyslexic individuals are not simply caused by reduced reading experience.

Some evidence also suggests that the relationship between naming performance and reading extends to adulthood. Jackson and McClelland (1979) found a significant correlation between performance on the Posner name identity task (B-b vs. B-d) and reading speed in college undergraduates.

There have been no training studies examining the relationship between naming speed and accuracy and later reading. Therefore, we cannot rule out the possibility that the observed relationship is not due to a third correlated factor, such as the other candidate deficits we have been discussing.

Even the standard picture-naming task requires several component processes, including visual perception and recognition, retrieval of the phonologic name code from LT memory (which assumes prior storage of the name in LT memory), and articulatory output. Some experimental work has focused on clarifying which of these components is deficient in dyslexic individuals, and the tentative conclusion is that the retrieval component is the most important.

Two studies have controlled for articulatory output by using a Posner task. The Posner task requires no articulatory output but does require name retrieval in the name identity condition. Ellis (1981) used the Posner name identity task with 10 to 15 year old dyslexic subjects and found that they were slower than control subjects only on the name identity (e.g., B-b) and not on the physical identity (e.g., R-R) condition. As already mentioned, a relationship between the name identity task and reading speed was found by Jackson and McClelland (1979). However, the Posner task uses letters for stimuli, and the task of naming letters is closer to reading and may differ in important ways from naming pictures. Therefore, a picture name-retrieval task that did not require articulatory output would be a more convincing test of this question.

As for visual perception and recognition, Wolf (1982) and Katz (1982) have presented evidence to show that these processes are not mainly responsible for the name retrieval problems of dyslexic individuals.

A final possibility is poorer prior storage of words *into* LTM. There has been little research in this area, but Nelson and Warrington (1980) found evidence of both verbal short-term and long-term memory impairments in a sample of dyslexic subjects. On the basis of these findings, they hypothesize two independent memory impairments in developmental dyslexia.

In summary, the evidence indicates that difficulty in retrieving phonologic name codes is a persistent and possibly intrinsic deficit in dyslexia. The longitudinal evidence is fairly convincing, though no longitudinal studies that carefully examine the relationship of naming, verbal STM, and phonemic awareness as predictors of later reading have been done. There is enough evidence to suggest that naming difficulty, especially on RAN-like tasks, might be considered as a possible marker phenotype in dyslexia.

Summary

Of the four candidate linguistic deficits, the strongest evidence emerged for phonemic awareness and transposition skills, followed by lexical retrieval skills. The evidence was weakest for a basic deficit in phoneme discrimination skills. It should be clear at this point that all these skills are closely interrelated, especially phoneme awareness, verbal STM, and lexical retrieval, and that the underlying deficit may be a factor that is common to all three. Ease of retrieving phonologic or phonetic codes, both for whole words and parts of words, from LTM might be such a factor. This would parsimoniously explain many of the results in both the verbal

STM and lexical retrieval literatures and possibly even some of the phoneme discrimination results. Such an underlying deficit could also account for the persistent deficit that dyslexic individuals have in reading nonsense words, where the phonology must be assembled from phonologic codes retrieved from LTM. At least on theoretical grounds, it does not fully account for what is required in phoneme awareness and transposition tasks, where the emphasis has been on the accessibility of phonologic codes to conscious awareness, but retrieval efficiency could affect accessibility.

Another question that must be asked about such an underlying factor (and about any of these candidate deficits) is whether they are plausibly a linguistic "primitive," which could be related eventually to the underlying neuroanatomy. In this regard, phoneme awareness and transposition skills appear to be weakest because they are metalinguistic skills that are heavily susceptible to environmental experience and training. For instance, Wallach, Wallach, and Dozier (1977) found immense social class differences in these skills among preschoolers, much of which must be due to how much exposure there is in the home to nursery rhymes and to rhyme and alliteration generally.

So far the existing research has not evaluated the diagnostic utility ences in group means may not translate into a diagnostic cutoff score with acceptable sensitivity and specificity. So before any of these deficits could be used as a marker phenotype, studies of diagnostic utility would have to be performed.

In addition, little research (except Denckla and Rudel, 1976a, and Tallal and Stark, 1982) has attempted to see which of these deficits is specific to dyslexia, rather than general to all LD or speech and language disordered children. More research is needed to fulfill the specificity criterion for a marker phenotype.

It is clear that additional research is needed to clarify the theoretical and empirical relationships among these somewhat ephemeral but clearly important linguistic processes. We lack a satisfactory theoretical model of their roles and relationships in normal language and reading development. One very helpful first step would be a longitudinal and training study that measured the relative contributions of all four linguistic skills, as well as IQ, to later reading and spelling ability. Such a study could clearly answer the question of which of these skills accounts for both the most outcome variance and the most unusual variance. The training portion would help evaluate which skill is most intrinsically related to reading development.

CONCLUSIONS

The chapter has been concerned with diagnosis and phenotype analysis in dyslexia, especially as it relates to family studies. Considerable progress has been made in both areas in the past ten years, and we are much closer to a "basic science" of reading and its disorders, which in turn will provide a sounder foundation for genetic studies. For genetic studies, the ideal outcome is the identification of a marker phenotype that appears early in development, persists, and is intrinsically related to dyslexia. We have shown that there are now two or three good candidates for a marker phenotype in dyslexia — specifically, phoneme awareness and segmentation skills, verbal short-term memory and lexical retrieval. Further research is needed to evaluate whether one or more of these simple linguistic skills will meet all the criteria for a marker phenotype.

Until a marker phenotype is established, those doing family studies must rely on more traditional diagnostic procedures. Our conclusions in this area were (1) that the most statistically sound definition of discrepancy in reading is one based on a regression equation; (2) that there is a trade-off between severity and specificity in the discrepancy level that is chosen; hence, genetic investigators may be well advised to include mild, subclinical cases in their affected group or avoid diagnosis altogether by using a continuous measure of the phenotype; (3) that self-reported reading history is valid but not perfectly diagnostic in adults; even so, it may be more desirable to classify adults with a positive history and normal test results as affected (i.e., compensated adults) than as normal; and (4) that an ideal diagnostic battery should include measure of nonword reading, speed and fluency for oral reading of running text, a good paragraph comprehension measure, and a test of written spelling, as well as a reading history questionnaire.

REFERENCES

Baddeley, A.D. (1978). The trouble with levels: A re-examination of Craik and Lockhart's framework for memory research. *Psychological Review, 85,* 139–152.

Baddeley, A.D., Thompson, N., and Buchanan, M. (1975). Word length and the structure of short-term memory. *Journal of Verbal Learning and Verbal Behavior, 14,* 575–589.

Bisanz, G.L., Das, J.P., and Mancini, G. (1984). Children's memory for phonemically confusable and non-confusable letters: Changes with age and reading ability. *Child Development, 55,* 1845–1854.

Bradley, L., and Bryant, P.E. (1978). Difficulties in auditory organization as a possible cause of reading backwardness. *Nature, 271,* 746–747.

Bradley, L., and Bryant, P.E. (1983). Categorizing sounds and learning to read — a causal connection. *Nature, 301,* 419–421.

Brady, S., Shankweiler, D., and Mann, V. (1983). Speech perception and memory coding in relation to reading ability. *Journal of Experimental Child Psychology, 35,* 345–367.

Cohen, R.L., Netley, C., and Clarke, M.A. (1984). On the generality of the short-term memory/reading ability relationship. *Journal of Learning Disabilities, 17*(4), 218–221.

Critchley, M. (1970). *The dyslexic child.* Springfield, IL: Charles C Thomas.

Decker, S.N., Vogler, G.P., and Defries, J. (in preparation). Validity of self-reported reading disability by parents of reading-disabled and control children.

Denckla, M.B., and Rudel, R. (1976a). Naming of pictured objects by dyslexic and other learning disabled children. *Brain and Language, 39,* 1-15.

Denckla, M.B., and Rudel, R. (1976b). Rapid "automatized" naming (R.A.N.): Dyslexia differentiated from other learning disabilities. *Neuropsychologia, 14,* 471-479.

Duffy, F.M., Denckla, M.B., Bartels, P.M., and Sandini, G. (1980). Dyslexia: Regional differences in brain electrical activity by topographic mapping. *Annals of Neurology, 7,* 412-420.

Eisenberg, L. (1978). Definitions of dyslexia: Their consequences for research and policy. In A.L. Benton and D. Pearl (Eds.), *Dyslexia: An appraisal of current knowledge* (pp. 29-43). New York: Oxford University Press.

Ellis, N.C. (1981). Visual and name coding in dyslexic children. *Psychological Research, 43,* 201-218.

Elston, R.C., and Namboodiri, K.K. (1980). Types of disease and models for their genetic analysis. *Schizophrenia Bulletin, 6*(2), 368-374.

Finucci, J.M., Isaacs, S.D., Whitehouse, C.C., and Childs, B. (1982). Empirical validation of reading and spelling quotients. *Developmental Medicine and Child Neurology, 24,* 733-744.

Finucci, J.M., Isaacs, S.D., Whitehouse, C.C., and Childs, B. (1984). Derivation and validation of a quantitative definition of specific reading disability for adults. *Developmental Medicine and Child Neurology, 26,* 143-152.

Godfrey, J.S., Syrdal-Lasky, A.K., Millay, K.K., and Knox, C.M. (1981). Performance of dyslexic children on speech perception tests. *Journal of Experimental Child Psychology, 32,* 401-424.

Hall, J.W., Ewing, A., Tinzmann, M.B., and Wilson, K.P. (1981). Phonetic coding in dyslexics and normal readers. *Bulletin of the Psychonomic Society, 17,* 177-178.

Huttenlocher, P.R., and Huttenlocher, J. (1973). A study of children with hyperlexia. *Neurology, 23,* 1107-1116.

Jackson, M.D., and McClelland, J.L. (1979). Processing determinants of reading speed. *Journal of Experimental Psychology (General), 108,* 151-181.

Jansky, J., and de Hirsch, K. (1972). *Preventing Reading Failure.* New York: Harper and Row.

Johnston, R. (1982). Phonological coding in dyslexic readers. *British Journal of Psychology, 73*(4), 455-460.

Jorm, A.F. (1979). The cognitive and neurological basis of developmental dyslexia: A theoretical framework and review. *Cognition, 7,* 19-33.

Jorm, A.F. (1983). Specific reading retardation and working memory: A review. *British Journal of Psychology, 74,* 311-342.

Katz, R.B. (1982). *Phonological deficiencies in children with reading disability: Evidence from an object-naming task.* Unpublished doctoral dissertion, University of Connecticut, Storrs.

Kidd, K.K. (1980). Genetic models of stuttering. *Journal of Fluency Disorders, 5,* 187-201.

Lassen, N.A., Ingvar, D.M., and Skinhoj, E. (1978). Brain function and blood flow. *Scientific American, 239,* 62-71.

Liberman, A.M., Harris, K.S., Hoffman, H.S., and Griffith, B.C. (1957). The discrimination of speech sounds within and across phoneme boundaries. *Journal of Experimental Psychology, 54,* 358-368.

Liberman, I.Y., Shankweiler, D., Fischer, F.W., and Carter, B. (1974). Explicit syllable and phoneme segmentation in the young child. *Journal of Experimental Child Psychology, 18,* 201–212.

Lieberman, P. (1983). *The biology and evolution of language.* Cambridge: Harvard University Press.

Mann, V.A. (1984). Longitudinal prediction and prevention of early reading difficulty. *Annals of Dyslexia, 34,* 117–136.

Mann, V.A., and Liberman, I.Y. (in press). Phonological awareness and verbal short-term memory: Can they presage early reading success? *Journal of Learning Disabilities.*

Mann, V.A., Liberman, I.Y., and Shankweiler, D. (1980). Children's memory for sentences and word strings in relation to reading ability. *Memory and Cognition, 8,* 329–335.

Mattingly, I.G. (1972). Reading, the linguistic process, and linguistic awareness. In J.F. Kavanaugh and I.G. Mattingly (Eds.), *Language by ear and by eye: The relationship between speech and reading.* Cambridge, MA: MIT Press.

McIntyre, M.C., and Dueckman-Krueger, A. (1983, February). Categorical perception in good and poor readers. Paper presented at the International Neuropsychological Society Meeting, Mexico City.

Morais, J., Cary, L., Algeria, J., and Bertleston, P. (1979). Does awareness of speech as a sequence of phones arise spontaneously? *Cognition, 7,* 323–331.

Nelson, H.E., and Warrington, E. (1980). An investigation of memory functions in dyslexic children. *British Journal of Psychology, 71,* 487–503.

Olson, R.K., Kliegl, R., Davidson, B.J., and Davies, S.E. (1984). Development of phonetic memory in disabled and normal readers. *Journal of Experimental Child Psychology, 37,* 187–206.

Olson, R.K., Kliegel, R., Davidson, B.J., and Foltz, G. (1985). Individual and developmental differences in reading disabilities. In T.G. Waller (Ed.), *Reading research: Advances in theory and practice, Vol. 4.* New York: Academic Press.

Pennington, B.F., Smith, S.D., McCabe, L.L., Kimberling, W.J., and Lubs, H.A. (1984). Developmental continuities and discontinuities in a form of familial dyslexia. In R. Emde and R. Harmon (Eds.), *Continuities and Discontinuities in Development.* New York: Plenum Press.

Rodgers, B. (1983). The identification and prevalence of specific reading retardation. *British Journal of Educational Psychology, 53*(3), 369–373.

Rozin, P., and Gleitman, L.R. (1977). The structure and acquisition of reading. II. The reading process and the acquisition of the alphabet principle of reading. In A.S. Reber and D.L. Scarborough (Eds.), *Toward a psychology of reading.* New York: Academic Press, 1972.

Rugel, R.P. (1974). WISC subtest scores of disabled readers. *Journal of Learning Disabilities, 7,* 57–64.

Rutter, M. (1978). Prevalence and types of dyslexia. In A.L. Benton and D. Pearl (Eds.), *Dyslexia: An appraisal of current knowldge.* (pp. 3–29). New York: Oxford University Press.

Rutter, M., and Yule, W. (1975). The concept of specific reading retardation. *Journal of Child Psychology and Psychiatry, 16,* 181–197.

Shankweiler, D. Liberman, I.Y., Mark, L.S., Fowler, C.A., and Fischer, F.W. (1979). The speech code and learning to read. *Journal of Experimental Psychology: Human Perception and Performance, 5,* 531–545.

Siegel, C., Waldo, M., Mizner, G., Adler, L.E., and Freedman, R. (1984). Deficits in sensory gating in schizophrenic patients and their relatives. *Archives of*

General Psychiatry, 41, 607–612.

Siegel, L.S., and Heaven, R.K. (in press). In S. Ceci (Ed.), Handbook of cognitive, social, and neuropsychological aspects of learning disabilities, Vol. 1, Hillsdale, NJ: Lawrence Erlbaum Associates.

Siegel, L.S., and Linder, B.A. (1984). Short term memory processes in children with reading and arithmetic disabilities. *Developmental Psychology, 20*(2), 200–207.

Smith, S.D., Pennington, B.F., McCabe, L.L., Kimberling, W.J., and Lubs, H.A. (in preparation). The cognitive phenotype in a form of familial dyslexia.

Stanovich, K.E. (1982). Individual differences in the cognitive processes of reading. II. Text level processes. *Journal of Learning Disabilities, 15*(9), 549–554.

Tallal, P. (1976). An investigation of rapid auditory processing in normal and disordered language development. *Journal of Speech and Hearing Research, 3,* 561–571.

Tallal, P. (1980). Auditory temporal perception, phonics, and reading disabilities in children. *Brain and Language, 9,* 182–198.

Tallal, P., and Piercy, M. (1973). Development aphasia: Impaired rate of nonverbal processing as a function of sensory modality. *Neuropsychologia, 11,* 389–398.

Tallal, P., and Piercy, M. (1974). Developmental aphasia: Rate of auditory processing and selective impairment of consonant perception. *Neuropsychologia, 13,* 69–74.

Tallal, P., and Piercy, M. (1975). Developmental aphasia: The perception of brief vowels and extended stop consonants.*Neuropsychologia, 13,* 69–74.

Tallal, P., and Stark, R.E. (1982). Perceptual/motor profiles of reading impaired children with or without concomitant oral language deficits. *Annals of Dyslexia, 32,* 163–176.

Thorndike, R.L. (1963). *The concepts of over- and under-achievement.* New York: Bureau of Publications, Teachers College, Columbia University.

Torgesen, J.K. (1982). The use of rationally defined subgroups in research on learning disabilities. In J.P. Das, R.F. Mulcahy, and A.E. Wall (Eds.), *Theory and research in learning disabilities* (pp. 111–113). New York: Plenum Press.

Torgeson, J.K., and Houck, G. (1980). Processing deficiencies in learning disabled children who perform poorly on the digit span task. *Journal of Educational Psychology, 72,* 141–160.

Vellutino, F.R. (1979). *Dyslexia: Theory and research.* Cambridge, MA: MIT Press.

Wallach, M., and Wallach, L. (1976). *Teaching all children to read.* Chicago: University of Chicago Press.

Wallach, M., Wallach, L., and Dozier, M. (1977). Poor children learning to read do not have trouble with auditory discrimination but do have trouble with phoneme recognition. *Journal of Educational Psychololgy, 69* (1), 36–39.

Wolf, M. (1982). The word-retrieval process and reading in children and aphasics. In K. Nelson (Ed.), *Children's language, Vol. III.* Hillsdale, NJ: Lawrence Erlbaum Associates.

Wolf, M. (1984). Naming, reading, and the dyslexias: A longitudinal overview. *Annals of Dyslexia, 34,* 87–116.

Chapter 5

Follow-up Studies of Developmental Dyslexia and Other Learning Disabilities

Joan M. Finucci

Much progress has been made in the past decade with respect to the availability of professionals in the field of education, psychology, and medicine who are able to give a differential diagnosis of developmental dyslexia and other learning disabilities. In addition, there is evident progress in the availability of both public and private school programs for teaching dyslexic and other learning disabled children. Parental awareness of learning disabilities and of their rights to secure an appropriate education for their children, even if handicapped, was facilitated by enactment in 1975 of Public Law 94–142, the Education for All Handicapped Children Act. But while the path to obtaining a diagnosis and appropriate schooling for their children has been made easier for parents, there still exist many questions in the minds of parents, teachers, other professionals, and especially the children themselves with respect to long-term prognosis. For parents and their children, the two most important questions generally relate to educational achievement and occupational attainment. Teachers, psychologists, and others ask also about general life-adjustment factors,

This work was supported by NIH grant HD 00486.

The comments of Drs. Barton Childs and Regina Cicci are gratefully acknowledged.

including adult reading habits and attitudes, mental health, self-esteem, and occupational satisfaction.

It is the purpose of this chapter to explore and review what is known currently about long-term prognosis and to examine some of the issues that should be considered in evaluating or conducting follow-up studies.

WHAT ARE FOLLOW-UP STUDIES?

As defined in this chapter, a follow-up study is any study that looks at one or more outcomes for at least one subject in light of one or more initial measures made on the same subject or subjects. Such projects are sometimes referred to as longitudinal if the period over which measurements are taken is at least several years. The initial measures might be the specific diagnosis of a condition, or they might be several of the characteristics that may be associated with a condition.

Within the category of follow-up studies we might distinguish three types: retrospective, prospective, and historical prospective (Mausner and Bahn, 1974). In a retrospective follow-up the researcher selects subjects with a particular condition, diagnosis, or outcome and sometimes subjects matched on characteristics other than the condition, diagnosis, or outcome and looks for measures taken in the past of factors that might have been predictive of current status. Examples of retrospective investigations are those that have examined the possibility that learning disability may be a precursor to juvenile delinquency (Poremba, 1975). Retrospective studies have a number of disadvantages. First, the subjects with the condition or outcome in question who are available for investigation may not be representative of the population of all such subjects. With respect to reading disability, the most disabled or least disabled may never find their way to an adult clinic or support group that serves as the source of subjects, and the most disabled may tend to ignore inquiries or requests for their participation. Second, the initial measures of interest to the investigator may not have been made or may have been made under highly variable conditions. Third, there may be no knowledge of events that may have affected outcome in the years intervening between the initial measures and the selection of subjects. The obvious advantage of such a method is that the outcome is known; the investigator does not have to wait for it to occur.

Prospective studies, on the other hand, lack some of the disadvantages of the retrospective approach. In the former, the investigator selects a group of subjects, makes initial measures on the subjects, and after a number of years, makes one or more outcome measures. Measures may also be made in intervening years. In some prospective studies, subjects are selected without regard to the presence or absence of a particular condition; the intent is to determine which of many possible variables might be determinants of the emergence of the condition. This type of investigation is exemplified by the NIH Collaborative Perinatal Project, in which 12 institutions collaborated to identify and follow up approximately 38,000 unselected infants to age 8. One component of that collaborative project was concerned with antecedents of learning disabilities, hyperactive-impulsive behavior, and the presence of soft neurologic signs (Nichols and Chen, 1981). The longitudinal study of Satz and his coworkers is another example of this type of approach (Fletcher and Satz, 1980; Satz, Taylor, Friel, and Fletcher, 1978). They examined 497 subjects; virtually all of the white male kindergarten pupils in a Florida county school system were included in the original sample. Measures made during kindergarten and in succeeding years were used as predictors of achievement outcomes at various points up to 6 years later.

The obvious advantage of the prospective method is that initial measures are made before the appearance of the condition under study, thereby preventing knowledge of the condition from biasing their ascertainment. In addition, this design allows for determination of incidence rates. Such a study also allows for the observation of many outcomes, associations among outcomes, and associations between predictor variables and outcomes. The obvious disadvantages are the great length of time and the larger number of subjects required, both of which affect cost, and the possibility that initial measures could bias outcome.

Prospective research might also be conducted by selecting subjects who fit a given diagnostic category and selecting a set of matched controls and by following up all pairs of subjects to determine if there is differential outcome. We know of no follow-up of learning disabilities that has truly followed this design. Rather, what might appear to be prospective studies of this type are, in fact, historical prospective studies.

The historical prospective method requires that a group be identified for whom a diagnosis of a particular condition was given in the past. The investigator in the present may or may not have been part of the group who made the original diagnosis. One of the distinctions between the historical prospective and a true prospective study is the time at which the decision is made to do the follow-up. One result is that in the former there may be greater attrition than in the latter, and, in addition, there may be less information available to explain why subjects are lost to follow-up. The obvious advantage over the retrospective method is that the early data relating to diagnosis have been previously assembled, thus allowing for more complete information with respect to initial measures. The advantage of the historical prospective approach over the prospective is that since the initial measures were made in the past, the waiting period required for measuring outcome has already transpired.

Sometimes the impetus for the historical prospective study comes from the availability of early records, before the development of a full-blown hypothesis. For instance, Robins (1966), in describing the genesis of her follow-up of children seen at a psychiatric clinic, noted that "the decision to undertake this piece of research grew out of the sudden availability of a population as represented in the complete records of a psychiatric clinic. . . . The clinic records appeared to be a treasure trove of research materials representing a first step in the study of the natural history of the development of adult antisocial behavior. . . . The antisocial children seen early in the clinic's history would now be fully mature and, if our predictions were correct, highly antisocial adults" (p. 13). In other cases, investigators have recognized that data gathered for other reasons could now be used to address new questions about outcome.

Examples of follow-ups of dyslexia or learning disabilities that follow the historical prospective approach are those of Rawson (1968); Spreen (1981, 1982); Finucci, Gottfredson, and Childs (1985); Gottfredson, Finucci, and Childs (1983); and Baker, Decker, and DeFries (1984). Rawson's study, probably one of the best known follow-up studies of dyslexic individuals, used as a subject group all of the 56 boys who had been in attendance for at least three elementary grade years at a small private school in Pennsylvania between 1930 and 1947. Twenty of the 56 had been classified as dyslexic. The school's records were available to the investigator, and follow-up was facilitated by the fact that the subjects were known both personally and clinically by her. Adult data, gathered by interviews with the subject, a close relative, or a friend, related primarily to educational and vocational achievement and were obtained when the age range of the subjects was from 26 to 40.

Spreen examined 203 learning disabled subjects from an original pool of 258 who had been seen at a clinic for neuropsychologic testing and educational counseling because of learning problems 4 to 12 years earlier. At the time of follow-up the mean age of the subjects was 18.7. Subjects were originally classified according to the degree of neurologic impairment: definite (n = 64), suggested (n = 82), or none (n = 57). A control group of 52 subjects without learning problems or evidence of neurologic impairment and matched with the other subjects for age, sex, and socio-economic status was also selected from secondary schools in the same area as those of the learning disabled subjects. At follow-up all subjects were interviewed about a range of issues, including school experiences and attitudes, employment history, health variables, behavioral problems, and involvement with police. In addition, school records were examined, behavior ratings were made by parents, and personality questionnaires were completed by the subjects.

The study of Gow School alumni (Gottfredson et al., 1983; Finucci et al., 1985) probably represents the largest follow-up with respect to both the number of subjects and the length of the follow-up period. In that investigation, 576 alumni of an independent secondary school for boys with dyslexia responded to a questionnaire that included items about education, occupations, adult habits and attitudes, and family characteristics. A wide array of baseline achievement and ability data was available for the respondents as well. In addition, a similar questionnaire was given to alumni of another independent school with a traditional college preparatory curriculum. The majority of subjects from both schools had completed their education and were well-established in their occupations.

In the study of Baker, Decker, and DeFries, a set of psychometric tests was readministered to 69 pairs of reading disabled children and matched controls who had been given the tests about five years earlier as participants in the Colorado Family Reading Study. This is one of the few studies in which the *same* tests were given at follow-up as were given initially.

THE MOTIVATION FOR FOLLOW-UP STUDIES

The foregoing has illustrated what follow-up studies are as well as describing the design of some. But we might explore futher why such investigations are important. In particular, we might consider why a chapter on this subject is appropriate for a book concerned with the genetics of learning disabilities.

The purposes of this kind of research are often reflected in the method. For instance, in the prospective design in which the original sample of subjects is unselected with respect to the presence of any condition (e.g., the Collaborative Perinatal Project), the purpose is generally to determine what factors may be predictive of any number of conditions that might emerge in the population. Given that some factors may be found to be important determinants of a condition, efforts may be made to reduce the presence of those factors. In studies that focus on groups given a specific diagnosis in the past, a frequent purpose is to determine outcomes after a period of time has elapsed and to investigate what, if any, factors may have influenced those outcomes. Some of those outcomes may relate to change in the condition itself (Baker, Decker, and DeFries, 1984; Fletcher and Satz, 1980; Frauenheim and Heckerl, 1983; Muehl and Forrell, 1973–74; Silver and Hagin, 1964). Other outcomes of interest may relate to adult adjustment (Finucci, et al., 1985; Gottfredson, Finucci, and

Childs, 1983; Preston and Yarington, 1967; Rawson, 1968; Spreen, 1981). Still other studies may examine changes in the condition as a function of treatment or remediation (Balow, 1965; Kline and Kline, 1975; Lovell, Byrne, and Richardson, 1963).

Another purpose of follow-up research has to do with examining the duration of characteristics, either hallmarks of the condition or ancillary characteristics. For instance, if the study focuses on developmental dyslexia, the interest might be in whether spelling difficulties are remediated concomitantly with oral reading difficulties; whether reading comprehension can improve in the presence of persistent oral reading difficulties; whether poor self-esteem and behavioral difficulties can be alleviated as achievement in reading improves; and whether IQ changes are evident if reading deficits remain untreated or as reading improves.

The purpose that is probably of most interest to those concerned with the genetics of learning disabilities is that of examining differential prognosis. When subgroups have been tentatively identified on the basis of behavioral or cognitive characteristics or according to familial patterns of transmission, we wish to know whether such varieties show differential prognosis. Such a finding helps to validate the subgroups. In another study we might divide subjects into groups according to outcome and use differential outcome as a first step in identifying subgroups. It is fairly clear that developmental dyslexia, for instance, is heterogeneous with respect to familial patterns of transmission (Finucci, Guthrie, Childs, Abbey, and Childs, 1976), cognitive characteristics (Decker and DeFries, 1981), and spelling error patterns (Finucci and Childs, 1983). Thus, it is unlikely that the genetics of developmental dyslexia will be elucidated unless homogeneous subgroups are identified in which genetic hypotheses might be tested, and differential prognosis is a potentially important characteristic for identifying meaningful subgroups.

WHAT HAS BEEN LEARNED FROM FOLLOW- UP STUDIES?

Herjanic and Penick (1972) made the first systematic review of investigations of adult outcomes of disabled readers. All of the studies reviewed were carried out before 1970, and three were unpublished doctoral dissertations. Despite the fact that the focus was on adults, the average age in seven of the nine studies examined was in the early to mid-twenties, an age at which it is still too early to say very much about occupational status. Herjanic and Penick concluded that the findings were equivocal with respect to developmental course and natural history of reading disability.

Among other problems, they cited the lack of controls, atypical samples of subjects, and inadequate measures of outcome as factors contributing to indecisive or contradictory results. They illustrated the possible influence of factors such as socioeconomic background (SES) and intelligence on outcome by noting that these two factors were more favorable in the studies of Rawson (1968) and Balow and Blomquist (1965). For instance, in the former, the 20 dyslexic subjects had a mean IQ of 123, and their fathers were, with one exception, college educated and in business or the professions; at follow-up, 90 percent of these dyslexic subjects had earned a bachelor's degree or better, and the same percentage were employed in professional positions.

In 1983, Schonhaut and Satz reviewed 18 follow-ups. They included only those that focused on children with primary reading–learning problems and excluded those concerned with children whose reading problems were of a secondary nature or in which ambiguous definitions of the disorders were used and those primarily concerned with the effects of remedial treatment of learning disabled children. Of the 18 studies, 8 had been included in the review of Herjanic and Penick (1972). In comparison with these reviewers, Satz and Schonhaut found marked variability in outcomes as well as in "sample selection, sample size, criterion assessment measures, comparison groups" and "follow-up intervals" (p. 543). Overall, without reference to the merit of each, they reported that 4 had favorable outcomes, 12 had unfavorable outcomes, and 2 had mixed outcomes.

Shonhaut and Satz also examined the quality of the separate studies. The five factors used to assess quality were length of follow-up period, sample size, method of sample selection, use of a control group, and adequacy of definition. In the 11 studies that had a follow-up period of at least 5 years, there was a balance between favorable and unfavorable outcomes. But there were more unfavorable than favorable outcomes for those studies that met the more rigorous levels of quality on the other four qualitative factors, each examined in turn.

Finally, a total score was assigned to each of the 18 studies based on how well they met each of the five listed criteria. When they examined the outcomes of the five "best," only one (Rawson, 1968) had a favorable result, whereas the other four (Howden, 1967; Rutter, Tizard, Yule, Graham, and Whitmore, 1976; Satz, Taylor, Friel, and Fletcher, 1978; Spreen, 1978) were unfavorable. Two of the major conclusions of the Schonhaut and Satz review were that children with early learning disabilities have a poor prognosis and that low SES is associated both with a higher probability of developing a learning disability and with poorer prognosis relative to middle or high SES.

Because the measures of all outcomes are not equally affected by various aspects of design (for instance, length of follow-up), the results of follow-up studies as they relate to specific outcomes will be described and evaluated in the following sections. For additional reviews the reader is referred to Spreen (1982) and Horn, O'Donnel, and Vitulano (1983).

Changes with Respect to Original Observations

A number of studies had as their purpose the determination of any change in factors that brought the child to the attention of schools, clinics, psychologists, or researchers in the first place. That is, the questions raised by the investigators had to do with whether *measured* characteristics of reading or learning disabilities are still present some years after the original diagnosis.

One of the earliest investigations is that of Silver and Hagin (1964) who reported on 24 children with specific reading disability in which both reading and perceptual tests were given at follow-up. The disabled readers, who had been in remedial classes, and 11 control subjects who were originally seen for behavioral difficulties were tested 10 to 12 years later, when the median age was about 19. In general, reading difficulties as measured by the WRAT persisted into adulthood, although fifteen (62 percent) of the disabled readers showed some improvement in reading skill. Those who achieved the best levels of reading as adults also tended to have fewer perceptual problems as adults, and subjects who had positive neurologic signs as children had the greatest perceptual and reading problems as adults. As a group, the disabled readers were poorer than the control group with respect to performance on perceptual tests both at the outset and at follow-up, and, although the disabled readers and control subjects were matched on IQ at the outset, the control subjects had higher IQs when examined later.

Muehl and Forrell (1973) reported on the reading performance in high school, when the average grade placement of the subjects was tenth grade, for 43 subjects whose average grade placement when first seen was fifth grade. Subjects were, on average, two years below grade placement in reading at the outset and were, on average, three grades retarded at follow-up. Only 4 percent were at an average or better reading level in high school as measured by the Iowa Tests of Educational Development. Of particular interest were some internal comparisons. Verbal IQ and age of diagnosis were found to be significant predictors of later reading skill, but the number of semesters in attendance at a reading clinic was not. In addition, the influence of SES on outcome was evidenced by the fact that the subjects with the best high school reading scores were more likely to have parents in professional occupations than were those who had the poorest performance in high school.

The report by Kline and Kline (1975) is one of the few that reveals rather positive results with respect to improvement in reading. They examined 216 children out of a total of 571 who were diagnosed as dyslexic (no quantitative definition was given) within 4 years after the diagnosis. Of 121 who were retested, 92 had received Orton-Gillingham remedial treatment and 29 had not. Of those who received the remediation, 95 percent showed some improvement and 64 percent were so improved as to be reading at grade level. Of the untreated group, the corresponding percentages were 45 percent and 17 percent, respectively. Similar results were obtained by telephone interview with parents who made judgments about improvement for 95 subjects. Forty-eight of these received Orton-Gillingham remedial techniques and 47 did not. In contrast to the results of Muehl and Forrell, length of treatment had a positive influence on subsequent reading scores.

There are considerable difficulties in evaluating these results. There is no information about the severity of the impairment at the outset; exact length of follow-up period is not known for either the treated or untreated groups; and it is not explicitly stated how the subjects who were retested were ascertained.

Both the studies by Satz and his colleagues (Fletcher and Satz, 1980; Satz, Friel, and Goebel, 1975; Satz, Taylor, Friel, and Fletcher, 1978) and Rutter and his colleagues (Yule, 1973; Rutter and Yule, 1975; Rutter, Tizard, Yule, Graham, and Whitmore, 1976) were given somewhat low ratings by Schonhaut and Satz (1983) because of the relatively short follow-up period. However, with respect to gains in achievement during school years, the studies are useful and informative because of the careful methods and large number of subjects.

The Satz studies that identified and tested children in kindergarten and followed them through grade 5 had as one of their major purposes the determination of early predictors of later achievement. Children were classified in both grades 2 and 5 into four reading criterion groups. Teachers' judgments of children as severely retarded in reading, mildly retarded, average, or superior were based on classroom reading level. For instance, at fifth grade, children were classified as severe if the reading level was at the third grade or below. Of 49 subjects who were classified as severe in second grade, 40 were given the same classification (by different teachers) in grade 5, and of 62 classified as mildly retarded readers in grade 2, 24 were severely retarded and 27 were mildly retarded in grade 5. That is, only 6 percent of those originally classified as severe and 18 percent of those originally classified as mild showed improvement relative to their classmates by grade 5. It should be pointed out, however, that although this work suggests an unfavorable prognosis in reading over 3 years for poor readers, it is not clear that these children had a *specific* reading disability. That is, their reading levels were only expressed relative to grade level and not to intelligence, and in fact, the severe group at grade 5 also showed a lag in mathematics skills of about 2½ years.

In 1964, Rutter and his colleagues conducted a survey of 9 to 11 year old children on the Isle of Wight. They defined the reading achievement of two groups as measured by the Neale Analysis of Reading Ability. A "reading backward" group included 155 subjects whose attainment in either accuracy or comprehension was 2 years, 4 months below the level predicted by age (i.e., they had low achievement in reading relative to age, regardless of intelligence). A "reading retarded" group included 86 subjects whose attainment in either accuracy or comprehension was 2 years, 4 months or below the level predicted by age and IQ (i.e., the disability in reading was not explicable by the child's general intelligence). There were 76 children common to both groups. When the children were tested at ages 14 to 15, slightly more than half of each group were still reading 2 standard deviations below the general population control group mean. Furthermore, the reading retarded group made less progress than the reading backward group in reading and in spelling. But the reading retarded group made greater progress in mathematics. Thus, these follow-up data on achievement measures point up the difference in prognosis between specific reading retardation and general reading backwardness.

Two more recent longitudinal studies have also focused on later achievement. Frauenheim and Heckerl (1983) examined the results of psychologic and educational tests of eleven men who as children had been diagnosed as dyslexic. The mean age at diagnosis was 10.5 years and at follow-up was 27 years. At diagnosis the group mean grade equivalent for the average of the Gates-McKillop Oral Reading Test and the Gates-MacGinitie Silent Reading Vocabulary was 1.9. At follow-up the mean grade equivalent on the same tests was 2.6, and only one subject scored as high as the fourth grade level. Performance on the Monroe-Sherman spelling test paralleled the reading scores. The group mean at outset was 1.4 and at follow-up, 2.1. In addition, only a slight increase was shown in arithmetic, from 3.1 to 4.6. These 11 subjects then had an obviously severe reading and spelling disability that persisted into adulthood despite the fact that all received special help in reading while in school, ranging from 5 to 20 semesters.

But again, we might speculate about whether dyslexia is an apt description for these subjects' difficulties. For instance, although these subjects had performance IQs clearly in the average or above average range, both at outset ($\bar{X} = 105$, range $= 97$ to 117) and at follow-up ($\bar{X} = 104$, range $= 92$ to 121), only two subjects had verbal IQs above 90 at the outset ($\bar{X} = 84$, range $= 77$ to 94), and a different two did at follow-up ($\bar{X} = 85$, range $= 78$ to 94). Also, the authors note some IQ test questions that provided particular difficulty. For instance, only two of the subjects could identify the month in which Labor Day occurs, only five could locate Brazil, and only one could identify the capital of Italy. These difficulties in concert with the arithmetic deficits suggests the possibility of general learning deficits rather than dyslexia.

In the study by Baker, Decker, and DeFries (1984), 69 children who were reading at half their grade level and who had a school-recorded IQ of at least 90 when identified and control children, matched on age, sex, and school district, were given psychometric tests approximately five years later. The average age in the first phase was 9.4 years and at follow-up was 14.8 years. IQ tests were administered by the investigators only during the second testing session, at which time the mean full scale IQs of the disabled and control groups were 103 and 116, respectively. There were significant differences between the disabled readers and the controls both at outset and at follow-up on all tests given: mathematics, word recognition, reading comprehension, spelling, two symbol processing tests, and one spatial reasoning test. The investigators noted that they did not find that the differences between the disabled subjects and the controls increased over time, as has been found in other studies (Trites and Fiedorowitz, 1976; Rutter, 1978). That is, the disabled and control children tended to develop at similar rates. As with the Satz studies, reading deficit was not expressed relative to IQ. Of interest would be whether, within the disabled group, there are some subjects who are like Rutter's retarded readers and others who are more like his backward readers, and, if so, whether the groups would show differential prognosis.

The research reviewed here is representative of projects in which achievement test results are examined at follow-up. The reader might also refer to Gottesman, Belmont and Kaminer (1975), Trites and Fiedorowicz (1976), and Rourke and Orr (1977), all of whom concluded that there is poor prognosis with respect to reading achievement for disabled readers. In general — Kline and Kline (1975) is one exception — studies have shown continued difficulties with reading and spelling for reading disabilities diagnosed in childhood.

Educational Attainment

Examination of educational attainment as an outcome measure necessarily requires a follow-up period that extends at least into the early 20's and preferably later. Few investigations have met this requirement. For instance, of the 24 follow-up studies of learning disabled persons reviewed by Horn, O'Donnell, and Vitulano (1983), four did not give a clear report of age at follow-up, and in only six of the other 20 studies was the mean (or median or mid-range) of age at follow-up at least 20. We will describe here the general findings about the educational attainment of young adults who as children had been diagnosed as dyslexic or learning disabled.

Robinson and Smith (1962) observed 44 subjects who attended a reading clinic 10 years earlier and reported good progress in educational attainment; more than half graduated from college, several were still in college, and some were pursuing graduate programs. However, although most received some remedial help in reading at some point during the intervening years, it was unclear how severely retarded in reading the subjects were at the outset. The median IQ at the outset was 120, probably a factor in the good outcome. Educational outcomes for the subjects in the Balow and Blomquist (1965) and the Preston and Yarington (1967) studies were comparable to those in the general population, although Preston and Yarington noted that schooling took disabled readers longer to complete because of significantly more grade failures. The median IQ in both of those studies was about 100. That 90 percent of the subjects studied by Rawson (1968) attained a bachelor's degree suggests the positive influence of their IQ ($\overline{X} = 123$) and SES (middle to high).

A wide range of educational achievement has been reported more recently, again probably related to socioeconomic factors and factors other than the reading or learning disabilities themselves. For instance, in the Frauenheim and Heckerl (1983) study of 11 subjects who had been given a diagnosis of dyslexia, nine completed grade 12 and two completed grade 10. None were reported to have received postsecondary education.

Bruck (1984) observed 101 learning disabled (LD) subjects, 50 peer-nominated controls, and 51 sibling controls. The control group had no history of learning disabilities. The average age at outset was 8 years and at follow-up, 21 years (range = 17 to 29). Learning disabled subjects were clinically diagnosed as having a primary problem in reading and spelling, and on the average each received 4.5 years of clinic or special school help for the learning problem. Mean IQ at the outset in the LD group was 103. Later interviews covered academic and occupational achievement, social and emotional adjustment, remediation or treatment received, and perception of current disabilities. In addition, all subjects were given reading and spelling tests at follow-up.

At the time of the interview, 10 percent had dropped out before completing high school, 32 percent completed high school or additional vocational training, 17 percent had dropped out of junior college or university, 31 percent were in junior college or university, and 11 percent had completed college. On average, they completed about 1½ fewer years of schooling than peer controls. These outcomes were significantly less favorable than those of the peer controls, but the investigator believed that the LD subjects had tended to nominate the highest achieving among their peers as controls. The educational achievement of the LD subjects was less than that of their normal learning siblings, but did not differ significantly from it. The author concluded that, although learning disabled subjects may require more time to complete their schooling than their nondisabled peers and continue to encounter difficulties with academic skills requiring rereading of texts and help in proofreading and editing, the prognosis for academic achievement is positive. She found that subjects with the most severe problems were the least likely to complete high school, but that once subjects entered a postsecondary academic stream, severity did not relate to the probability of program completion.

Finucci, Gottfredson, and Childs (1985) studied the alumni of the Gow School, an independent boarding school in New York state for boys with specific reading disability. The school includes grades 7 to 12 and offers a college preparatory curriculum and a special course called "reconstructive language" aimed at remediating written language disabilities. There were 965 boys who had attended the school between 1940 and 1977, and addresses were available for 672 of these. There were 579 (86.2 percent) who responded to either a mail or telephone questionnaire with items covering educational and occupational attainments, current reading habits and attitudes, and educational and reading history in the family.

Upon entrance to the school, approximately 97 percent of the 551 respondents with available test scores had Stanford-Binet IQs greater than 100, and the mean for these 551 subjects was 118, of 488 respondents for whom there were Gray Oral Reading and Morrison-McCall Spelling test scores, 78 percent had achievement quotients on the two tests at or below .80, and an additional 16 percent had quotients between .81 and .90. The mean for these 488 respondents for reading and spelling quotients was .73. Thus, all but a few of these subjects had average or higher IQs and moderate to severe reading and spelling disabilities. (See Finucci, Isaacs, Whitehouse, and Childs, 1982, for a discussion of reading and spelling quotients.) Comparisons of entry data for respondents and nonrespondents show no differences between the two groups. The average age at follow-up was about 37 years.

Many of the analyses of educational outcome data discussed here are confined to those 468 respondents who were not students at the time for the survey. Of that number, 236 (50.4 percent) had received at least a bachelor's degree, and of those, 36 (7.7 percent of the 468) had received a graduate degree. An additional 180 (38.5 percent) had some college or technical training beyond high school. If the analyses are confined to the 396 alumni who left Gow before 1970 and therefore have completed or are near completion of postsecondary education, 229 (57.8 percent) had received a bachelor's degree.

Table 5–1 shows a distribution of major fields of study for Gow alumni who graduated from college, for a sample of men who attended

Table 5-1.   Percentage Distributions of College Majors for Gow Alumni Who Graduated from College and for Other Groups

Major	Gow Alumni*	Gilman Alumni†	Late 1950s‡	Late 1970s§	1970-71‖	1978-79¶
Liberal Arts, social sciences, education	40.4	66.3	29.1	27.2	47.2	39.6
Mathematics, engineering, sciences	6.5	17.8	31.5	35.4	28.1	31.9
Business	42.6	5.6	23.2	24.5	22.1	25.3
Fine arts, vocational	10.4	10.3	3.7	3.5	2.7	3.4
Other or not classified	—	—	12.7	9.3	—	—

*n = 230

†= 359

‡Data of Eckland reported in Polachek (1978): major fields of 410 male college graduates, predominantly white, who were high school seniors in 1955.

§Data of Research Triangle Institute–National Longitudinal Study Survey reported in Polachek (1978): intended major of 999 men who were college freshmen in academic year 1972–73.

‖Data reported by Roemer (1983) from Earned Degrees Conferred 1970–71. U.S. Department of HEW, Office of Education (white men, earned Bachelor's degrees 1970-1971).

¶Data reported by Roemer (1983) from Earned Degrees Conferred 1978–79. U.S. Department of HEW, Office of Education (white men, earned Bachelor's degrees, 1978–79).

the Gilman School in Baltimore during the period 1940 to 1977, and for four other samples. The Gilman School is an independent college preparatory school with a good record of placing its graduates in highly selective colleges. The fathers of the Gilman and Gow alumni included in these samples had approximately equivalent SES as determined by the amount of education required in their respective occupations.

In comparison to all other groups, the Gow men were overrepresented in business fields and underrepresented in mathematics, engineering, and science fields. The small percentage of alumni in the latter group was consistent over time; 5.3 percent of alumni graduating from Gow during the period 1940–1959 and 6.9 percent of alumni graduating in 1960 or after majored in those fields. This was somewhat surprising in light of the frequently cited anecdotal information about good visuo-spatial skills and high performance IQs in many dyslexic subjects. Perhaps subjects with those skills choose to put them in good use in fine arts and vocational fields where the reading demand in school is less. The 10.4 percent of Gow alumni who graduated from college in these latter fields is higher than the percentages in that category for other groups except Gilman.

Like the subjects in the Bruck investigation, Gow men who graduated from college took longer than Gilman alumni to complete their schooling. One third of the Gow men, as opposed to 11 percent of the Gilman men, attended 5 or more years of college before attaining their bachelor's degree. In addition, of the men who did graduate from college, 28 percent of the Gow alumni versus 17 percent of the Gilman alumni either delayed entering college or dropped out for one or more years. But 80 percent of the Gow men who graduated from college did so within six years of their high school graduation.

Finally, of measures taken while the Gow alumni were at the school, achievement quotients determined from reading comprehension and spelling test scores obtained at entry to the school, reconstructive language grades, and average grades in all courses were the best predictors of which subjects obtained a bachelor's degree. That is, there was a direct relationship between the scores on these tests at school and educational outcomes. The boys with milder dyslexia did well; severe dyslexia is more likely to be a serious handicap in attaining a college degree.

Additionally, in contrast with results found in the general population (Sewall and Houser, 1975), there was no relationship between the fathers' and sons' educational attainment. That is, the 151 sons of fathers with graduate degrees and 127 sons of fathers with less than a bachelor's degree were just as likely to obtain a bachelor's degree. Neither was the IQ of the Gow alumnus predictive of his educational attainment, in contrast to a usual population finding.

Both Bruck (1984) and Finucci and coworkers (1985) concluded that the more severe the disability at the outset, the more limited the educational attainment. But it is clear that college is not out of the question for properly motivated children with dyslexia or other learning disabilities. Choice of major field of study is probably a crucial issue in success, and the time required for degree attainment can be expected to be longer than for non-disabled subjects. Socioeconomic status is a strongly determining factor in the determination of educational attainment in both disabled and nondisabled populations. The dyslexic individual is at somewhat of a disadvantage in regard to whatever level of expectation is dictated by his SES and IQ.

Occupational Attainment

In the long run, possibly the outcome of most interest to disabled subjects and parents alike is that of occupation. As noted by Gottfredson and colleagues (1984), "a man's occupation to a great extent represents who he is in society. . .it influences the expectations others have of him as well as the income and life style he provides his family." Because settling into an occupation generally occurs after completion of one's education, even less is known about the occupational attainment of dyslexic individuals and other learning disabled subjects than is known about their educational attainments.

Among the early studies, subjects observed by Rawson (1968) had the highest levels of occupational attainment; all but two of the 20 dyslexic subjects obtained professional positions. Subjects followed by Robinson and Smith (1962), Balow and Blomquist (1965), and Preston and Yarington (1967) who completed their education obtained employment in a wide range of occupations, professional as well as semiskilled and skilled. In all three of these projects the authors suggested that occupational outcome was at least as good as that represented in the general population, but in none was the follow-up long enough to see the subjects well established in their ultimate occupations.

Spreen (1982) found that the occupational attainment of learning disabled children was poorer than that for control children. Within his learning disabled groups, the greater the degree of neurologic impairment in childhood, the less likely subjects were to be in skilled employment, and consequently their earnings were lower in comparison to those of other learning disabled subjects or controls.

Among the subjects seen by Bruck (1984), in whom the average age was only 21.1 years, 385 of the subjects were still students at follow-up, 52 percent were employed, and 11 percent were unemployed, that is, out of school and looking for a job. The percentage unemployed differed across age groups. Sixteen percent of the late adolescents (ages 17 to 21) but only four percent of the young adults (ages 22 to 29) were unemployed. These figures were comparable to those for sibling controls, but among the peer controls many more, 75 percent of the total group, were still students.

Gottfredson et al. (1983) examined the adult occupations of a large sample of Gow School alumni who responded to the questionnaire described earlier (Finucci et al., 1985). Table 5–2 shows the distribution of occupations for 339 Gow alumni, 387 Gilman School alumni, their fathers, and the U.S. white male population in general.

The largest major category of work for the Gow men is managerial work. They were as likely to be in this category as their fathers and more likely to be in this category than were the other three gourps. In contrast, they were about as likely to be in the professional category as white men in general, but much less likely to be in this category than were the other three groups. The Gow men in professional or technical occupations were more likely to be school teachers, technicians, designers, or computer specialists rather than lawyers or physicians, who were well represented among

Table 5-2.   Percentage Distributions of Men in Broad Occupational Categories, Gow and Gilman Alumni, Their Fathers, and White Men in General

	Gow Alumni	Gilman Alumni	Gow Fathers	Gilman Fathers	White Men in General
Professional / technical	17.7	53.0	31.2	48.4	15.0
Managerial	49.6	32.6	53.0	39.6	11.9
Sales	15.3	9.8	11.5	9.6	7.3
Farming	3.2	.8	1.5	.8	3.0
Other	14.2	3.9	2.7	1.6	62.8
N	339	387	330	376	*

*Calculated from data on white men age 16 and over in the 1970 experienced civilian labor force. N is approximately 2,118,250.

the Gilman alumni and the fathers of both groups. Thus, the Gow men in professions were underrepresented in the most reading-intensive jobs.

Because the Gow men had relatively high levels of SES and IQ, Gottfredson and colleagues predicted that they would have relatively high-level jobs. This prediction was supported, since well over 80 percent of the subjects were in white collar jobs. The results of a path analysis showed that much of the difference between Gow and Gilman men could be accounted for by differences in educational attainment. Severity of dyslexia restricted occupational attainment to a large extent by placing limitations on educational attainment. But it is important to recognize that most of these subjects were drawn from middle to upper SES levels who had bene-fited from special schooling. If dyslexia limits the educational attainment and restricts the occupational attainment of these subjects who had such opportunity, it can hardly fail to place limits on dyslexic people who do not have such advantages.

It is of particular interest to dyslexic individuals, their parents, and vocational advisors that many dyslexic people found career success in pres-tigious positions that were less reading-intensive than other positions having similar pay and responsibility. For instance, Gottfredson and coworkers (1983) found that many dyslexic individuals were engaged in management occupations in which nonacademic competencies such as taking initiative and responsibility or being persuasive were important.

Other Aspects

In addition to acheivement testing and educational and occupational attainment, a number of other outcomes have been studied, though incon-sistently. Some recent studies are discussed here.

Spreen (1981), in structured interviews of 203 learning disabled adolescents and 52 control subjects and in interviews with the parents of both groups, examined delinquency through questions related to encounters with police, specific offenses, and resulting penalties. There was no increased likelihood of encounters with police or an excess of offenses for the learning disabled group as compared with the control group. There were, however, somewhat more severe penalties for those learning disabled subjects with no evidence of neurologic impairment than for those who had neurologic impairment or for control subjects. Spreen's results, obtained in a historical prospective study, are in contrast to those of previous retrospective studies that had shown an association between learning disabilities and delinquency.

Bruck (1984) also examined asocial or deviant behavior that appeared in the learning disabled and peer controls after entrance to high school. She used two measures. One was a measure of delinquent acts, such as assault, larceny, disorderly conduct, driving without a license, and drug possession, and along with these she recorded whether they resulted in jail, involved police, or did not involve police. The second measure related to the frequency of alcohol and drug intake. The LD subjects were involved in almost twice as many delinquent acts as their peer controls (27 percent for LD and 14 percent for peer controls), but these proportions do not differ significantly. The nonsignificant excess of delinquent acts by the LD subjects tended to result in no police involvement. Three percent of the LD subjects and 2 percent of the peer controls had been involved in acts resulting in jail. The groups did not differ in the percentage of heavy drug use (12 percent of the LD subjects and 8 percent of the peer controls) or in the percentage of heavy alcohol use (5 percent of the LD subjects and 6 percent of the peer controls).

Spreen (1982) also reported on the personal and emotional adjustment of the learning disabled and control subjects based on data from a behavior rating scale completed by parents and a personality questionnaire completed by the subjects themselves. The learning disabled subjects reported a greater number of signs of personal maladjustment and more antisocial behavior than the control groups even when confounding variables such as age, sex, and IQ were taken into account, and maladjustment was greater for those LD subjects who showed the most neurologic impairment at diagnosis. In addition, female LD subjects showed poorer emotional and social adjustment than did male subjects. Bruck (1984) also examined psychosocial adjustment based on interview data coded independently by a psychiatric social worker, family therapist, and clinical psychologist following similar guidelines. Four areas on which ratings were made were family relationships, same-sex peer relationships, opposite-sex peer relationships, and an overall psychologic adjustment rating reflecting personal and emotional well-being.

There were no overall differences between LD subjects and peer controls on the first three measures, although within the LD group, women experienced family problems significantly more often than did men, and there was a trend for LD women to date less frequently than the female controls. There were, however, significantly more overall psychologic adjustment problems for the LD subjects than for the peer controls. The difference between the two groups could be accounted for mainly by differences between the late adolescents (ages 17 to 21) rather than between the young adults (ages 22 to 29) and by differences between the LD and control women rather than between the LD and control men.

Other outcomes for the Gow men were also studied by Finucci and colleagues (1985). These include their adult attitudes, perceptions, and habits that relate to reading and spelling, a comparison of their reading habits with those of their wives and friends, and the prevalence of reading disabilities in their children. Almost half (48 percent) of the Gow alumni over the age of 25 considered their current spelling ability to be either below average, poor, or terrible rather than average or above average. This figure compares with 10 percent of the Gilman alumni who reported their adult spelling to be that bad. Furthermore, this perception of spelling ability among the Gow alumni was related to severity of dyslexia at the time of entry to the school. More than 80 percent of subjects whose average reading and spelling quotient was below .60 reported their adult spelling to be no better than below average, whereas fewer than 20 percent of the alumni whose quotients were greater than .80 gave similar responses. Responses to a question about present attitude toward reading were only slightly better; 36 percent of the Gow alumni gave an unfavorable response compared with 14 percent of the Gilman alumni, and again those with the lowest scores at school gave the least favorable answers.

In addition, 68 percent of the Gow men who were married reported reading less than their wives, while 52 percent reported reading less than their friends. Fewer of the Gilman men reported reading less than their wives or friends, 45 percent and 26 percent, respectively, but the pattern is the same. It is important to remember that for both groups these are self-report data, and it may be easier for men to admit that they read less than their wives than that they read less than their (presumably male) friends.

Alumni from both schools were asked about reading disability in their siblings and offspring. Nineteen percent of the Gow men compared with only 7 percent of the Gilman men who had a sibling reported at least one affected. Of those with offspring of at least school age, 36 percent of the Gow men compared with 15 percent of the Gilman men reported at least one affected. In both groups, brothers were reported affected more often than sisters and sons more often than daughters. Admittedly, these data are based on variable or estimated diagnoses by alumni using different types of information, but the large differences in percentage undoubtedly reflect to some extent the familial nature of developmental dyslexia.

ISSUES FOR FURTHER CONSIDERATION

Despite the large number of the investigations reviewed, certain aspects of such studies could be improved upon. We will address several issues in turn.

Definition and Other Measures at Outset

Herjanic and Penick (1972) noted in their review that it was "rare to find studies distinguishing between mild and severe reading disorders" (p. 407). One of the reasons for this lack of distinction is that many investigators made. no attempt to define dyslexia or specific learning disabilities in quantitative terms or even in good qualitative terms. For instance, of the 18 projects reviewed by Schonhaut and Satz (1983), only five were considered to have used objective, well-defined criteria. It is our position that a measure of discrepancy between expected and observed achievement should be specified. Studies that did not meet these criteria were that of Rutter and associates (1976) and the Gow School study (Gottfredson et al., 1983, 1984; Finucci et al., 1984a). Those that report only achievement deficits relative to grade level and not to IQ or general ability or that report only group achievement and group IQ measures ignore the specific nature of dyslexia or other "specific" learning disabilities. Specification of tests and procedures used in defining dyslexia also allows one to make comparisons and assess possible explanations for differences in outcome across studies.

Other important measures to make at the outset include intelligence and socioeconomic status. These are important not only as descriptors of the total group, but also as possible predictors of outcome within the group. An additional characteristic that has been given little attention at outset is that of self-esteem. In particular, it would be of interest to know whether changes in self-esteem scores are a function of changes in achievement scores or educational and occupational successes or failures, or both.

The results of the Spreen (1981, 1982) and Bruck (1984) studies, which showed poorer psychologic adjustment at follow-up for girls than for boys, illustrate one other variable which should be given greater attention, that of the sex of the subject. Because dyslexia and other specific learning disabilities affect more boys than girls, some investigations have been restricted to boys. In others, although sex ratios may be reported, results are not analyzed with respect to sex. In the light of the aforementioned results, it would seem important not only to make an effort to include girls in the study sample, but to evaluate results as a function of sex of the subject.

Length of Follow-up

Of all the reports reviewed here, only the Gow School study and the Rawson studies included follow-ups of subjects who were well established in occupations. This is due in part to the relatively recent widespread recognition of learning disabilities. Longer follow-up periods would also allow examination of mental health status and marital stability at mid-life.

Means of Follow-up

The studies of Spreen (1981, 1982) and of Bruck (1984) provide good models for ascertaining follow-up data. In both, sufficient numbers of the original study group and their parents were still accessible to the investigators as young adults. Thus, rather than collecting only mail or telephone questionnaire data, subjects and parents were interviewed personally, which provided the opportunity for more reliable ascertainment of responses to questions in sensitive areas relating to behavioral and psychologic adjustment. In addition, Bruck took the opportunity to administer achievement measures to her subjects at follow-up, thereby obtaining more uniform information than would be obtained using follow-up achievement data in records from a variety of schools.

Recognition of Heterogeneity

Yule (1973) and Rutter and Yule (1975) examined outcome (achievement scores at follow-up) in the light of the diagnosis. What was demonstrated was differential prognoses for specifically disabled readers versus generally backward readers. This approach should be applied to subgroups within a group of specifically disabled learners. For instance, much has been done to characterize subgroups of developmental dyslexia (Boder, 1973; Mattis, French, and Rapin, 1975; Decker and DeFries, 1981; Finucci, Isaacs, Whitehouse, and Childs, 1983). Whether such subgroups differ in the success of their adult adjustment has not been studied. One might hypothesize that subgroups that differ in underlying deficits (for instance, language-based cognitive deficits versus visuo-spatial perceptual deficits) would differ in the nature of their educational and occupational pursuits.

Use of Previously Assembled Data

A final note concerns the suggestion that researchers take advantage of previously assembled study groups or study data. In a recent editorial, Kolata (1984) described how investigators in other fields of science have used materials collected for other purposes in "a new kind of epidemiology." For instance, Willett and MacMahon (1984) used stored blood samples of subjects selected from among 10,940 participants in a study of hypertension to study the relationship between certain vitamins or carotenoids in the blood and the development of cancer. The subjects of Willett's research were those who developed cancer within 10 years of the start of the study, together with controls matched on a number of variables. As Kolata points out, the appeal of such studies is their cost effectiveness. Care must be taken, however, that data to be used were carefully assembled in the first place and that sufficient information was gathered to identify subjects of interest within the larger study group.

The subjects of the Collaborative Perinatal Study may be a population from which a sample of subjects should be followed. Although they were not completely representative of the United States population, IQ and SES data are available for them. Those identified as learning disabled at age 7 are now in their late teens and early twenties, and it would be of interest to know the type and success of any remediation given to those subjects, their educational achievement and psychologic adjustment to date, and the influence of IQ, SES, and initial severity on outcome.

SUMMARY

Several follow-up studies of both dyslexia and other learning disabilities have been carried out since the 1950s. The focus of many has been on whether subjects show improvement over time in reading and other academic skills. In general, reading deficits are not completely remediated, but IQ and SES exert a positive effect on remedial success. Fewer studies have followed subjects far enough into adulthood to obtain good data on educational and occupational attainment or social and marital adjustment. The Gow study suggests that given good socioeconomic circumstances and educational training, dyslexic individuals can prosper in professional positions that are not the most reading-intensive, particularly management positions. One area that has not yet been studied adequately is the long-term effects of dyslexia on psychologic adjustment.

REFERENCES

Baker, L.A., Decker, S.H. and DeFries, J. (1984). Cognitive abilities in reading-disabled children: A longitudinal study. *Journal of Child Psychology and Psychiatry, 25,* 111–117.

Balow, B. (1965). The long-term effect of remedial reading instruction. *The Reading Teacher, 9,* 581–586.

Balow, B., and Blomquist, M. (1965). Young adults ten to fifteen years after severe reading disability. *Elementary School Journal, 66,* 44–48.

Boder, E. (1973). Developmental dyslexia: A diagnostic approach based on three atypical reading-spelling patterns. *Developmental Medicine and Child Neurology, 15,* 663–687.

Bruck, M. (1984). The adult functioning of children with specific learning disabilities: A follow-up study. In I. Sigel (Ed.), *Advances in applied developmental psychology.* Norwood, NJ: Ablex Publishing.

Decker, S., and DeFries, J.C. (1981). Cognitive ability profiles in families of reading-disabled children. *Developmental Medicine and Child Neurology, 23,* 217–227.

Finucci, J.M., and Childs, B. (1983). Dyslexia: Family studies. In C.L. Ludlow and J.A. Cooper (Eds.), *Genetic aspects of speech and language disorders.* New York: Academic Press.

Finucci, J., Guthrie, J., Childs, A., Abbey, H., and Childs, B. (1976). The genetics of specific reading disability. *Annals of Human Genetics, 40,* 1–23.

Finucci, J.M., Isaacs, S.D., Whitehouse, C.C., and Childs, B. (1982). Empirical validation of reading and spelling quotients. *Developmental Medicine and Child Neurology, 24,* 733–744.

Finucci, J.M., Isaacs, S.D., Whitehouse, C.C., and Childs, B. (1983). Classification of spelling errors and their relationship to reading ability, sex, grade placement, and intelligence. *Brain and Language, 20,* 340–355.

Finucci, J.M., Gottfredson, L.S., and Childs, B. (1985). A follow-up study of dyslexic boys. *Annals of Dyslexia, 35,* 117–136.

Fletcher, J.M. and Satz, P. (1980). Developmental changes in the neuropsychological correlates of reading achievement: a six-year longitudinal follow-up. *Journal of Clinical Neuropsychology, 2,* 23–37.

Frauenheim, J.G., and Heckerl, J.E. (1983). A longitudinal study of psychological and achievement test performance in severe dyslexic adults. *Journal of Learning Disabilities, 16,* 339–347.

Gottesman, R.L. Belmont, I., and Kaminer, R. (1975). Admission and follow-up status of reading-disabled children referred to a medical clinic. *Journal of Learning Disabilities, 8,* 642–650.

Gottfredson, L.S., Finucci, J.M., and Childs, B. (1983). *The adult occupational success of dyslexic boys: A large-scale, long-term follow-up.* (Report No. 334) Baltimore: Johns Hopkins University, Center for Social Organization of Schools.

Herjanic, B.M., and Penick, E.C. (1972). Adult outcomes of disabled child readers. *The Journal of Special Education, 6,* 397–410.

Horn, W.F., O'Donnell, J.P., and Vitulano, L.A. (1983). Long-term follow-up studies of learning disabled persons. *Journal of Learning Disabilities, 16,* 542–555.

Howden, M.E. (1967). *A nineteen-year follow-up study of good, average, and poor readers in the fifth and sixth grades.* Doctoral dissertation, University of Oregon, Eugene.

Kline, C., and Kline, C. (1975). Follow-up study of 211 dyslexic children. *Bulletin of the Orton Society, 25,* 127–144.

Kolata, G. (1984) A new kind of epidemiology. *Science, 224,* 481.

Lovell, K., Byrne, C., and Richardson, B. (1963). A further study of the educational progress of children who had received remedial education. *British Journal of Educational Psychology, 33,* 3–9.

Mattis, S., French, J.H., and Rapin, I. (1975). Dyslexia in children and young adults: Three independent neuropsychological syndromes. *Developmental Medicine and Child Neurology, 17,* 150–163.

Mausner, J.S., and Bahn, A.K. (1974). *Epidemiology.* Philadelphia: W.B. Saunders.

Muehl, S., and Forrell, E.R. (1973–74). A follow-up study of disabled readers: Variables related to high school reading performance. *Reading Research Quarterly, 9,* 110–123.

Nichols, P., and Chen, T.C. (1981). *Minimal brain dysfunction: A prospective study.* Hillsdale, NJ: Lawrence Erlbaum Associates.

Polachek, S. (1978). Sex differences in college major. Industrial and Labor Relations review, 31, 498–508.

Poremba, C.D. (1975). Learning disabilities, youth and delinquency: Programs for intervention. In H. Myklebust (Ed.), *Progress in learning disabilities, Vol. III.* New York: Grune & Stratton.

Preston, R.C., and Yarington, D.J. (1967). Status of fifty retarded readers eight years after reading clinic diagnosis. *Journal of Reading, 11,* 122–129.

Rawson, M.B. (1968). *Developmental language disability: Adult accomplishments of dyslexic boys.* Baltimore: Johns Hopkins Press.

Robins, L.N. (1966). *Deviant children grown up.* Baltimore: Williams & Wilkins.

Robinson, H.M., and Smith, H.K. (1962). Reading clinic clients — ten years later. *Elementary School Journal, 63,* 22–27.

Roemer, R. (1983). Changing patterns of degree selection among women: 1970–78. *Research in Higher Education, 18,* 435–454.

Rourke, B.P., and Orr, R.R. (1977). Prediction of the reading and spelling performances of normal and retarded children: A four-year follow-up. *Journal of Abnormal Child Psychology, 5,* 9–20.

Rutter, M. (1978). Prevalence and types of dyslexia. In Benton, A., and Pearl, D. *Dyslexia: An appraisal of current knowledge.* pp. 5–28. New York: Oxford University Press.

Rutter, M., and Yule, W. (1975). The concept of specific reading retardation. *Journal of Child Psychology and Psychiatry, 16,* 181–197.

Rutter, M., Tizard, J., Yule, W., Graham, P., and Whitmore, K. (1976). Research report: Isle of Wight studies 1964–1974. *Psychological Medicine, 6,* 313–332.

Satz, P., Friel, J. and Goebel, R.A. (1975). Some predictive antecedents of specific reading disability: A three-year follow-up. *Bulletin of the Orton Society, 25,* 91–110.

Satz, P., Taylor, H.G, Friel, J., and Fletcher, J.M. (1978). Some developmental and predictive precursors of reading disabilities: A six-year follow-up. In A. Benton and D. Pearl (Eds.), *Dyslexia: An appraisal of current knowledge.* New York: Oxford University Press.

Schonhaut, S., and Satz, P. (1983). Prognosis for children with learning disabilities:

A review of folow-up studies. In M. Rutter (Ed.), *Developmental neuropsy-chiatry* (pp. 542–555). New York: Guilford Press.

Sewall, W.H., and Hauser, R.M. (1975). *Education, occupation, and earnings: Achievement in early career.* New York: Academic Press.

Silver, A.A., and Hagin, R.A. (1964). Specific reading disability: Follow-up studies. *American Journal of Orthopsychiatry, 34,* 95–102.

Spreen, O. (1978). *Learning disabled children growing up.* Final report to Canada Health and Welfare, Mongraph University of Victoria.

Spreen, O. (1981). The relationship between learning disability, neurological impair-ment, and delinquency: Results of a follow-up study. *The Journal of Nervous and Mental Disease, 169,* 791–799.

Spreen, O. (1982). Adult outcomes of reading disorders. In R.N. Malatesha and P.G. Aaron (Eds.), *Reading disorders: Varieties and treatments* (pp. 473–498). New York: Academic Press.

Trites, R., and Fiedorowicz, C. (1976). Follow-up study of children with specific (or primary) reading disability. In R. Knights and D.J. Bakker (Eds.), *The neuropsychology of learning disorders: Theoretical approaches.* Baltimore: University Park Press.

Willett, W.C., and McMahon, B. (1984). Diet and cancer: An overview. Part I. *New England Journal of Medicine, 310,* 633–638.

Yule, W. (1973). Differential prognosis of reading backwardness and specific read-ing retardation. *British Journal of Educational Psychology, 4,* 244–248.

PART III

GENETIC DISORDERS WITH LEARNING DISABILITIES: GENOTYPE-PHENOTYPE RELATIONSHIPS

Chapter 6

How Do Genes Influence Behavior? Some Examples from Mutant Mice

Richard S. Nowakowski

The question posed in the title of this chapter can be answered in two words: "not directly." By this is meant that it is unlikely that we shall ever discover a specific gene that codes for a specific behavior. This is simply because genes do not code for a complicated phenotype like a behavior per se, but rather, at the simplest level of conceptualization, they code for a gene product, usually a peptide (Stent, 1981). Thus, in order to understand how genes might influence behavior, we must first understand how genes modify the substrate of behavior, i.e., how the modification of a gene product leads to a change in the structure and function of the nervous system. In addition, we must learn how specific aspects of the structure and function of the nervous system influence behavior. Thus, in order to arrive at an understanding of how a particular gene exerts its influence on a particular behavior, it will be necessary to analyze a cascade of events extending from the nature of the modifications in the affected gene product, through an understanding of the developmental events affected (e.g., which kinds of cells and in which part of the brain), to a precise understand-

---

The research described in this chapter was supported by NSF Grant BNS-8120050, NIH Grant NS21922, NIH Biomedical Research Support Grant 5S07RR05386, and a grant from the Vaughn Stroke Research Fund.

125

ing of how these developmental events have affected the structure (i.e., "wiring") of the mature brain and how these structural changes will change the ability of the nervous system to process the information it confronts, and ending with an understanding of how these functional changes will produce changes in behavior.

Needless to say, it will take considerable study to reach this level of analysis for even one genetic influence, but progress toward this goal is being made on a variety of fronts. In my laboratory, the strategy being used is to identify mutations in the mouse that modify the structure of the nervous system and then attempt to go "backward" in development and analyze the earlier events in the cascade outlined previously; we then also go "forward" toward the behavioral end of the cascade. This chapter briefly reviews the current state of knowledge regarding the influence of genes on the structure of the nervous system, using examples from mutant mice to illustrate particular points. The scope of this article will be limited to mutations that affect neuronal migration in the cerebral cortex because these are probably the most relevant for learning disabilities (Duffy, McAnulty, and Schachter, 1984; Galaburda and Kemper, 1979; Galaburda, Sherman, and Geschwind, 1983; Galaburda, 1984; Kemper, 1984).

GENERAL ADVANTAGES OF THE MOUSE FOR GENETIC ANALYSIS

Two questions that readers of this book might ask are (1) is it easier to study genetic effects in mice? and (2) is it easier to study learning disabilities in mice? The simple answers to these questions are "yes" and "no"; i.e., the mouse presents considerable advantages to the geneticist, but it has a limited behavioral repertoire. However, in my view the advantages offered by the mouse are not available anywhere else and outweigh the disadvantages considerably. The two major advantages of the laboratory mouse for genetic analysis are (1) the availability of a large pool of mutations, many of which have already been assigned loci on the linkage map of the mouse (Festing, 1979; M.C. Green, 1981); and (2) the availability of a large number of inbred strains (Festing, 1979; M.C. Green, 1981). Inbred strains are useful tools because they provide a resource of specimens that are essentially genetically homogeneous, and therefore the effects of a particular genotype can be analyzed on numerous specimens with identical genetic backgrounds. This is particularly useful when studying the development of a phenotype or any condition that might change over time. Another useful feature of inbred strains of mice is that they are a source of genetic variability in the form of polymorphisms. The difference between a mutation and a genetic polymorphism is simply a matter of degree. If the phenotype produced by a change at a particular genetic locus is in some way detrimental, it is usually termed a mutation. If, however, the phenotype is benign, it is usually termed a polymorphism. (Usage of these terms, however, is not rigid, and one is often used when the other might be expected. Both clearly represent genetic variability, and there is probably no reason at the molecular level to distinguish one from the other.) Finally, inbred strains can be used to analyze polymorphisms by actually producing new inbred strains from already existing ones. The derivation of these new strains, called recombinant inbred strains, is described in the following section.

RECOMBINANT INBRED STRAINS

A set of recombinant inbred (RI) strains is a collection of inbred strains that are closely related, in that all the genes they carry are derived from the genomes of two "progenitor" strains. They are a powerful genetic tool and were originally developed for studying allelic differences at the histocompatibility loci (Bailey, 1971, 1981). The diagram in Figure 6–1 illustrates the breeding scheme utilized by Bailey to make the CXB series, which was the first set of RI strains intentionaly produced (Bailey, 1971)

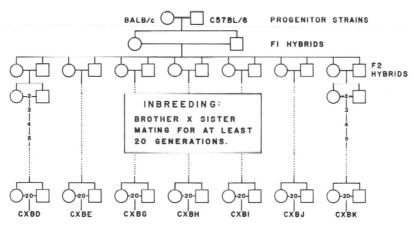

Figure 6–1. The derivation of a set of recombinant inbred strains from two progenitor strains. See text for details. (From Nowakowski, R.S. [1984]. The mode of inheritance of a defect in lamination in the hippocampus of the BALB/c mouse. *Journal of Neurogenetics, 1,* 249–258.) Modified from Bailey (1971).

and which has been extensively studied (Bailey, 1981). The first step was to produce F1 hybrids by mating a female of one of the progenitor strains with a male from the other progenitor strain. (In the case of the CXB series, a female BALB/cAnNBy and a male C57BL/6JNBy were used [Bailey, 1981].) Next, F2 hybrids are produced by mating two F1 hybrids. (This is the step where the recombinaton of the genes from the two progenitor strains begins to occur.) Finally, the F2 hybrids are inbred in order to return the newly recombined genes to a homozygous state. During the inbreeding process, genetic recombination continues to occur in each of the recombinant lines, but with each successive generation additional homozygosity is produced, and the opportunity for recombination is reduced (E.L. Green, 1981). At least 20 generations of brother × sister mating are necessary before a train is considered to be inbred. Once a set of RI strains has been produced, traits that differ in the two progenitor strains can be analyzed in each strain of the set. This typing of a trait produces a *strain distribution pattern,* which provides evidence about whether a particular trait is determined by a single genetic locus or by several loci, about the allelism (or nonallelism) of the trait of interest with other traits, and even some linkage data. Basically, concordance of the strain distribution pattern of two traits provides evidence that the two traits may be either linked or pleiotropic effects of the same locus, whereas the lack of concordance (i.e., even a single deviation) is conclusive proof that the traits are under separate genetic control (Bailey, 1981). A more extensive description of the production and utilization of RI strains, a listing of some of the available RI strains, and a listing of the strain distribution patterns for a variety of loci in the CXB series can be found in Bailey (1981).

SELECTION FOR GENETIC VARIABILITY

Basically, genetic variability in mice is detected in one of two ways. First, mutations may occur spontaneously (or may be induced) in a stock of inbred mice. It has been estimated that in mice less than one gene per generation mutates (Fitch and Atchley, 1985; Schlager and Dickie, 1967). Although this is a low rate of mutation, if (1) the mutant gene is dominant or if it is recessive and forced to homozygosity by inbreeding (i.e., it is fixed) and (2) it produces a *detectable* new phenotype that is different from the other members of that stock, it may be spotted by an astute investigator or animal caretaker or selected for through the use of some screening procedure. This is the way most of the neurologic mutations of the mouse have been found. Second, several inbred strains may be tested for a difference in a particular trait. If a difference is found, then the appropriate genetic tests, using RI strains or Mendelian crosses, or both, are done to determine if the strain difference is influenced by one or more than one genetic locus. The presumption that the gene(s) influencing the trait in question was (were) fixed during the inbreeding process. An example of a useful neurologic mutation found in this way is the *hippocampal lamination defect* (gene symbol: *Hld*) gene. Further details about the discovery, anatomy, genetics, and development of the mice carrying this gene are given later in this chapter.

HOW DO NEURONS MIGRATE?

During the normal development of the cerebral cortex, young neurons are generated in proliferative zones that line the lateral ventricles; the newly produced neurons then migrate across a broad intermediate zone and past previously generated neurons to reach their final position at the top of the cortical plate (Angevine, 1965; Nowakowski and Rakic, 1979, 1981; Sidman and Rakic, 1973). Rakic (1972) discovered that during their migration the young neurons are intimately apposed to radially aligned glial fibers that apparently provide guidance for the young neurons as they traverse the intermediate zone and the deep portions of the cortical plate, which contains the cell bodies of the previously generated neurons. The process of neuronal migration (Fig. 6–2) can be divided into three phases: (1) a "starting phase," during which a neuroblast becomes a young neuron that then acquires an apposition to the radial glial cell and a polarity away from the proliferative zone; (2) a "locomotory phase," during which the young neuron must maintain its apposition to the radial glial fiber and its polarity; and (3) a "stopping phase," during which the young neuron deapposes from the radial glial fiber and differentiates into a mature neuron. At present, it is unresolved whether the successful completion of a migration requires that a migrating neuron interact with the various constituents of its environment or if its relationship to the guiding radial glial fiber provides sufficient information during all three phases of the life history of the migrating neuron. The approach being used in this laboratory is to try to answer these questions by exploiting the availability of mutations that affect the migration of neurons during the development of the cerebral cortex of the mouse.

AVAILABLE MUTATIONS IN MICE

Potentially, mutations could affect any portion of the migratory process, so initial investigations have been directed at mutations that affect

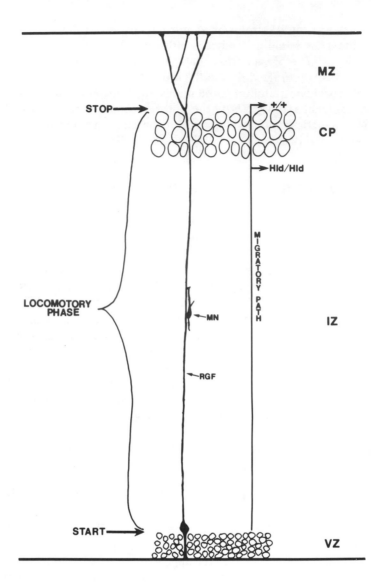

Figure 6-2. Schematic diagram of the migration path of young neurons in area CA3c of the developing hippocampus. A migrating neuron *(MN)* goes through three "phases": (1) It must leave the ventricular zone *(VZ)* and *start* its migration; (2) it must propel itself across the intermediate zone *(IZ)* and through the cortical plate *(CP)* using a radial glial fiber *(RGF)* as a guide; and (3) it must recognize that it has reached its final position at the top of the cortical plate *(CP)* at the border with the marginal zone *(MZ)* and detach itself from the radial glial fiber *(RGF)* and *stop* migrating. The arrows and bracket on the left-hand side of the diagram indicate the portions of the hemispheric wall in which each of these phases

the position of neurons in the mature nervous system. The rationale is that these mutations may affect the position of young neurons either by acting on the normal signal for stopping or by disrupting the locomotory phase of migration. At present, there are three single gene mutations and one documented strain difference (mode of inheritance unknown) that have been shown to affect neuronal migration in the cerebral cortex (Table 6–1). The best studied of these are *reeler* (gene symbol: *rl*), an autosomal recessive mutation located on chromosome 3 of the mouse linkage map (Caviness and Rakic, 1978; Pinto-Lord and Caviness, 1979; Pinto-Lord, Evrard, and Caviness, 1982), and *hippocampal lamination defect* (gene symbol: *Hld*), an autosomal dominant mutation.

DISCOVERY OF THE HIPPOCAMPAL LAMINATION DEFECT (Hld) MUTATION

In a survey of the mossy fiber distribution in the hippocampus and dentate gyrus of various inbred strains of mice, Barber, Vaughn, Wimer, and Wimer (1974) discovered that the pattern of mossy fibers in the hippocampal pyramidal cell layer of BALB/cJ mice is *qualitatively* different from that of any of seven other inbred stains of mice examined. The difference described by Barber and coworkers (1974) is that the BALB/cJ mice essentially lack an *infra*pyramidal mossy fiber layer but have a well-developed *intra*pyramidal mossy fiber layer instead. This pattern of lamination of the hippocampus can be examined using the Timm's sulphide silver method as a histochemical method (Danscher, 1981) to detect the heavy metals (probably zinc) found in the synaptic boutons of the mossy fibers (i.e., the axons of the dentate gyrus granule cells). With this histochemical method the terminal fields of mossy fibers are intensely strained so that they appear as dark-brown to black laminae above and below a pale pyramidal cell layer (Fig. 6–3). As can be seen in Fig. 6–3B, in the BALB/cByJ mouse there are numerous pyramidal cells (indicated by the arrow) below an *intra*pyramidal mossy fiber layer. In contrast, in the C57BL/6J mouse (Fig. 6–3A) there are almost no cells below the mossy fibers, which form

---

occur. The normal stopping point of late-generated migrating neurons in the + / + is indicated by the arrow on the top of the cortical plate. The stopping point of the late-generated pyramidal cells in the *Hld / Hld* mouse is indicated by the arrow on the bottom of the cortical plate. *CP*, cortical plate; *IZ*, intermediate zone; *MN*, migrating neuron; *MZ*, marginal zone; *RGF*, radial glial fiber; *VZ*, ventricular zone. From Nowakowski, R.S. (1985). Neuronal migration in the hippocampal lamination defect (*Hld*) mutant mouse. In H.J. Marthy (Ed.), *NATO Advanced Study Institute on cellular and molecular control of direct cell interactions in developing systems*. New York: Plenum Press.

Table 6-1.   Mutations Affecting Neuronal Migration in the Cerebral Cortex

Mutant	Mode of Inheritance	Affected Area of CNS
Hippocampal lamination defect (provisional gene symbol: *Hld*)	Autosomal dominant or codominant	CA3c of hippocampus
NZB mice	Unknown	Islands of ectopic neurons in layer I of cerebral cortex; some disruption of underlying white matter
Reeler mouse (gene symbol: rl or rl^{orl})	Autosomal recessive	Widespread; affects cerebral and cerebellar cortex, tectum, thalamus, inferior olive, and perhaps elsewhere
Shaker-short tail (gene symbol: sst or sst^J)	Autosomal recessive	Heterotopic cells in dentate gyrus and hippocampus. Other defects are widespread in both cerebral and cerebellar cortex

an *infra*pyramidal synaptic field. Subsequently, Vaughn, Matthews, Barber, Wimer, and Wimer (1977) showed that in the BALB/cJ mouse the late-generated cells reside in the deepest portions of the hippocampal pyramidal cell layer, abnormally positioned below the *intra*pyramidal mossy fiber layer. This is in contrast to other observations in the normal mouse (Angevine, 1965), rat (Bayer, 1980), and monkey (Rakic and Nowakowski, 1981) that have shown that the early-generated neurons are located in the deep portion of the pyramidal cell layer and that the late-generated cells are located in the superficial portion. Thus, in comparison both with a "normal" inbred strain of mice (e.g., C57BL/6J) and with other species, the pyramidal cell layer of area CA3c in BALB/cJ mice is inverted in terms of the relative positions of early-generated and late-generated neurons, and the distribution of pyramidal cells and of mossy fibers in BALB/cJ mice can be considered to be "abnormal." This reversal from the normal pattern suggests that neuronal migration to area CA3c of the hippocampus of BALB/cJ is perturbed and that late-generated neurons fail to migrate past the previously generated ones (Nowakowski, 1984a; Nowakowski and Davis, 1985).

INHERITANCE OF *Hld*

Barber and coworkers (1974) suggested that the qualitative difference between the BALB/c mouse and mice of other inbred strains reflects an

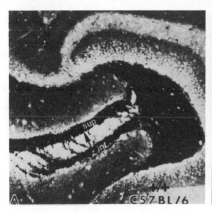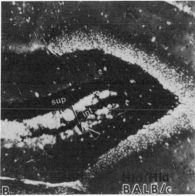

Figure 6-3. Photomicrographs of Timm's stain preparations of area CA3c and the adjacent dentate gyrus in the normal (+ / +) mouse (A) and in the *Hld* mutant mouse *(B)*. In these preparations, the axons of the granule cells (usually called mossy fibers) of the stratum granulosum of the dentate gyrus (SG) are stained black owing to their high content of heavy metals.

A, In area CA3c of the + / + mouse, the mossy fibers divide into two bundles such that the pyramidal cell layer (pcl) is sandwiched between a *supra*pyramidal mossy fiber bundle *(sup)* that runs along its superficial face and an *infra*pyramidal mossy fiber bundle *(inf)* that runs along its inferior face. Within the pyramidal cell layer, the early-generated neurons occupy the deeper layers and the late-generated neurons occupy the more superficial layers (indicated by the arrow and *E* for early-generated and *L* for late-generated).

B, In area CA3c of the *Hld / Hld* mouse, there is a population of neurons (arrows in *B*) below the *intra*pyramidal mossy fiber bundle *(int)*. These neurons are the late-generated neurons that in the + / + mouse would occupy the superficial-most portion of the pyramidal cell layer just below the *supra*pyramidal mossy fiber bundle (Vaughn, Matthews, Barber, Wimer, and Wimer, 1977). Note that the positions of the early-generated neurons and late-generated neurons are essentially the reverse of those found in the + / + mouse (indicated by the arrow and *E* for early-generated and *L* for late-generated). *inf, infra*pyramidal mossy fiber layer; *int, intra*pyramidal mossy fiber layer; *pcl,* pyramidal cell layer; *SG,* stratum granulosum of the dentate gyrus; *sup, supra*pyramidal mossy fiber layer. From Nowakowski, R.S. (1985). Neuronal migration in the hippocampal lamination defect (*Hld*) mutant mouse. In H.J. Marthy (Ed.), *NATO Advanced Study Institute on cellular and molecular control of direct cell interactions in developing systems.* New York: Plenum Press.

underlying difference at a single genetic locus. To test this idea and to determine the mode of inheritance of this strain difference, the distribution of mossy fibers was examined in mice of different genetic compositions (Nowakowski, 1983, 1984b).

The lamination of area CA3c of the hippocampus was examined in several different experimental conditions:

1. In males and females of both the BALB/cJ and C57BL/6J inbred strains.
2. In both kinds of F1 hybrids, CB6F1 hybrids that are made by crossing a BALB/cJ female with a C57BL/6J male and B6CF1 hybrids that are the result of a cross of a C57BL/6J female and a BALB/cByJ male.
3. In BALB/cByJ and C57BL/6J mice that were fostered to females of the other strain before receiving their first meal.
4. In each of the seven inbred strains that constitute the CXB series of recombinant inbred strains (Bailey, 1981). The derivation of the CXB series of recombinant inbred strains was explained previously.
5. In F2 hybrids made by crossing two CB6F1 hybrids (i.e., in CB6F2 hybrids).

For each of these experimental situations the lamination of the pyramidal cell layer was classified as "BALB/c-like" or as "B6-like." As described before, the distinguishing characteristic of the BALB/c-like pattern is the presence of pyramidal neurons sandwiched between a layer of mossy fibers and the stratum oriens, as seen in the Timm's strain (Nowakowski, 1983, 1984).

The results are summarized in Table 6–2. Both CB6F1 and B6CF1 hybrids have the BALB/c-like pattern, indicating that the gene responsible is not recessive; i.e., it is either dominant or codominant. This same pattern was always found in both male and female CB6F1 hybrids and also in both male and female B6CF1 hybrids. Since the X-chromosome of a B6CF1 male is derived from the C57BL/6J mother and the X-chromosome of a CB6F1 male is derived from the BALB/cJ mother and both these males show the BALB/c-like hippocampal lamination, these results indicate that the gene responsible is not on the X-chromosome. This interpretation is supported by the results of the cross-fostering experiments. For both of these experimental situations, the pattern of pyramidal cell layer lamination was always the same as that of normally raised mice of the same genotype. This experiment also rules out the transmission of the BALB/c-like pattern by means of a factor in the mother's milk.

Of the seven recombinant inbred strains, five (CXBD, CXBG, CXBH, CSBI, and CXBK) have a BALB/c-like pattern of pyramidal cell layer lamination, and two (CXBE and CSBJ) have B6-like patterns. The strain distribution pattern obtained from the analysis of the CXB series of recombinant inbred strains is not concordant with any of the approximately 200 strain differences so far reported for the two progenitor strains, BALB/c and C57BL/6 (Bailey, 1981; B.A. Taylor, personal communication). This

Table 6-2. Single Gene Inheritance of Hippocampal Lamination Defect

Genetic Condition or Experimental Treatment	Pattern of Hippocampal Lamination
BALB/cJ or BALB/cByJ	BALB/c-like
C57BL/6J	B6-like
CB6F1 hybrids	BALB/c-like
B6CF1 hybrids	B6-like
BALB/cByJ fostered to C57BL/6J at birth	BALB/c-like
C57BL/6J fostered to BALB/cByJ at birth	BALB/c-like
CXBD (RI strain)	BALB/c-like
CXBE (RI strain)	B6-like
CXBG (RI strain)	BALB/c-like
CXBH (RI strain)	BALB/c-like
CXBI (RI strain)	BALB/c-like
CXBJ (RI strain)	B6-like
CXBK (RI strain)	BALB/c-like
CB6F2 hybrids	7 of 9 are BALB/c-like

is conclusive proof that the BALB/c pattern of hippocampal pyramidal cell lamination is not the pleiotropic effect of another, already described allelic difference between the two progenitor strains (Bailey, 1981). The fact that only two phenotypes are apparent for the distribution of mossy fibers in the seven CXB recombinant inbred strains indicates strongly ($p < 0.008$) that only one genetic locus is involved in determining the trait (Bailey, 1981), although the unlikely possibilities that there exist two or more unlinked genes that produce the same phenotype or that two or more closely linked genes are involved cannot be eliminated.

In all, nine CB6F2 mice were examined, and seven of them showed the BALB/c-like pattern. These data are most consistent with inheritance by a dominant or co-dominant autosomal gene ($X^2 = 0.037$). There are also significantly ($X^2 = 13.37$; $p < 0.005$) more BALB/c-like phenotypes than would be expected if the gene were recessive or if an interaction of genes at several unlinked loci were required to produce the BALB/c phenotype.

Therefore, it seems most probable that only a single autosomal dominant (or codominant) gene is involved in determining the BALB/c-like phenotype of pyramidal cell layer lamination. The provisional name "hippocampal lamination defect" and gene symbol *Hld* are suggested (Nowakowski, 1983, 1984b). This name was chosen to reflect the fact that the lamination of the pyramidal cell layer of the BALB/cJ mouse is qualitatively different from that observed in other inbred strains (Barber and colleagues, 1974) and in other species (Bayer, 1980; Rakic and Nowakowski, 1981).

ANATOMY OF NORMAL (+ / +) AND MUTANT (*Hld/Hld*) HIPPOCAMPUS

In the + / + hippocampus the pyramidal cells of area CA3c are sandwiched between two bundles of mossy fibers, a *supra*pyramidal mossy fiber layer (*sup* in Fig. 6–3A) and an *infra*pyramidal mossy fiber layer (*inf* in Fig. 6–3A). Within the pyramidal cell layer of area CA3c of the + / + mouse (Fig. 6–3A), the early-generated neurons (i.e., those generated before embryonic day 14, E14) occupy the deep portions and the late-generated neurons (i.e., those generated on E15 or E16) occupy the superficial portions. The small arrow in the pyramidal cell layer in Fig. 6–3A indicates this "inside-to-outside spatiotemporal gradient" in neuron position. (For a complete discussion of the concept of spatiotemporal gradients, see Angevine, 1965.) In the pyramidal cell layer of area CA3c of the *Hld / Hld* mouse (Fig. 6–3B), the early-generated cells are found about the *intra*pyramidal mossy fiber layer (*int* in Fig. 6–3B), whereas the late-generated cells are found below the *intra*pyramidal mossy fiber layer. The small arrow in the pyramidal cell layer in Fig. 6–3B indicates that this is an "outside-to-inside spatiotemporal gradient" in neuron position, which is the reverse of that found in the + / + mouse. It is important to note that the reversal in relative position found in area CA3c of the *Hld/Hld* mouse is not present in area CA1 (Vaughn et al., 1977).

DEVELOPMENT OF NORMAL + / + AND MUTANT (*Hld/Hld*) HIPPOCAMPUS

The goal of the experiments presented here is to determine (1) *when* during development and (2) *where* along the migratory pathway the migration of the late-generated pyramidal neurons in the *Hld / Hld* mouse is disrupted (Nowakowski, in press). This has been done by comparing the migration paths of late-generated neurons in *Hld / Hld* and + / + hippocampus. In addition, the migration of the late-generated neurons destined for area CA3c of the *Hld / Hld* hippocampus has been compared to the migration of late-generated neurons destined for area CA1. To follow the migrating neurons from their site of origin in the ventricular zone to their final position in the cortical plate, tritiated thymidine (^{3}H–TdR) was injected into pregnant mice either at embryonic day 13 (E13) or E14 to label the early-generated pyramidal cells or at E15 or E16 to label the late-generated pyramidal cells (for the rationale behind this approach see Nowakowski, in press; Nowakowski and Rakic, 1981). The labeled offspring were then sacrificed after various survival times ranging from 1 hour after ^{3}H–TdR injection to postnatal day 7 (P7). All animals were sacrificed under deep anesthesia by intracardiac perfusion with a mixed aldehyde fixative, and their brains were processed for autoradiography (Rakic and Nowakowski, 1981). The *Hld / Hld* mice were all of the BALB/cByJ inbred strain, and the + / + mice were all of the C57BL/6J inbred strain (Nowakowski, 1984b).

Migration of Late-Generated Pyramidal Cells

In Figure 6–4A the position of the late-generated neurons in the + / + mouse at P0 is shown, whereas in Figure 6–4B the position of the late-generated neurons in the *Hld / Hld* mouse at P0 is shown. In both + / + and *Hld / Hld* mice the labeled late-generated migrating neurons are still confined to the intermediate zone and appear to have completed only about one half of their migration. Thus, in contrast to the early-generated pyramidal cells (Nowakowski, in press), the late-generated pyramidal cells have *not* reached their final position in either CA3 or CA1 by the day of birth (P0). Note, however, that since the late-generated pyramidal cells were generated on embryonic day 16, only about 3 days have elapsed since these cells began their migration and that, on the basis of the rate of migration of the early-generated pyramidal cells, the expected arrival time of the late-generated pyramidal cells is not until P3.

By P3 the late-generated pyramidal cells have *not* reached their final position at the top of the cortical plate in CA3 (Fig. 6–5A and C) but they have reached the top of the cortical plate in CA1 (Fig. 6–5B and D). Comparison of Figures 6–5A and C shows that the migratory progress of the late-generated neurons to area CA3c is similar in + / + and *Hld / Hld* hippocampus and that in both the normal and mutant mouse the labeled migrating neurons are still in the intermediate zone below the developing cortical plate. In contrast, Figures 6–5B and D show that the late-generated neurons destined for area CA1 are at the top of the cortical

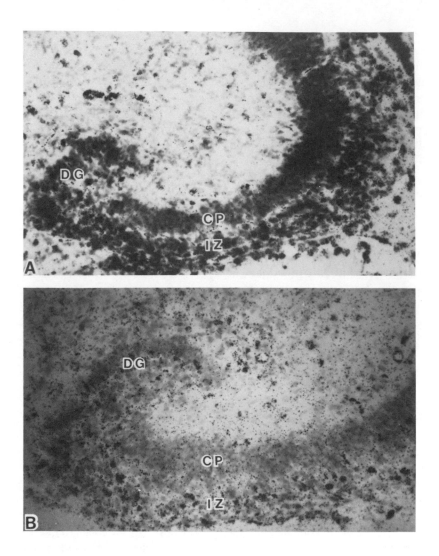

Figure 6-4. Two autoradiograms illustrating the progress of the migration of late-generated neurons in +/+ *(A)* and *Hld/Hld (B)* mice. In *A*, the hippocampus of a +/+ pup that was exposed to ^{3}H-thymidine on E16 and sacrificed on P0 is shown. In *B*, the hippocampus of an *Hld/Hld* pup that was exposed to ^{3}H-thymidine on E16 and sacrificed on P0 is shown. In both the +/+ *and the Hld/ Hld* mice, the migrating neurons are still found below the cortical plate *(CP)* in the intermediate zone *(IZ)*. *CP,* cortical plate; *DG,* dentate gyrus; *IZ,* intermediate zone; *VZ,* ventricular zone. From Nowakowski, R.S. (1985). Neuronal migration in the hippocampal lamination defect (*Hld*) mutant mouse. In H.J. Marthy (Ed.), *NATO Advanced Study Institute on cellular and molecular control of direct cell interactions in developing systems.* New York: Plenum Press.

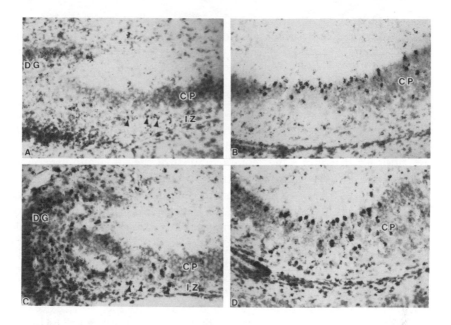

Figure 6–5.   Four autoradiograms illustrating the progress of the migration of late-generated neurons to area CA3c of +/+ *(A)* and *Hld/Hld (C)* mice and to area CA1 of +/+ *(B)* and *Hld/Hld (D)* mice. In *A* and *B*, areas CA3c and CA1 of the hippocampus of a +/+ pup that was exposed to ³H-thymidine on E16 and sacrificed on P3 is shown. In *C* and *D*, areas CA3c and CA1 of the hippocampus of an *Hld/Hld* pup that was exposed to ³H-thymidine on E16 and sacrificed on P3 is shown. In area CA3c of both the +/+ and the *Hld/Hld* mice, the migrating neurons *(arrowheads)* are still found below the cortical plate *(CP)* in the intermediate zone *(IZ)* or in the lowermost portions of the cortical plate. In contrast, however, in area CA1 of the both the +/+ and the *Hld/Hld* mice, the late-generated neurons are already at the top of the cortical plate *(CP)*. *CP*, cortical plate; *DG*, dentate gyrus; *IZ*, intermediate zone. From Nowakowski, R.S. (1985). Neuronal migration in the hippocampal lamination defect (*Hld*) mutant mouse. In H.J. Marthy (Ed.), *NATO Advanced Study Institute on cellular and molecular control of direct cell interactions in developing systems.* New York: Plenum Press.

plate in both normal *(B)* and mutant *(D)*. Thus, the CA1 neurons have completed their migration in about 6 days and also before the CA3 neurons have. The late-generated CA3 pyramidal cells do not reach their final position at the top of the cortical plate until P5 (not illustrated). At this stage, the migrating late-generated neurons in the *Hld/Hld* mouse are still in the same position as they were at P3 (Fig. 6–5B). Thus, in the +/+

mouse the late-generated pyramidal cells migrating to area CA3c need about 8 days to complete their migration, whereas in the *Hld / Hld* mouse the late-generated pyramidal cells migrating to area CA3c complete their abbreviated journey in about 6 days.

The major difference observed between the migration of young neurons to area CA3c in the *Hld / Hld* mouse as compared with the + / + mouse is that the migrating neurons in the mutant traverse most of the intermediate zone but stop migrating at the inferior border of the cortical plate (Fig 6–2) without traversing through the cortical plate to their normal position. Therefore, they complete most of their migration successfully; moreover, they arrive at the inferior border of the cortical plate at the same time as coevally generated neurons in the + / + mouse, indicating that they migrate at approximately the normal speed. This means that the influence of the *Hld* locus on the migration of the late-generated pyramidal cells occurs at a particular time and place during development (i.e., on P3 just below the cortical plate). Thus, it seems likely that *Hld* influences the stopping point of migration and does not act, for example, by slowing down the rate of migration of young neurons moving to area CA3c.

The fact that only the late-generated neurons destined for area CA3c of the hippocampus are abnormally positioned, whereas late-generated pyramidal cells destined for other subdivisions of the hippocampus (e.g., CA1) reach their final positions successfully, is perhaps the most remarkable aspect of the laminar reorganization produced by the *Hld* mutation. Thus, whatever stops the migration to area CA3c must not affect the neurons migrating to area CA1. The experiments described (Nowakowski, in press) have shown that one difference between these two populations of neurons is the *time* of arrival at their final position. Thus, the late-generated neurons in the normal (+ / +) mouse require approximately 8 days to reach their final position in area CA3, but only about 6 days to reach their final position in the area CA1. Obviously, an event occurring during the 2 day interval between the arrival of the late-generated neurons in area CA1 and the arrival of the coevally generated neurons destined for area CA3c could affect area CA3c without affecting area CA1. It should also be noted, however, that the migration path of the late-generated neurons destined for area CA3 lengthens considerably during the period that the neurons are migrating, whereas the migration path of the neurons destined for area CA1 does not change significantly (Fig. 6–6). Presumably, the change in the distance from the ventricular zone to the cortical plate of area CA3 lengthens as a result of the growth of the fimbria. It seems likely that this increase in the length of the migratory pathway contributes to the difference between the arrival times of CA3 and CA1 neurons to their final position at the top of the cortical plate and, therefore, that the difference in arrival times at their final position may simply reflect the differences in migratory distances. In other words, the difference in migratory distance may contribute to the *Hld* phenotype by permitting some unknown factor to inhibit neuronal migration to CA3c during the additional time it takes these pyramidal cells to reach their final destination.

DENDRITIC ARBORIZATION OF ABNORMALLY POSITIONED NEURONS

Cells A and B of Figure 6-7 illustrate the dendritic arborization of two neurons from area CA3c of *Hld / Hld* mice that are considered to be abnormally positioned (i.e., late-generated) because their cell bodies were located below the *intra*pyramidal mossy fiber layer. It is clear that the overall shape and form of these pyramidal neurons are essentially normal, in that they have a single large dendrite emerging from the apex of the soma. The apical dendrite typically bifurcates a short distance above the soma, usually within the stratum pyramidale itself. The orientation of the abnormally positioned cells is always radial, and no horizontally or obliquely oriented examples were seen. The characteristic dendritic excrescences, indicating the points of synaptic contacts with mossy fiber synaptic boutons (Blackstad, 1975), are found on the apical dendrites of the abnormally positioned pyramidal cells as they pass through both the *intra*pyramidal mossy fiber layer and the *supra*pyramidal mossy fiber layer. Usually, the *intra*pyramidal mossy fibers terminate on the abnormally positioned pyramidal cells below the point of bifurcation of the apical dendrite. The *supra*pyramidal mossy fibers usually terminate above the point of bifurcation, and usually each branch of the apical dendrite has a set of thorns.

In addition to the dendritic excrescences, some of the abnormally positioned pyramidal cells in the *Hld / Hld* hippocampus have short, fine-caliber dendritic branches that emerge from the apical dendrite in the vicinity of the points of contact of the *intra*pyramidal mossy fibers. These fine-caliber dendritic branches appear to be similar to tertiary dendrites and usually extend for a distance of 100 to 200 μm. (The arrows on cell B in Figure 6-7 indicates such projections.) These fine-caliber dendrites usually are oriented in the same plane as the mossy fibers, but they can be directed either up through the pyramidal cell layer or down toward the stratum oriens. Dendritic excrescences were not observed on these fine-caliber branches, even though in some instances they were observed to run parallel to the mossy fibers for a relatively long distance (cell B in Fig. 6-7).

Cell C in Figure 6-7, which has its cell body positioned such that it is embedded in the *intra*pyramidal mossy fiber layer, has dendritic excrescences on both its apical dendrites (at two points corresponding to where it passes through the two mossy fiber layers) and its basal dendrites. Cell C in Figure 6-7 also has a short length of fine-caliber dendrite emerging

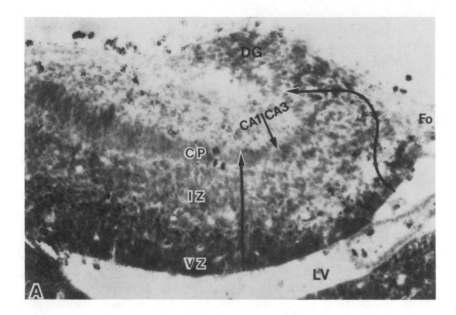

Figure 6-6. Photographs of the hippocampus of the mouse at E16 *(A)*, when the late-generated neurons are just beginning their migration, and at P3 *(B)*, when the late-generated neurons are close to finishing their migration. The arrows extending from the ventricular zone to the top of the cortical plate indicate the approximate migration path of neurons migrating to area CA3c and to area CA1. (The approximate boundary between CA3 and CA1 is indicated.) Note that the length of the migration path to area CA3c increases considerably, presumably because

from its apical dendrite in the vicinity of the *intra*pyramidal mossy fiber contacts. Cell D in Figure 6-7, which is considered to be a "normally" positioned, early-generated neuron because its cell body is situated *between* the two mossy fiber layers, has dendritic excrescences both on its apical dendrites as they pass through the *supra*pyramidal mossy fiber layer and on its basal dendrites as they pass through the *intra*pyramidal mossy fiber layer. Cell D is, therefore, representative of what has been seen in this study for normally situated neurons of area CA3c of the hippocampus in both *Hld / Hld* and + / + mice and has been shown in normal rats and mice by other authors (Amaral, 1978; Lorente de No, 1934).

During the development of the hippocampus, all pyramidal cells are generated in a ventricular zone lining the medial wall of the lateral ventricle (Nowakowski, 1984b, in press; Nowakowski and Rakic, 1981). During normal development, the pyramidal cells migrate through the intermediate zone

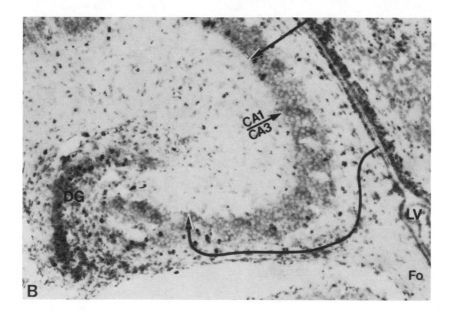

of the growth of the fornix *(Fo)*, whereas the length of the migration path to area CA1 remains approximately the same and may even get shorter. *CP*, cortical plate; *DG*, dentrate gyrus; *Fo*, fornix; *IZ*, intermediate zone; *LV*, lateral ventricle; *VZ*, ventricular zone. From Nowakowski, R.S. (1985). Neuronal migration in the hippocampal lamination defect *(Hld)* mutant mouse. In H.J. Marthy (Ed.), *NATO Advanced Study Institute on cellular and molecular control of direct cell interactions in developing systems.* New York: Plenum Press.

and past the previously generated pyramidal cells in the developing cortical plate before taking up their position at the superficial-most border of the cortical plate (Nowakowski and Rakic, 1979, 1981). In the *Hld / Hld* mouse, however, the late-generated pyramidal cells migrate through the intermediate zone, but they fail to migrate past the previously generated pyramidal cells that occupy the developing cortical plate (Nowakowski, 1984b, in press). This means that the abnormally positioned pyramidal cells in *Hld / Hld* do not reside in a completely normal milieu in terms of the types of environmental factors that are presumably important for shaping dendritic trees and axonal arbors. It is perhaps important to point out that in interpreting the data from the mutant mice, equal emphasis must be given to both the normal and abnormal aspects of the cell morphology because information about both is essential for insight into what does and does not influence the shape of dendritic trees during normal development.

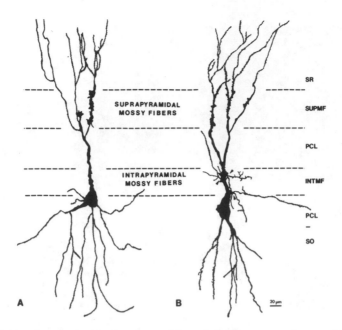

Figure 6-7. Camera lucida drawings of four Golgi impregnated pyramidal cells from area CA3c of the hippocampus of the *Hld / Hld* mouse. The somata of both cell A and cell B are positioned below the *intra*pyramidal mossy fiber layer. The arrowheads on cell B indicate the point of emergence of the fine-caliber dendritic branches from the apical dendrite. The soma of cell C straddles the *intra*pyramidal mossy fiber layer; the arrowhead on cell C indicates the point of emergence of the fine-caliber dendritic branches from the apical dendrite. The soma of cell D is between the *intra*pyramidal mossy fiber layer and the *supra*pyramidal mossy

FACTORS INTRINSIC TO THE PYRAMIDAL CELLS

Apical Dendrites

With the exception of the distribution of dendritic excrescences and the presence of the fine-caliber dendritic branching (discussed later), the overall shape and form of the dendritic trees of the abnormally positioned hippocampal pyramidal cells appears to be relatively normal: The apical dendrites extend through the pyramidal cell layer and branch extensively in the stratum radiatum and stratum lacunosum-moleculare, and the basal dendrites also appear normal. The bifurcation point of the apical dendrites does not appear to be affected. It is interesting to note that the incidence of pyramidal cells with unusual or oblique orientations is apparently *not* increased in *Hld / Hld* hippocampus. This is different from the increase in frequency of unusually oriented pyramidal cells in the hippocampus

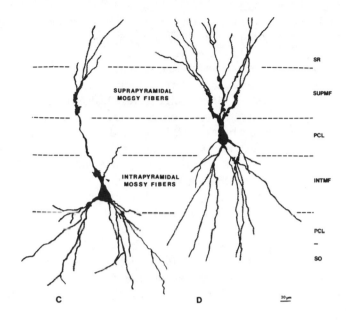

fiber layer; cells in this position invariably have essentially normal dendritic trees. See text for details. *INTMF, intra*pyramidal mossy fiber layer; *PCL,* pyramidal cell layer; *SO,* stratum oriens; *SUPMF, supra*pyramidal mossy fiber layer; *SR,* stratum radiatum. Modified from Nowakowski, R.S., and Davis, T.L. (in press). Dendritic arbors and dendritic excrescences of abnormally positioned neurons in area CA3c of mice carrying the mutation "hippocampal lamination defect." *Journal of Comparative Neurology, 239,* 267–275.

and neocortex of the reeler mouse (Pinto-Lord and Caviness, 1979; Stanfield and Cowan, 1979a). These observations indicate that in the *Hld / Hld* mouse the abnormally positioned pyramidal cells retain not only the ability to make the characteristic bifurcated dendritic tree of the CA3c pyramids (Lorente de No, 1934) but also the ability to orient their apical dendrites radially in the cortex.

FACTORS EXTRINSIC TO THE PYRAMIDAL CELLS

Dendritic Excrescences

The distribution of the dendritic excrescences upon the abnormally positioned cells in the *Hld / Hld* mouse indicates that these abnormally positioned cells receive input from both the *supra*pyramidal mossy fiber layer and the *intra*pyramidal mossy fiber layer. However, the distribution of the mossy fibers on the dendrites of the abnormally positioned cells in *Hld / Hld* does not correspond to that seen in the + / + mouse for populations of neurons generated at corresponding periods of development. In Figure 6–8, a schematic diagram illustrates the differences in the distribution of dendritic excrescences on area CA3c pyramidal cells that are generated at comparable times in *Hld / Hld* and + / + mice. In the + / + mouse, the late-generated area CA3c neurons are positioned at the border of the pyramidal cell layer with the *supra*pyramidal mossy fiber layer, where they receive synaptic input from the *supra*pyramidal mossy fibers on their apical dendrites and input from the *infra*pyramidal mossy fibers on their basal dendrites. In contrast, in the *Hld / Hld* mouse the late-generated area CA3c neurons are situated at the inferior border of the pyramidal cell layer below the *intra*pyramidal mossy fiber layer but above the stratum oriens. These late-generated neurons receive input from both the *intra*pyramidal mossy fibers and the *supra*pyramidal mossy fibers at two separate portions of their apical dendrites and apparently receive little or no mossy

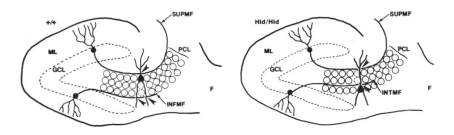

Figure 6–8.   A schematic drawing of the differences in the inputs of the mossy fibers onto late-generated pyramidal cells in the area CA3c of normal *(+ / +)* mouse and *Hld / Hld* mouse. In each diagram the neuron with the blacked-in dendrites represents a late-generated pyramidal cell. The arrowheads indicate the points of synaptic contact between the mossy fibers and the dendrites of the pyramidal cells. See text for further details. *F,* fimbria; *GCL,* granule cell layer of the dentate gyrus; *INFMF, infra*pyramidal mossy fiber layer; *INTMF, intra*pyramidal mossy fiber layer; *ML,* molecular layer of the dentate gyrus; *PCL,* pyramidal cell layer; *SO,* stratum oriens; *SUPMF, supra*pyramidal mossy fiber layer; *SR,* stratum radiatum. Modified from Nowakowski, R.S., and Davis, T.L. (in press). Dendritic arbors and dendritic excrescences of abnormally positioned neurons in area CA3c of mice carrying the mutation "hippocampal lamination defect." *Journal of Comparative Neurology, 239,* 267–275.

fiber input on their basal dendrites. In other words, for both $+/+$ and *Hld/Hld* mice the occurrence of dendritic excrescences, as seen in Golgi preparations, corresponds to the distribution of mossy fiber boutons, as seen with the Timm's stain (Barber et al., 1974; Nowakowski, 1984a) or electron microscopy (Nowakowski, unpublished observations; Vaughn et al., 1977). Another interesting feature of the distribution of dendritic excrescences on the abnormally positioned pyramidal cells is that they are absent from the basal dendrites of these cells. This is, perhaps, to be expected because in Timm's-stained preparations mossy fibers have not been observed to leave the *intra*pyramidal mossy fiber bundles and travel to the vicinity of the basal dendrites of these cells (Barber et al., 1974; Nowakowski, 1984a).

RELATIONSHIP TO NEURONAL MIGRATION

The apparent failure of the *intra*pyramidal mossy fibers to terminate on the basal dendrites of the late-generated CA3c pyramidal cells indicates that in the hippocampus of the *Hld/Hld* mouse the developmental processes that lead to the disruption of neuron position are distinct from those that control the synaptic specificity of the mossy fiber termination upon the dendrites of the pyramidal cells. In addition, the fact that the inversion in pyramidal cell layer lamination is only present where the *infra*pyramidal mossy fibers are located (Nowakowski, unpublished observations; Vaughn et al., 1977) indicates that the mossy fibers may play some role in influencing the position the late-generated pyramidal cells assume. One clue to the existence of a possible relationship of the mossy fibers to the migratory pyramidal cells comes from the fact that in *Hld/Hld* the disruption of the migration of neurons to area CA3c occurs at approximately postnatal day 3 or 4 (Nowakowski, 1984b, 1985). If this period corresponds to the time span during which the mossy fibers grow into area CA3c, then it is possible that the mossy fibers could interact with the migrating neurons. At present, however, the issue of whether or not the *intra*pyramidal mossy fibers are present at the time the late-generated pyramidal cells are migrating is unresolved. Some of the granule cells of the *infra*pyramidal limb of the dentate gyrus are generated as early as embryonic day 13 (Angevine, 1965), but the mossy fibers themselves do not become stainable with Timm's stain until about postnatal day 6 (Cunny and Nowakowski, 1983; Stanfield and Cowan, 1979b). Further experiments are in progress to determine whether the final position of the migrating pyramidal cells in *Hld/Hld* is influenced by the ingrowth of the *infra*pyramidal mossy fibers.

WHAT ARE THE EFFECTS OF *Hld* LOCUS
ON BEHAVIOR?

Presuming that the organization of the mossy fibers within the *supra*pyramidal and *intra*pyramidal bundles of *Hld/Hld* is preserved (Gaarskjaer, 1978, 1981) and that electrotonic conduction through the dendrites predominates (Rall, 1969; Turner and Schwartzkroin, 1983), the different distribution of mossy fiber inputs upon the dendrites of the late-generated CA3c pyramidal cells in *Hld/Hld* as opposed to +/+ would predict that the effect of mossy fiber input on the generation of action potentials in the pyramidal cells would be different in these two inbred strains of mice. Moreover, it is clear (see Fig. 6–8) that the distance from the cell body of the early-generated pyramidal cells to the point of synaptic contact with the *supra*pyramidal mossy fibers must be reduced in *Hld/Hld* because of the absence of the normally interposed, late-generated neurons, suggesting that the early-generated pyramidal neurons of *Hld/Hld* and +/+ may also be affected differently by mossy fiber activity. Another influence on the normal functioning of the hippocampus may arise from the fact that many of the abnormally positioned pyramidal cells in area CA3c of the *Hld/Hld* hippocampus have numerous fine-caliber dendritic branches emerging from the apical dendrite in the vicinity of the point of contact of the mossy fibers. It is reasonable to infer that whatever afferents terminate on these fine-caliber brances modify the normal functional relationships of the pyramidal cells. It also seems likely that the abnormal position of the late-generated pyramidal cells could lead to abnormalities in other, as yet unexplored, afferent systems and perhaps in efferent systems (e.g., Schaffer collaterals). Thus, it is possible that the reorganization of hippocampal circuitry produced by *Hld* and its subsequent effect(s) on information processing could be the basis for some of the behavioral differences that have been reported to exist between BALB/c and other inbred strains of mice (Schwegler and Lipp, 1981, 1983). At present, a battery of behavioral tasks that have been traditionally used to test hippocampal functions are being used to determine if the *Hld* locus affects behavior (Peeler and Nowakowski, in preparation). Eventually, more sophisticated behavioral and electrophysiologic methods (Berger, 1984) will be used to analyze the behavioral effects of the structural changes in the *Hld* hippocampus.

CONCLUSIONS AND PROSPECTS

Of more than 100 known neurologic mutations of the mouse (M.C. Green, 1981; Sidman, Green, and Appel, 1965), the *Hld* mutation is the only one that apparently affects a single small subdivision of cortex. The fact that in a single subdivision of the CNS, a single gene affects both the position attained by migrating neurons (Nowakowski, 1984b; Vaughn et al., 1977) and the establishment of connectivity of a population of axons (Nowakowski and Davis, 1983, 1985) indicates that the *Hld* mutation may be a useful tool for future studies of the cell biology of neuronal migration and neuronal specificity. Further studies of the details of the reorganization of area CA3c produced by the *Hld* mutation and of other regions of the CNS by other mutations that affected neuronal migration should provide additional insight into the relative importance of intrinsic and extrinsic factors on the ultimate shape of dendritic and axonal arborizations and some insight into the similarities and differences in the "rules" obeyed by differentiating neurons in various regions of the CNS. The identification of a gene that specifically affects only a small part of the cortex may be of significance in contributing to our understanding of the relationships between the lamination of cortical structures and behavior (Schwegler and Lipp, 1981, 1983) and how cortical subdivisions arise during development. Finally, the fact that *Hld* affects only a single subdivision of the hippocampus suggests that other genes might affect other small subdivisions of the central nervous system. In fact, there is some fairly good evidence suggesting that such genes do exist (Robinson, Fox, and Sidman, submitted for publication; Wimer and Wimer, 1985a,b). If there are similar genetic influences on single neocortical subdivisions, they could influence, rather specifically, behaviors associated with specific cortical areas. Although the identification of such hypothetical genes will be difficult, the groundwork laid by the ongoing analysis of the influence of the *Hld* locus on hippocampal development, anatomy, and function will be of significance in determining the range of reorganizational responses possible from the developing brain.

REFERENCES

Amaral, D.G. (1978). A Golgi study of cell type in the hilar region of the hippocampus in the rat. *Journal of Comparative Neurology, 182,* 851–914.

Angevine, J.B., Jr. (1965). Time of neuron origin in the hippocampal region: An autoradiographic study in the mouse. *Experimental Neurology* (Suppl. 2), 1–71.

Bailey, D.W. (1971). Recombinant-inbred strains. An aid to finding identity, linkage and function of histocompatibility and other genes. *Transplantation, 11,* 426–428.

Bailey, D.W. (1981). Recombinant inbred strains and bilineal congenic strains. In H.L. Foster, J.D. Small, and J.G. Fox (Eds.), *The mouse in biomedical research, Vol. I* (pp. 223–239). New York: Academic Press.

Barber, R.P., Vaughn, J.E., Wimer, R.E., and Wimer, C.C. (1974). Genetically-associated variations in the distribution of dentate granule cell synapses upon the pyramidal cell dendrites in mouse hippocampus. *Journal of Comparative Neurology, 156,* 417–434.

Bayer, S.A. (1980). Development of the hippocampal region in the rat. I Neurogenesis examined with ^{3}H-thymidine autoradiography. *Journal of Comparative Neurology, 190,* 87–114.

Berger, T.W. (1984). Long-term potentiation of hippocampal synaptic transmission affects rate of behavioral learning. *Science, 224,* 627–629.

Blackstad, T.W. (1975). Electron microscopy of experimental axonal degeneration in photochemically modified Golgi preparations: A procedure for precise mapping of nervous connections. *Brain Research, 95,* 191–210.

Caviness, V.S., Jr., and Rakic, P. (1978). Mechanisms of cortical development: A view from mutations in mice. *Annual review of Neuroscience, 1:* 297–326.

Cunny, H.C., and Nowakowski, R.S. (1983). The development of mossy fibers in the hippocampus of C57Bl/BJ and BALB/cByJ mice. *Journal of the Mississippi Academy of Science, 28,* 34.

Danscher, G. (1981). Histochemical demonstration of heavy metals. A revised version of the sulphide silver method suitable for both light and electron microscopy, *Histochemistry, 71,* 1–16.

Duffy, F.H., McAnulty, G.B., and Schachter, S.C. (1984). Brain electrical activity mapping. In N. Geschwind and A.M. Galaburda (Eds.), *Cerebral dominance: The biological foundations* (pp. 53–74). Cambridge, MA: Harvard University Press.

Festing, M.F.W. (1979). *Inbred strains in biomedical research.* New York: Oxford University Press.

Fitch, W.M., and Atchley, W.R. (1985). Evolution in inbred strains of mice appears rapid. *Science, 228,* 1169–1175.

Gaarskjaer, F.B. (1978). Organization of the mossy fiber system of the rat studied in extended hippocampi. II. Experimental analysis of fiber distribution with silver impregnation methods. *Journal of Comparative Neurology, 178,* 73–88.

Gaarskjaer, F.B. (1981). The hippocampal mossy fiber system of the rat studied with retrograde tracing techniques. Correlation between topographic organization and neurogenetic gradients. *Journal of Comparative Neurology, 203,* 717–735.

Galaburda, A.M. (1984). Anatomical assymetries. In N. Geschwind and A.M. Galaburda (Eds.), *Cerebral dominance: The biological foundations* (pp. 11–25). Cambridge, MA: Harvard University Press.

Galaburda, A.M., and Kemper, T. (1979). Cytoarchitectonic abnormalities in developmental dyslexia: A case study. *Annals of Neurology, 6,* 94–100.

Galaburda, A.M., Sherman, G.F. and Geschwind, N. (1983). Developmental dyslexia: Third consecutive case with cortical anomalies. *Society for Neuroscience Abstracts, 9,* 940.

Green, E.L. (1981). *Genetics and probability in animal breeding experiments.* London: Macmillan.

Green, M.C. (1981). *Genetic variants and strains of the laboratory mouse.* Stuttgart: Gustav Fischer Verlag.

Kemper, T.L. (1984). Asymmetrical lesions in syslexia. In N. Geschwind and A.M. Galaburda (Eds.), *Cerebral dominance: The biological foundations* (pp. 75–89). Cambridge, MA: Harvard University Press.

Lorento de No, R. (1934). Studies on the structure of the cerbral cortex. II. Continuation of the study of the ammonic system. *J.F. Psych. Neurol., 46,* 113–117.

Nowakowski, R.S. (1983). Single gene inheritance of an abnormality in lamination in area CA3c of the hippocampus of BALB/c mice. *Society for Neuroscience Abstracts, 9,* 833.

Nowakowski, R.S. (1984a). The migration of pyramidal cells to area CA3c of the hippocampus of mice carrying the mutation "hippocampal lamination defect." *Society for Neuroscience Abstracts, 10,* 47.

Nowakowski, R.S. (1984b). The mode of inheritance of a defect in lamination in the hippocampus of the BALB/c mouse. *Journal of Neurogenetics, 1,* 249–258.

Nowakowski, R.S. (in press). Neuronal migration in the hippocampal lamination defect (*Hld*) mutant mouse. In H.J. Marthy (Ed.), *NATO Advance Study Institute on cellular and molecular control of direct cell interactions in developing systems.* New York: Plenum Press.

Nowakowski, R.S., and Davis, T.L. (1983). A Golgi study of abnormally positioned neurons in area CA3c of BALB/c mice. *Anatomical Record, 205,* 145A.

Nowakowski, R.S., and Davis, T.L. (1985). Dendritic arbors and dendritic excrescences of abnormally positioned neurons in area CA3c of mice carrying the mutation "hippocampal lamination defect." *Journal of Comparative Neurology, 239,* 267–275.

Nowakowski, R.S., and Rakic, P. (1979). The mode of migration of neurons to the hippocampus: A Golgi and electron microscopic analysis in foetal rhesus monkey. *Journal of Neurocytology, 8,* 697–718.

Nowakowski, R.S., and Rakic, P. (1981). The site of origin and route and rate of migration of neurons to the hippocampal region of the rhesus monkey. *Journal of Comparative Neurology, 196,* 129–154.

Pinto-Lord, M.C., and Caviness, V.S., Jr. (1979). Determinants of cell shape and orientation: A comparative Golgi analysis of cell-axon interrelationships in the developing neocortex of normal and reeler mice. *Journal of Comparative Neurology, 187,* 49–70.

Pinto-Lord, M.C., Evrard, P., and Caviness, V.S., Jr. (1982). Obstructed neuronal migration along radial glial fibers in the neocortex of the reeler mouse: A Golgi-EM analysis. *Developmental Brain Research, 4,* 379–393.

Rakic, P. (1972). Mode of cell mignation to the superficial layers of fetal monkey neocortex. *Journal of Comparative Neurology, 145:* 61–83.

Rakic, P., and Nowakowski, R.S. (1981). The time of origin of neurons in the hippocampal region of the rhesus monkey. *Journal of Comparative Neurology, 196,* 99–128.

Rall, W. (1969). Time constants and electronic lengths of membrane cylinders and neurons. *Biophysical Journal, 9,* 1483–1508.

Robinson, S.M., Fox, T.O., and Sidman, R.L. (submitted for publication). A genetic variant in the morphology of the medial preoptic area.

Schlager, G., and Dickie, M.M. (1967). Spontaneous mutations and mutation rates in the house mouse. *Genetics, 57,* 319–330.

Schwegler, H., and Lipp, H.P. (1983). Hereditary covariations of neuronal circuitry mossy fiber distribution and two-way avoidance performance in mice and rats? *Neuroscience Letter, 23,* 25–30.

Schwegler, H., and Lipp, H.P. (1983). Heriditary covariations of neuronal circuitry and behavior: Correlations between the proportions of hippocampal synaptic fields in the regio inferior and two-way avoidance in mice and rats. *Behavioral Brain Research, 7,* 1–38.

Sidman, R.L., and Rakic, P. (1973). Neuronal migration with special reference to developing human brain: A review. *Brain Research, 62,* 1–35.

Sidman, R.L. Green, M.D., and Appel, S.H. (1965). *Catalog of the neurological mutants of the mouse.* Cambridge, MA: Harvard University Press.

Stanfield, B.B., and Cowan, W.M. (1979a). The morphology of the hippocampus and dentate gyrus in normal and reeler mice. *Journal of Comparative Neurology, 185,* 393–422.

Stanfield, B.B., and Cowan, W.M. (1979b). The development of the hippocampus and dentate gyrus in normal and reeler mice. *Journal of Comparative Neurology, 185,* 423–460.

Stent, G.S. (1981). Strength and weakness of the genetic approach to the development of the nervous system. In W.M. Cowan (Ed.), *Studies in developmental neurobiology: Essays in honor of Viktor Hamburger* (pp. 288–321). New York: Oxford University Press.

Turner, D.A., and Schwartzkroin, P.A. (1983). Electrical characteristics of dendrites and dendritic spines in intracellularly stained CA3 and dentate hippocampal neurons. *Journal of Neuroscience, 3,* 2381–2394.

Vaughn, J.E., Matthews, D.A., Barber, R.P., Wimer, C.C., and Wimer, R.E. (1977). Genetically associated variations in the development of hippocampal pyramidal neurons may produce differences in mossy fiber connectivity. *Journal of Comparative Neurology, 173,* 41–52.

Wimer, R.E., and Wimer, C.C. (1985a). Animal behavior genetics: A search for the biological foundations of behavior. *Annual Review of Psychology, 36,* 171–218.

Wimer, R.E., and Wimer, C.C. (1985b). Three sex dimorphisms in the granule cell layer of the hippocampus in house mice. *Brain Research, 328,* 105–109.

Chapter 7

Multiple Anomaly Syndromes and Learning Disabilities

Robert J. Shprintzen and
Rosalie B. Goldberg

The study of learning disabilities is deeply rooted in the numerous fields of behavioral science. Psychologists, speech pathologists, educational specialists, reading specialists, and other behavioral scientists were the first professionals to look at learning disabilities in a systematic way. Researchers from these fields are trained to analyze human behavior. In its simplest terms, human behavior may be defined as something that a person does. In the behavioral scheme of things, raising one's arm, sitting down, thinking, blinking the eye, and singing are all human behaviors and may all be modified by behavioral techniques. Therefore, learning disabilities may be regarded as a behavioral disorder because they represent something abnormal that a person is doing. A learning disability is a behavioral disorder in much the same way as a twitch of the eye, a lisp, a phobia, or bulemia.

The proliferation in the study of learning disabilities coincides chronologically with the early growth of the fields of clinical genetics, dysmorphology, and syndromology. These new fields were less a study of what individuals did, but rather more a study of what people were. Dsymorphologists relied upon the study of an individual's phenotype, genotype, karyotype, history, and laboratory tests to find out the biologic root causes of an individual's abnormalities. An individual's behavioral repertoire was generally discussed in relation to specific syndromes that would predictably be associated with certain functional disorders such as mental retardation, "dementia," "affectionate" behavior, or a "cocktail party" manner. Such behavioral features of syndromes were generally mentioned as interesting observations or as secondary manifestations of central nervous system anomalies (as in Down syndrome and Williams syndrome) or chemical imbalances (as in Lesch-Nyhan syndrome and Hurler syndrome). On only rare occasions were behavioral features considered to be of major value in differential diagnosis (as in Lesch-Nyhan syndrome).

In establishing diagnoses, syndromologists and dysmorphologists must depend upon "hard" features. "Hard" features can be defined as those that are objectively measurable and not open to subjective interpretation. Radiographs, anthropometrics, karyotypes, electrocardiograms, and myriad other examination techniques can be employed to provide such "hard" evidence. If these tests were repeated on multiple occasions on the same child on the same day by a large number of trained professionals, the results would presumably be comparable, if not the same.

Learning disabilities and other cognitive disorders do not present the same "hard" data as physical examination features. The diagnosis of such impairments is reached only after extensive testing and some degree of examiner interpretation. It is little wonder, therefore, that many clinicians would be reluctant to accept such "subjective" evidence as a "hard" feature. In fact, child neurologists regard learning disabilities or language impairment to be "soft signs" of CNS impairment. Perhaps there is the perception that performance on these tests is largely influenced by the intellectual environment at home (including the amount of stimulation received) and intangibles such as "motivation." In other words, cognitive performance may largely be determined by environmental influences and not as directly related to structure as are, for example, myopia, microcephaly, or orbital hypertelorism.

In this chapter we discuss the possibility, in fact the desirability, of including information about learning disabilities and other cognitive disorders as the type of "hard" diagnostic evidence needed for syndrome identification. This is done within the framework of discussing several syndromes that have such cognitive impairment as an identifiable feature or, stated differently, as an identifiable anomaly.

LEARNING DISABILITIES AS ANOMALIES

What is an anomaly? An anomaly may be defined as any deviation from normal structure, form, or *function* that is interpreted to be abnormal (Siegel-Sadewitz and Shprintzen, 1982). Anomalies that occur as parts of syndromes have several properties that are well understood by syndromologists. First, no anomaly associated with a given syndrome occurs in every single case of that syndrome. Stating the same thing in a slightly different way, no anomaly is pathognomonic of a given syndrome. There are simply no obligatory findings. For example, even though Crouzon syndrome is a "syndrome of craniosynostosis," it is possible to express the gene for Crouzon syndrome and have no evidence of craniosynostosis. Second, all anomalies show variable expression. Any anomaly frequently associated with a given syndrome will not always be expressed in equal degree for every case of that syndrome. For example, ear anomalies occur very frequently in Treacher Collins syndrome. Some patients have a severe grade III microtia with a 60 to 70 dB conductive hearing loss, whereas others may have relatively normal-appearing auricles with only slight thinning of the helical rims and perhaps a 20 dB conductive hearing loss. Actually, both of these properties of anomalies represent the same principle, that of variable expression. Variability of expression implies a range of severity from very severe to clinical absence of the anomaly (hence the lack of pathognomonicity). Learning disabilities and other cognitive disorders have these same properties.

For example, the Steinert syndrome often has learning disabilities as a feature in the population seen at the Center for Craniofacial Disorders, even when the onset of this form of muscular dystrophy occurs in early adolescence. But even though cognitive defects may be *expected* to occur with frequency, a percentage of patients with this autosomal dominant condition have no evidence of any learning impairment whatsoever.

Variable expression is particularly well demonstrated by the velo-cardio-facial syndrome. Specific learning disabilities have been reported in all known cases to date. Recent data (Golding-Kushner, Weller, and Shprintzen, 1985) indicate that cognitive functioning is variably affected, ranging from mild mental retardation in approximately 40 percent of reported cases to above-average IQ scores with deficits in abstraction that affect performance in mathematics and reading comprehension in several others. The fact that variability of expression in the velo-cardio-facial syndrome results in mental retardation at one end of the spectrum and specific learning disabilities in mathematics and reading comprehension at the other indicates the strong likelihood of a firm biologic, structural basis for such cognitive impairments. It also implies that mental retardation and at least some learning disabilities may represent different points on a continuum. In other words, mental retardation versus learning disabilities (within the same syndrome) may differ only in degree of severity, rather than being separate and distinct entities.

LEARNING DISABILITIES AS A FREQUENTLY
EXPRESSED ANOMALY

There are a sizable number of syndromes that have learning disabilities and other cognitive deficiencies as frequent, though by no means pathognomonic, findings. Many of these syndromes have major and minor craniofacial anomalies as well and are therefore often ascertained through craniofacial centers. Discussion in this chapter is limited to such syndromes and largely focuses on those with which we have had considerable experience.

The learning disabilities found in some of these syndromes may be a secondary feature. In other words, all organs related to congitive functioning are structurally normal. More precisely, the central nervous system (CNS) itself is not anomalous. However, other anomalies expressed by a mutant gene or a deformational process may have an adverse effect on an otherwise normal CNS. Examples of this phenomenon include Crouzon syndrome, Treacher Collins syndrome, achondroplasia syndrome, ADAM sequence, facio-auriculo-vertebral sequence, Pierre Robin sequence, Stickler syndrome, and Hunter syndrome. An abnormal chromosome constitution or the embryopathic effect of a teratogen would not be expected to yield such a secondary effect, for reasons that are discussed later.

In other syndromes, learning disabilities and other cognitive disorders are primary features. When learning disabilities occur as a primary feature, it may be assumed that they are etiologically related to a morphologic abnormality within the CNS. The reason it is necessary to assume this relationship is that for minor cognitive impairments such as learning disabilities and language impairment, specific structural anomalies of the brain have not yet been firmly established. This is precisely why the term "soft sign" was coined. Therefore, in the absence of detailed anatomic evidence of a structural CNS malformation related to learning disabilities, it might be best to think of learning disabilities as a primary feature when the examiner is convinced that they are not secondary. Mutant genes, an abnormal chromosome constitution, and embryopathic effects of teratogens may all result in learning disabilities as a primary part of a syndrome. In fact, the majority of chromosomal syndromes result in a variety of cognitive deficiencies, most often severe. All of the known teratogens also consistently cause a variety of CNS malformations, with subsequent cognitive deficiencies ranging from mild to severe.

It is difficult, if not impossible, to differentiate those syndromes in which learning disabilities are secondary features from those in which they are primary features based upon the analysis of the cognitive distrubances alone. It is essential to regard the cognitive dysfunction within the gestalt of the syndromic entity in order to understand its etiology. This is of extreme importance because in many syndromes in which the learning disability is a secondary feature, it may prove to be preventable. This is only occasionally true of syndromes in which cognitive defects are a primary finding. Primary cognitive defects can only be prevented in syndromes related to maternal metabolic abnormalities, such as fetal iodine deficiency effects (endemic cretinism) (Connolly, Pharoah, and Hetzel, 1979; Smith, 1982) or in instances in which the use of teratogens is monitored during a pregnancy.

SYNDROMES WITH LEARNING DISABILITIES AS A SECONDARY FEATURE

As stated previously, it is essential to identify those syndromes in which cognitive dysfunction is a secondary feature. In instances in which secondary effects on the CNS occur largely in the postnatal period, proper medical or surgical intervention may possibly be applicable to prevent them. The recognition of these syndromes must occur at the earliest possible time. Because learning disabilities are usually not diagnosed until school age, by that time it may be too late to reverse the problem.

Crouzon Syndrome

Crouzon syndrome is one of the more easily recognized congenital malformation syndromes, unless the expression is very mild. Descriptions of this syndrome are numerous and are best summarized by Gorlin, Pindborg, and Cohen (1976) and Cohen (1975, 1979, 1980). It is generally regarded to be a syndrome of craniosynostosis because one of the most frequent findings in the syndrome is premature fusion of the cranial bones. It is generally recognized that early craniectomies will prevent the increased intracranial pressure that could result in secondary CNS damage with its subsequent cognitive defects. The exact frequency of mental retardation in Crouzon syndrome is not known because of the ascertainment biases involved in looking at this relatively rare syndrome. It is assumed to be relatively low by most clinicians. What is more poorly understood is the frequency of less severe cognitive deficiencies, including learning disabilities and language impairment.

Among the population at the Center for Craniofacial Disorders (CCFD), there is approximately a 25 percent incidence of some learning impairment among adult patients with Crouzon syndrome who did not have craniectomies as children but who did evidence increased intracranial pressure. In the patients who did have early craniectomies, there has been only one instance of either mental retardation or learning disabilities. Of course, there is an ascertainment bias in this group, in that none were referred from institutions for the retarded or similar settings. However, it should be pointed out that in other syndromes of craniosynostosis, cognitive deficiencies do occur even after early craniectomy. For example, in our patients with Apert syndrome, there is a 100 percent incidence of either mental retardation or learning disabilities and a 100 percent incidence of significant language delay in spite of early craniectomy and careful follow-up for increased intracranial pressure. In patients with Apert syndrome in whom we have found no evidence of secondary brain constriction, we have still seen cognitive impairment. As a result, we have concluded that the cognitive impairment seen in Apert syndrome is likely to be a primary effect of the mutant gene rather than secondary to craniosynostosis. It is therefore incorrect to regard Apert syndrome as equivalent to Crouzon syndrome with syndactyly. Similarly, Shprintzen and Goldberg (1982) reported on a syndrome of craniosynostosis with severe mental retardation as a primary feature even though early craniectomies had been performed.

The finding of cognitive dysfunctions in Crouzon syndrome at any age should alert the astute clinician to the possibility that the patient has increased intracranial pressure that can be reversed surgically. A case study illustrates this principle. A patient was referred to CCFD at 5 years of age with the diagnosis of Crouzon syndrome (Fig. 7–1). She was from a rural area of the Midwest that did not have a nearby craniofacial center.

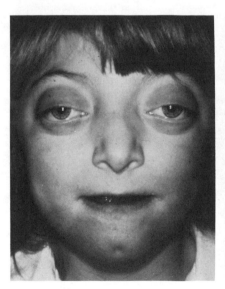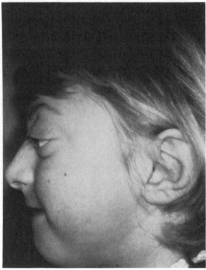

Figure 7-1.   Lateral and frontal photographs of 5 year old girl with Crouzon syndrome.

The syndrome was not recognized immediately at birth. In fact the initial facial expression of the syndrome was very mild. Therefore, early craniectomies were not performed. History and examination of all first-degree relatives revealed that this was a new mutation, thus also confounding the diagnosis. History also revealed that the patient had a patent anterior fontanel throughout the first year of life.

When seen at CCFD at 5 years, 3 months of age, examination revealed a head circumference of 50 cm (25th centile) with mild acrocephaly. Height and weight were at the 90th centile. There was moderately severe exorbitism, mild orbital hypertelorism, and moderate midfacial hypoplasia. There were no extracranial anomalies. Skull radiographs (Fig. 7–2) showed evidence of "digital impressions" in the calvarium, indicating some degree of increased intracranial pressure. Ophthalmologic examination showed 20/50 vision bilaterally, exotropia, and hyperopia. Neurologic evaluation showed a mildly ataxic gait, poor fine motor coordination and short attention span. Psychometric evaluation confirmed the short attention span, mild overactivity, but an above-average IQ. Because of evidence of increased intracranial pressure and its secondary effect on fine motor control, as well as the need for a reduction of the exorbitism, craniofacial

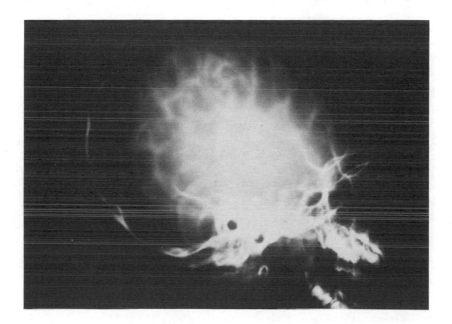

Figure 7–2. Skull films of patient in Figure 7–1 showing signs of increased intracranial pressure.

surgery was performed. Surgery consisted of a frontal bone advancement that would relieve the intracranial pressure, improve the contour of the cranium, and resolve the supraorbital aspect of the exorbitism (Fig. 7–3). At the same time, the lateral orbital rims were advanced (Fig. 7–4). The lower orbital rims (the upper maxilla) were advanced separately in a second procedure. At the time of surgery, intracranial pressure was found to be 2.5 times higher than normal (Fig. 7–5). Following surgery, all neurologic and fine motor impairments resolved completely.

Though this case is anecdotal, it does illustrate that the CNS-related problems experienced by this patient were secondary to the craniosynostosis and were amenable to treatment. If only the neurologic "soft signs" of this patient had been observed, they might have been treated symptomatically (more specifically, educationally), and the opportunity to intervene surgically might have been lost. However, the soft signs together with the physical findings and an understanding of the natural history of Crouzon syndrome led to a "gestalt" type of diagnostic decision.

Treacher Collins Syndrome

Nearly 50 percent of the patients with Treacher Collins syndrome at CCFD have cognitive disorders, ranging from moderate mental retardation

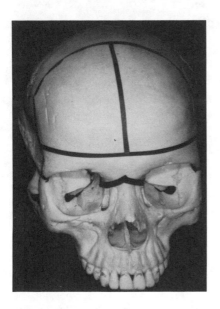
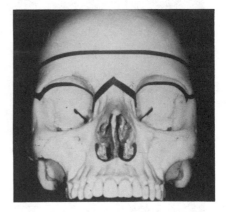

Figure 7–3.   Representation of osteotomies made in patient shown in Figure 7–1.

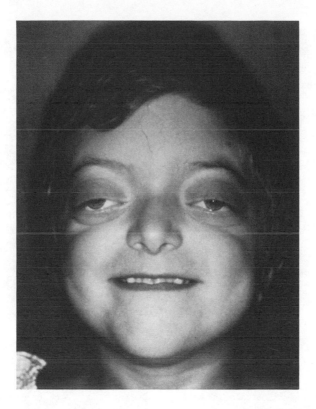

Figure 7-4. Patient shown in Figure 7-1 after frontal bone and upper orbital advancement.

to learning disabilities. It is unclear at present whether all instances of cognitive dysfunction have the same causation or whether there are several reasons for such problems. However, it is known that in many cases of Treacher Collins syndrome, learning deficiencies are secondary to chronic obstructive apnea throughout childhood. Several studies have found that the pharyngeal airway is severely reduced in size in Treacher Collins syndrome (Sher, Shprintzen, and Thorpy, in press; Shprintzen, 1982; Shprintzen, Croft, Berkman, and Rakoff, 1979). As a result of upper airway compromise, both obstructive sleep apnea (Johnston, Taussig, Koopman, Smith, and Bjelland, 1981; Sher et al., in press; Shprintzen, 1982; Shprintzen et al., 1979) and chronic apnea during wakefulness (Sher et al., in press; Shprintzen, 1982) have been reported.

A well-known complication of obstructive apnea is decreased cognitive functioning, including poor school performance (Frank, Kravath, Pollak, and Weitzman, 1983; Goldstein et al., in press; Guillemenault, Eldridge;

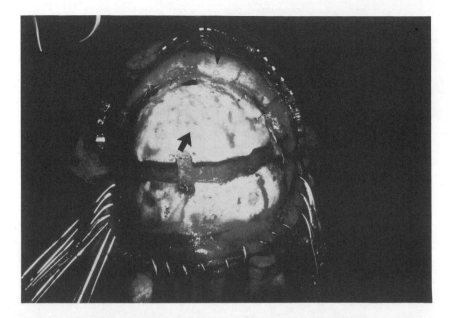

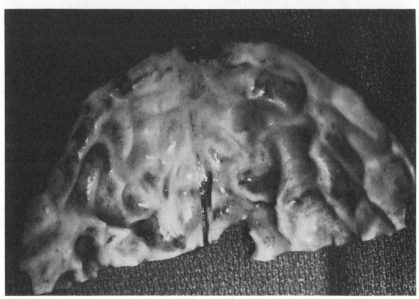

Figure 7-5. Intraoperative appearance of the frontal bone of the patient shown in Figure 7-1 at the time of craniectomy and frontal bone advancement showing the impressions of the cerebral convolutions on the interior surface of the calvarium caused by increased intracranial pressure.

Simmons, and Dement, 1976), mental dullness (Kravath, Pollak, and Borowiecki, 1977), hyperactivity (Frank et al., 1983), and learning disabilities, neurologic dysfunction, and developmental delay (Brouillette, Fernbach, and Hunt, 1982). The effect of continuous oxygen deprivation on a developing central nervous system can only be speculated. It is, however, well recognized that early reversal of apnea can reverse poor learning skills (Goldstein et al., 1985; Guillemenault et al., 1976). Thus, recognition of poor cognitive function in children with Treacher Collins syndrome should lead the astute clinician to obtain a detailed history of respiratory patterns during both sleep and wakefulness.

It is also possible that in some cases of Treacher Collins syndrome, there is a congenital brain anomaly. Approximately 40 percent of CCFD's patients with Treacher Collins syndrome have a primary microcephaly. Many of these patients are mildly mentally retarded; the remainder have learning disabilities. It is thought that the structural facial anomalies in Treacher Collins syndrome are caused by insufficient neural crest migration. Might the observed microcephaly be etiologically related to the same tissue deficiency that caused insufficient ectomesenchymal tissue proliferation? Or is it related to chronic hypoxia? We only know that all of the individuals for whom information was available had normal head circumferences at birth and that all had histories of constant or episodic apnea.

Achondroplasia Syndrome

Though primarily regarded as a syndrome of short stature secondary to skeletal dysplasia, the achondroplasia syndrome also has significant craniofacial dysmorphology associated with it. The typically reported craniofacial findings associated with achondroplasia include megalocephaly, small foramen magnum, frontal bossing, depressed nasal root, and midfacial hypoplasia. Intelligence is typically reported to be normal (Smith, 1982). However, learning disabilities and poor performance in school are not uncommon in achondroplasia in spite of normal intellect. Brain anomalies have not been demonstrated in achondroplasia. The implication is that cognitive impairments are secondary to the craniofacial anomalies expressed by the autosomal dominant gene for achondroplasia. It has been demonstrated that the foramen magnum in achondroplasia is small (Warkany, 1971). In fact, the entire basicranium is abnormally small, probably related to some degree to premature synostosis of the basicranial sutures. Mild dilatation of the ventricles is not uncommon (Cohen, Rosenthal, and Matson, 1967). Actually, the small size of the foramen magnum in achondroplasia syndrome is secondary to the severely abnormal morphology of the basicranium, not dissimilar to that seen in Apert syndrome. Neurologic disorders secondary to the cranial anomalies have been observed and may be quite variable (Cohen et al., 1967).

Individuals with achondroplasia syndrome also have an increased risk of obstructive apnea (Goldstein et al., 1985). As previously discussed in relation to Treacher Collins syndrome, achondroplasia syndrome is another disorder in which the effects of prolonged hypoxia are potentially dangerous to normal cognitive development. A recent case report has documented an improvement in intellect and school performance following tracheostomy in a child with achondroplasia syndrome.

ADAM Sequence

The ADAM sequence is actually a series of embryonic and fetal disruptions caused by early amniotic rupture. This early rupture causes compresson of the developing embryo and subsequent morphogenetic problems. Probably the best recognized morphogenetic problems are the combination of craniofacial and limb defects. Encephaloceles, anencephaly, and hydrocephalus have been observed in association with this disorder (Smith, 1982). It was previously referred to as the "amniotic band syndrome" (Cohen, 1978) but more recently has been referred to by the acronym ADAM (amniotic disruptions, amputations, mutilations) (Keller et al., 1978). Smith (1982) has labeled this type of disruption as the "early amnion rupture spectrum." We consider any cognitive effects of this disorder to be secondary because they are not likely to be an intrinsic part of the child.

In our experience, a variety of cognitive dysfunctions can occur associated with the ADAM sequence. In its most severe form of expression, mental retardation can occur if the brain has been severely compressed. More frequent, however, have been language delay and specific learning disabilities. In the clinical population seen at most craniofacial or cleft palate centers, intellect will most likely be normal, but more minor expressions of cognitive impairment may become evident as language and learning abilities develop. It should be stressed that the degree of cognitive impairment has no apparent relationship to the degree of facial deformation.

Lysosomal Storage Diseases

There are a large number of inherited disorders of metabolism in which secondary changes occur within the central nervous system because of the storage of undegraded metabolities in neuronal tissues. These include all of the mucopolysaccharidoses, mucolipidoses, sphingolipidoses, and gangliosidoses. While the brains of such patients are intrinsically normal, the subsequent tissue changes secondarily cause cognitive disorders. Many of these syndromes have severe mental retardation or early death as a feature (Tay-Sachs syndrome, Leroy I-cell syndrome, Hurler syndrome, Hunter syndrome, Type I generalized gangliosidosis, and Sanfilippo syndrome). However, several of these storage disorders have little or no associated mental retardation, but do have a higher than expected frequency of speech and language delay and learning disabilities. These lysosomal disorders include Morquio syndrome, Maroteaux-Lamy syndrome, Scheie syndrome, Hurler-Scheie compound syndrome, and pseudo-Hurler syndrome.

Clefting and Oral Teratoma

This reportedly rare syndrome involves the herniation of a congenital teratoma through the basicranium, between the developing palatal shelves, thus preventing the shelves from fusing (Gorlin et al., 1976). The teratoma must be surgically removed and the cranial defect repaired. All of the patients at our center with this syndrome have learning disabilities but normal intellect. It is unclear whether the cognitive impairment is secondary to the deformation of the brain by the teratoma or secondary to the surgical trauma. Hypoxia is also a potential complication. The learning disabilities expressed in this syndrome are varied and may depend on the site of the insult.

Other Syndromes

The preceding syndromes represent only a partial list of those in which learning disabilities and other cognitive impairments can occur secondary to a variety of insults to the central nervous system. Table 7-1 lists an additional series of syndromes in which secondary complications can cause minor cognitive disorders. The syndromes are listed according to the mechanism for the insult to the CNS.

SYNDROMES WITH LEARNING DISABILITIES AS A PRIMARY FEATURE

There are many more syndromes that have learning disabilities expressed as a primary feature than as a secondary finding. In many of these syndromes, learning disabilities exist on a continuum with other cog-

Table 7-1.   Syndromes with Learning Disabilities as a Secondary Feature

Syndromes with High Risk for Hypoxia
Crouzon syndrome
Pfeiffer syndrome
Stickler syndrome
Facio-auriculo-vertebral sequence
Pierre Robin deformation sequence (oligohydramnios type)
Treacher Collins syndrome
Nager syndrome
Achondroplasia syndrome
Spondyloepiphyseal dysplasia syndrome
Clefting and oral teratoma

Syndromes with Secondary Impingement on CNS Tissue
Achondroplasia syndrome
ADAM sequence
Crouzon syndrome
Pfeiffer syndrome
Saethre-Chotzen syndrome
Maroteaux-Lamy syndrome
Morquio syndrome
Pseudo-Hurler syndrome
Scheie syndrome
Hurler-Scheie compound syndrome
Clefting and oral teratoma

nitive impairments, such as mental retardation. It is logical to assume that most syndromes with cognitive dysfunction as a frequent finding would be likely to show learning disabilities in at least some individuals who have the mildest expression of CNS anomaly. For example, though essentially all individuals with Down syndrome are mentally retarded, some individuals with the common disorder have intellects that measure within normal limits (by statistical definition). Yet all of these individuals are certainly learning impaired. With this point in mind, it would be beyond the scope of this chapter to describe all syndromes in which learning disabilities might be found. Instead, several syndromes that have a characteristically high frequency of learning disabilities are described, and others are tabulated.

Velo-cardio-facial Syndrome

Velo-cardio-facial syndrome was largely delineated by the consistency of observations of specific learning disabilities within a subpopulation of children with cleft palate. Delineated by Shprintzen and associates (1978), other reports have continued to provide an increasing amount of information about both the physical and behavioral characteristics of this common syndrome of clefting (Golding-Kushner et al., 1985; Shprintzen et al., 1981; Smith, 1982; Williams, Shprintzen, and Goldberg, 1985; Young, Shprintzen, and Goldberg, 1980). This syndrome is perhaps the most common syndrome of clefting, and Shprintzen, Siegel-Sadewitz, Amato, and Goldberg (1985) reported that it makes up 4.7 percent of the total cleft population at the Center for Craniofacial Disorders but, even more significant, 8.1 percent of their cleft-palate-only population. This syndrome is an autosomal dominant genetic disorder (Williams et al., 1985) with numerous clinical features. The clinical features of this syndrome include cleft of the secondary palate, congenital heart disease (including VSD, right-sided aortic arch, or tetralogy of Fallot), retrognathia secondary to a flat basicranium (Arvystas and Shprintzen, 1984), characteristic facies (prominent nose, malar flatness, "allergic shiners," down-turned oral commissures), minor auricular anomalies, infantile hypotonia, relatively small stature, inguinal and umbilical hernias, and Pierre Robin malformation sequence. Either learning disabilities or mental retardation have been documented in all cases reported.

The cognitive aspects of velo-cardio-facial syndrome are quite distinctive and are as much of the diagnostic profile as the physical findings. It has been established that the cognitive deficiencies are not secondary to either infantile hypoxia or the congenital heart anomalies (Shprintzen et al., 1981). Golding-Kushner and coworkers (1985) reported on the psychometric and language findings in 26 patients with velo-cardio-facial syndrome. In preschool years, all children were noted to have normal or borderline normal IQ scores, but performance on IQ tests deteriorated in school-age years and in adolescence. The reason for this deterioration was felt to be a specific weakness in abstract reasoning skills. In preschool children, IQ measures do not depend on abstract reasoning, but measure the concrete rote learning skills of young children. These concrete skills remain intact in individuals with velo-cardio-facial syndrome, but they fail to develop more robust abstraction abilities. Therefore, as these children grow older, their intellectual skills seem to deteriorate according to test scores, though this is merely an artifact of their specific learning disabilities. Academic testing showed that intellectual skills such as matching letters, reading words, and recalling a string of numbers were age appropriate. However, despite adequate sight reading, reading comprehension was very poor. Another area consistently deficient was mathematical ability. In other words, children with velo-cardio-facial syndrome were found to learn rote materials in a relatively normal manner, but were unable to apply a learned method or process to new stimuli and situations. Also of note was that all subjects failed perceptual and graphomotor screening tests. Language testing on the Illinois Test of Psycholinguistic Abilities showed that the weakest areas were in auditory association and visual association, two subtests requiring abstraction skills. The rote memory subtests such as auditory sequential memory had robust scores.

Golding-Kushner and colleagues (1985) also noted a characteristic personality profile in this syndrome. It consisted of a bland affect, poor social interaction, and impulsive and disinhibited behavior. These children tended to be very affectionate, and they did not display any bizarre behaviors. Although this personality profile is fairly consistent with children who have moderate or severe mental retardation, it should be pointed out that the majority of patients with velo-cardio-facial syndrome are not mentally retarded, and only one reported case of 60 described to date in the literature was moderately retarded. Perhaps this type of personality associated with the learning disabilities points out all the more strongly the likelihood of an underlying brain malformation (as yet undiscovered) in this syndrome.

Steinert Syndrome

This myotonic form of muscular dystrophy is a relatively common autosomal dominant genetic disorder with extremely variable expression. The variability of expression is manifested both by the age of onset and the degree of neuromuscular abnormality. Etiologic heterogeneity has been suggested, differentiating the early-onset form (showing up at birth or shortly after) from the late-onset form (Bundey and Carter, 1972). It is generally believed that the early-onset form is almost always maternally transmitted. Cognitive disorders are similarly variable.

Mental retardation can occur in Steinert syndrome. In our experience, the more severe cognitive disorders are seen in the early-onset expressions of this syndrome. Milder cognitive impairments, specifically learning disabilities, are seen frequently in the late-onset form. We have been presented with patients who were presumed to be normal in early childhood. Some form of neuromuscular symptom developed in early adolscence (usually between 12 and 16 years of age). Very often, the first symptom is a late onset of a speech disorder, such as hypernasality or mild dysarthria. Other first-noticed symptoms include ptosis, muscle weakness in the arms or hands, and deterioration of school performance. Though these symptoms may prompt referral to appropriate professionals, it is often found in a careful review of the patient's history that minor manifestations of the disorder may have been expressed several years earlier. For example, there is a characteristic facies associated with the syndrome (vertical maxillary excess; steep mandibular angle; skeletal open-bite; narrow, high-arched palate; prominent beaked nose; and mask-like expression). This characteristic growth pattern could not possibly result from a late-onset myotonia in adolescence. It may therefore be assumed that the effects of muscle weakness are gradual or precede overt pathologic symptoms.

To date, all patients we have seen with a clinically apparent onset of Steinert syndrome in early adolescence have shown evidence of learning disabilities. In fact, teachers' reports of deteriorating school performance have usually predated other overt signs of the disorder. The learning problems tend to be a generalized deterioration of learning skills rather than a specific area of deficiency. The decreased adequacy of learning may be accompanied by other behavioral problems, such as personality disturbance. It should be noted that in milder expressions of the syndrome, there may be no clinically detectable evidence of learning disorder or other cognitive impairment.

Neurofibromatosis

This common autosomal dominant genetic disorder is only one of several syndromes that have hamartomas as a major clinical finding. The majority of syndromes have a variety of associated central nervous system disorders, such as the Sturge-Weber sequence, Bloch-Sulzberger syndrome, tuberous sclerosis, Gorlin syndrome, and LEOPARD syndrome. This neurocutaneous disorder has widely variable expression. Cited among its phenotypic spectrum has been a relatively high incidence of mental retardation (Borberg, 1957; Fienman and Yakovac, 1970). However, Carey, Laub, and Hall (1979) pointed out that in these earlier reports, no distinction was made among individuals who were mentally retarded, learning disabled, or developmentally delayed. Carey and associates (1979) reported that 11.4 percent of their series of 131 cases had learning disabilities, in addition to another 9.9 percent who were mentally retarded. Our own series of patients were referred to us because of hypernasal speech (Pollack and Shprintzen, 1981), and learning disabilities were also reported among this sample. We have now seen a larger sample of individuals with neurofibromatosis and learning disabilities. In general, a major impairment to learning appears to be related to an attention deficit with easy distractability. Those patients with learning disabilities tend to have IQ scores in the 70s and 80s, perhaps indicating that their learning problems represent a generalized decrease in cognitive abilities on a continuum with mental retardation. In our sample, all patients were noted to have macrocephaly. Carey and associates (1979) reported that 25 percent of their patients with neurofibromatosis who were mentally retarded had macrocephaly.

As discussed by Pollack and Shprintzen (1981), the reason for the problems associated with neurofibromatosis remains unclear. A central nervous system abnormality of some type may be hypothesized, but its exact nature remains a mystery.

Fetal Alcohol Syndrome

Though this syndrome is not genetic, it is quite commonly seen in many birth defects clinics. It is well recognized in its severe form, but only recently is it becoming recognized in its milder expressions. Part of the problem with recognizing the full phenotypic spectrum of the teratogenic effects of ethanol is that the diagnosis is entirely dependent upon a confirmed history of maternal alcohol abuse. We have seen many patients in whom fetal alcohol effects were suspected based upon phenotypic analysis, but alcohol abuse was denied.

Of course, it is also possible that the confusing overlap of the phenotype in fetal alcohol syndrome with the phenotypes of many other conditions obfuscates appropriate diagnosis. However, when certain phenotypic features are found in a patient associated with a variety of cognitive defects, the effects of maternal alcohol ingestion during pregnancy must be suspected and therefore explored. These phenotypic findings include cleft palate or submucous cleft palate, poorly defined philtrum and cupid's bow, horizontal maxillary excess with class II malocclusion, micrognathia, short palpebral fissures, flattened nasal root, strabismus, the characteristic palmar crease, and digital anomalies. We have seen several patients in whom these findings occurred in association with learning disabilities and in whom maternal abuse of alcohol was confirmed. In one patient with submucous cleft palate, learning disabilities, horizontal maxillary excess, flattened philtrum, and strabismus, maternal alcohol abuse was confirmed. The child had an IQ measured in the 90s but an attention deficit and learning disabilities. Both of his parents were noted to be of superior intellect with no evidence of learning problems. Thus, in spite of an IQ that was not abnormal, his cognitive status could certainly be regarded as unexpected because of his parents' superior achievement and therefore a teratogenic symptom.

Other Syndromes

Table 7–2 provides a partial list of syndromes in which learning disabilities are a primary feature, with a frequency greater than that expected in the normal population. Siegel-Sadewitz and Shprintzen (1982) provides another useful reference for cognitive impairments.

DIAGNOSTIC SIGNIFICANCE

As mentioned at the beginning of this chapter, the understanding of specific learning disability profiles, along with language data and other psy-

Table 7-2.   Syndromes with Learning Disabilities as a Primary Feature

Aarskog syndrome
Apert syndrome
Ataxia-telangiectasia syndrome
BBB syndrome (hypertelorism-hypospadias)
Beckwith-Wiedemann syndrome
Carpenter syndrome
Dubowitz syndrome
Facio-auriculo-vertebral sequence
Fetal alcohol syndrome
G syndrome
Holoprosencephaly sequence (lobar type)
Langer-Giedion syndrome
LEOPARD syndrome
Neurofibromatosis
Oto-palato-digital syndrome
Prader-Willi syndrome
Shprintzen-Goldberg syndrome
Steinert syndrome
Velo-cardio-facial syndrome

chometric data, will help professionals delineate new syndromes and differentiate those that have already been described. At the time of this writing, profiles of specific learning skills and detailed psychometric data are available for very few syndromes. However, even the limited data available today can help in the process of differential diagnosis. For example, as discussed by Shprintzen and coworkers (1981), there is a good deal of phenotypic overlap between the velo-cardio-facial syndrome and tricho-rhino-phalangeal syndrome, Langer-Giedion syndrome, Stickler syndrome, fetal alcohol syndrome, cerebro-costo-mandibular syndrome, persistent left superior vena cava syndrome, and Steinert syndrome. Using the data provided by Golding-Kushner and associates (1985), which specifically describe the learning, language, psychologic, and behavioral features of velo-cardio-facial syndrome, differential diagnosis becomes a conclusive process. Of the syndromes being considered in differential diagnosis, the cognitive profile of velo-cardio-facial syndrome is quite distinct from that of the other syndromes that have cognitive deficits. For example, although fetal alcohol syndrome has varying degrees of cognitive impairment, the deficits are more global, with all areas of cognitive functioning tending to be depressed. This is not the case in velo-cardio-facial syndrome, in which rote learning is unaffected, but reading comprehension and math present problems.

Obviously, the use of cognitive data depends on a concerted effort from appropriate professionals. Rich sources of data are literally untapped. The study of congenital anomalies is one that cuts across many professions. Clearly, learning specialists, psychologists, and speech-language pathologists must be involved with increasing frequency.

FUTURE SOURCES OF DATA

The number of syndromes in which learning disabilities can be found as a clinical feature are far more numerous than can be delineated here. There will undoubtedly be many additions to the already growing list of such syndromes. These will come from several different sources.

One source will be new syndromes that will be delineated in the future. The description of new congenital malformation and deformation syndromes seems to be growing at an exponential rate. More professionals from the behavioral sciences are becoming interested in the process of syndrome delineation. These new scientists will help to meld their knowledge of learning disorders to the process of clinical genetics, thus making learning analyses as important a part of diagnosis as anthropometric measurements.

Another source of additional syndromic associations with learning disabilities will be the recognition of milder expressions of syndromes that in their severe states have mental retardation as a feature. We described such a case of fetal alcohol syndrome previously, and undoubtedly others will come to light as the phenotypic spectra of newly delineated syndromes expand.

Improved medical care will also foster a better understanding of learning disabilities. The majority of attention to date has been paid to surgical and medical intervention to attend to acute problems. As acute problems become more easily resolved, time and energy can be spent in pursuing chronic problems that may be less obvious to an examining physician.

CONCLUSIONS

At this time, there is not much information in the scientific literature about the specificity of learning disabilities to individual syndromes. As this information becomes available, however, the diagnosis of learning disabilities and other cognitive deficiencies will be as important to syndromic diagnosis as radiographs and physical examinations. In fact, learning disabilities, language disorders, and intellectual impairment may be a valuable asset to syndrome differentiation. If the concept of cognitive dysfunctions being caused by some disorder of the central nervous system is accepted, then cognitive impairments provide evidence of such disorders, which currently escape detection by even the most sophisticated CT scan. Undoubtedly, some day this biologic link will become defined as NMR and other new tools are applied. But for now, learning disabilities deserve our appropriate attention as a key piece to the diagnostic puzzle.

REFERENCES

Arvystas, M., and Shprintzen, R.J. (1984). Craniofacial morphology in the velo-cardio-facial syndrome. *Journal of Craniofacial Genetics and Developmental Biology, 4,* 39–45.

Borberg, A. (1951). Clinical and genetic investigations into tuberous sclerosis and Recklinghausen's neurofibromatosis. *Acta Psychiatrica Neurologica, 71* (Suppl. 71). pp 3–239.

Brouillette, R.T., Fernbach, S.K. and Hunt, C.E. (1982). Obstructive sleep apnea in infants and children. *Journal of Pediatrics, 100,* 31–40.

Bundey, S., and Carter, C.L. (1972). Genetic heterogeneity for dystrophia myotonica. *Journal of Medical Genetics, 9,* 311–315.

Carey, J.C., Laub, J.M., and Hall, B.D. (1979). Penetrance and variability in neurofibromatosis: A genetic study of 60 families. *Birth Defects Original Articles Series, 15*(5B), 271–281.

Cohen, M.E., Rosenthal, A.D., and Matson, D.D. (1967). Neurological abnormalities in achondroplastic children. *Journal of Pediatrics, 71,* 367–376.

Cohen, M.M., Jr. (1975). An etiologic and nosologic overview of craniosynostosis syndromes. *Birth Defects Original Article Series, 11*(2), 139–189.

Cohen, M.M., Jr. (1978). Syndromes with cleft lip and cleft palate. *Cleft Palate Journal, 15,* 306–328.

Cohen, M.M., Jr. (1979). Craniosynostosis and syndromes with craniosynostosis: Incidence, genetics, penetrance, variability, and new syndrome updating. *Birth Defects Original Article Series, 15*(5B), 13–63.

Cohen, M.M., Jr. (1980). Perspectives on craniosynostosis. *Western Journal of Medicine, 132,* 507–513.

Connolly, K.J., Pharoah, P.O.D., and Hetzel, B.S. (1979). Fetal iodine deficiency and motor performance during childhood. *Lancet, 2*(8153), 1149–1151.

Fienman, N.L., and Yakovac, W.C. (1970). Neurofibromatosis in childhood. *Journal of Pediatrics, 76,* 339–346.

Frank, Y., Kravath, R.E., Pollack, C.P., and Weitzman, E.D. (1983). Obstructive sleep apnea and its therapy: Clinical and polysomnographic manifestations. *Pediatrics, 71,* 737–742.

Golding-Kushner, K., Weller, G., and Shprintzen, R.J. (1985). Velocardiofacial syndrome: Language and psychological profiles. *Journal of Craniofacial Genetics and Developmental Biology, 5,* 259–266.

Goldstein, S.J., Shprintzen, R.J., Wu, R.H.K., Thorpy, M.J., Hahm, S.Y., Marion, R., Sher, A.E., and Saenger, P. (1985). Achondroplasia and obstructive sleep apnea: Correction of apnea and deficient sleep entrained growth hormone release by tracheostomy. *Birth Defects Original Articles Series, 21(2),* 93–102.

Gorlin, R.J., Pindborg, J.J., and Cohen, M.M., Jr. (1976). *Syndromes of the head and neck* (2nd ed.). New York: McGraw-Hill.

Guillemenault, C., Eldridge, F.K., Simmons, F.B., and Dement, W.C. (1976). Sleep apnea in eight children. *Pediatrics, 58,* 23–31.

Johnston, C., Taussig, L.M., Koopman, C., Smith, P., and Bjelland, J. (1981). Obstructive sleep apnea in Treacher-Collins syndrome. *Cleft Palate Journal, 18,* 39–44.

Keller, H., Neuhauser, G., Durkin-Stamm, M.V., Kaveggia, E.G., Schaaff, A., and Stigmann, F. (1978). "ADAM complex" (amniotic deformity, adhesions, mutilations)—A pattern of craniofacial and limb defects. *American Journal of Medical Genetics, 2,* 81–98.

Kravath, R.E., Pollak, C.P., and Borowiecki, B. (1977. Hypoventilation during sleep in children who have lymphoid airway obstruction treated by nasopharyngeal tube and T and A. *Pediatrics, 59,* 865–871.

Pollack, M., and Shprintzen, R.J. (1981). Velopharyngeal insufficiency in neurofibromatosis. *International Journal of Pediatric Otorhinolaryngology, 3,* 257–262.

Sher, A.E., Shprintzen, R.J., and Thorpy, M.J. (in press). Endoscopic observations of obstructive sleep apnea in children with anomalous upper airways: Predictive and therapeutic value. *International Journal of Pediatric Otorhinolaryngology.*

Shprintzen, R.J. (1982). Palatal and pharyngeal anomalies in craniofacial syndromes. *Birth Defects Original Article Series, 18*(1), 53–78.

Shprintzen, R.J., and Goldberg, R.B. (1982). A recurrent pattern syndrome of craniosynostosis associated with arachnodactyly and abdominal hernias. *J Craniofacial Genet Devel Biol, 2,* 65–74.

Shprintzen, R.J., Croft, C.B., Berkman, M.D., and Rakoff, S.J. (1979). Pharyngeal hypoplasia in the Treacher Collins syndrome. *Archives of Otolaryngology, 105,* 127–131.

Shprintzen, R.J., Siegel-Sadewitz, V.L., Amato, J., and Goldberg, R.B. (1985). Anomalies associated with cleft lip, cleft palate, or both. *American Journal of Medical Genetics, 20,* 585–596.

Shprintzen, R.J., Goldberg, R.B., Lewin, M.L., Sidoti, E.J., Berkman, M.D., Argamaso, R.V., and Young, D. (1978). A new syndrome involving cleft palate, cardiac anomalies, typical facies, and learning disabilities: Velo-cardio-facial syndrome. *Cleft Palate Journal, 15,* 56–62.

Shprintzen, R.J., Goldberg, R.B., Young, D., Wolford, L. (1981). Velo-cardio-facial syndrome: A clinical and genetic analysis. *Pediatrics, 67,* 167–172.

Siegel-Sadewitz, V.L., and Shprintzen, R.J. (1982). The relationship of communication disorders to syndrome identification. *Journal of Speech and Hearing Disorders, 47,* 338–354.

Smith, D.W. (1982). *Recognizable patterns of human malformation* (3rd ed.). Philadelphia: W.B. Saunders.

Warkany, J. (1971). *Congenital malformations.* Chicago: Year Book Medical Publishers.

Williams, M.A., Shprintzen, R.J., and Goldberg, R.B. (in press). Male-to-male transmission of the velo-cardio-facial syndrome: A case report and review of 60 cases. *J Craniofacial Genet Devel Biol.*

Young, D., Shprintzen, R.J., and Goldberg, R.B. (1980). Cardiac malformations in the velo-cardio-facial syndrome. *American Journal of Cardiology, 46,* 643–647.

Chapter 8

Cognitive Development of Children with Sex Chromosome Abnormalities

Bruce G. Bender,
Mary H. Puck,
James A. Salbenblatt, and
Arthur Robinson

Sex chromosome abnormalities (SCA) are genetic disorders associated with a variety of developmental problems, including learning disorders (LD). The study of SCA provides a unique opportunity to increase understanding of genetic and developmental features of LD. Most research on the genetics of LD involves cross-sectional or retrospective study of children in order to trace familial patterns of transmission of problems of unknown cause. In contrast to such heterogeneous samples, children with LD and the same SCA share a single genetic factor. The possibility of identifying a LD subtype of specific genetic causation is thus greatly increased, especially when the study is prospective (Pennington, Bender, Puck, Salbenblatt, and Robinson, 1982). Longitudinal evaluations of children with SCA may elucidate the relationship between physical and cognitive development and help to establish the processes by which SCA is associated with LD. This knowledge in turn may increase understanding of the role of the sex chromosomes in normal cognitive development.

This study was supported in part by grant 5R01–HD10032 from the USPHS; grant RR–69 from the General Clinical Research Centers Program of the Division of Research Resources, NIH; and The Genetic Foundation.

CHROMOSOME ABNORMALITIES

Before 1956, the precise number of chromosomes present in each cell had not been established. We now know that humans normally have 46 chromosomes divided into 23 pairs or homologs, two of which are sex chromosomes (Tjio and Levan, 1956). The chromosomal constitution of normal males and females is 46, XY and 46, XX, respectively (Figs. 8-1 and 8-2).

Abnormalities of chromosome number (aneuploidy) result from an abnormal segregation of the chromosomes (nondisjunction) occurring either in gametogenesis (meiotic nondisjunction) or as a postzygotic phenomenon (mitotic nondisjunction). In the former case, all cells of the conceptus will be aneuploid, whereas in the latter event there may be two or more populations of cells that will vary in their chromosomal constitution, a situation called mosaicism.

Sex Chromosome Disorders

Chromosome abnormalities occur in one of 200 newborns. Approximately half of these are SCA. The most common SCAs occur when a male has an extra X or Y chromosome or when a female has an extra X or, in

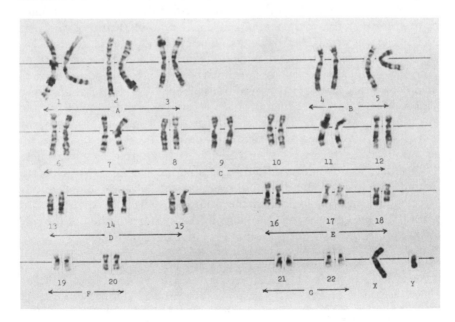

Figure 8-1.   Normal male karyotype displaying XY sex chromosome constitution.

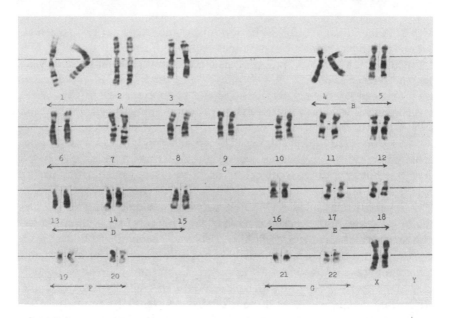

Figure 8-2. Normal female karyotype displaying XX sex chromosome constitution.

the case of X monosomy, is missing all or part of an X: 47,XXY, 47,XYY, 47,XXX, 45,X, 46,XXp-, 46,XXq-, respectively. Two or more extra sex chromosomes are rare. SCA mosaicism can include a variety of cell line combinations such as 45,X/46,XX; 45,X/46,XX/47,XXX, and so on.

With the exception of the 45,X karyotype (Turner syndrome), X and Y aneuploidy is rarely identified at birth because affected individuals appear normal. Aneuploidy of the autosomes, on the other hand, is usually accompanied by readily identifiable physical and developmental problems, including mental retardation. Early studies of individuals with SCA have been necessarily limited to retrospective analyses of adult patients, a biased form of ascertainment. There developed, however, sufficient data to establish that newborns with SCA have an increased risk of impaired cognitive development. In the last two decades, newborn screening has established incidence rates for SCA and has also provided unbiased samples for careful comparative study of physical, intellectual, and emotional development.

THE DENVER STUDY OF CHILDREN WITH SCA

The Denver study (Robinson, Puck, Pennington, Borelli, and Hudson, 1979) is one of nine groups from five countries following children with SCA identified at birth (Robinson, Lubs, and Bergsma, 1979; Stewart, 1982). In Denver, amniotic membranes obtained from placentas of 40,000 consecutive newborns at two hospitals were examined during the 10-year period between 1964 and 1974 (Robinson and Puck, 1967). Any discrepancy between laboratory findings and the phenotypic sex of the babies was confirmed by chromosome analysis or karyotyping of peripheral blood cells. Of 68 infants with SCA thus identified, 46 became the basic sample for data presented in this chapter (Table 8–1). (Eight infants died in the neonatal period, seven children declined to participate, two initially joined the study but later chose to drop out, and five discontinued after moving out of state.)

Regularly scheduled physical and developmental evaluations, psychologic testing, and extensive interviews with parents and children constitute the research protocol. School reports and academic evaluations are integrated into the clinical records. Siblings who share similar genetic and environmental background serve as controls. All family members participate in the research program, thus reducing the special attention that could otherwise be experienced as discomfort by the identified child. In order to prevent overrepresentation of single characteristics shared by large families, only one male and one female sibling were included as controls from any one family.

Early development of these children has been reported elsewhere (Bender, Fry, et al., 1983; Bender, Puck, Salbenblatt, and Robinson, 1984a, 1984b; Eller, Frankenburg, Puck, and Robinson, 1971, Pennington, Puck, and Robinson, 1980; Puck, Tennes, Frankenburg, Bryant, and Robinson, 1975; Robinson, Puck, Pennington, Borelli, and Hudson, 1979; Tennes, Puck, Bryant, Frankenburg, and Robinson, 1975; Tennes, Puck, Orfanakis, and Robinson, 1977). The results reported here will summarize accumulated data pertaining to cognition and school experiences. The Denver sample of 48 children with SCA is one of the largest in existence. However, the number of subjects in each karyotype group remains small, and generalizations are made cautiously. Discussion includes results from other longitudinal studies of SCA.

INTELLIGENCE

Although only two children with SCA are clearly mentally retarded, the Full Scale intelligence score of the group of 38 nonmosaic propositi is significantly lower than that of the controls by an average of 14 points on the Wechsler Intelligence Scale for Children. Variability is considerable. Twenty-two scores are in the statistically defined average range of ±1

Table 8-1.   Denver Study Subjects

Karyotype	Number of Subjects	Mean Age	Age Range
47,XXY	14	12.0	10–19
47,XYY	4	10.5	10–13
47,XXX	11	15.5	12–19
45,X and Partial X Monosomy			
45,X	6	12.9	10–18
46,XXq-	2	15.0	12–17
45,X/46,X,r(X)	1	11.3	—
Female Mosaics			
45,X/46,XX/47,XXX	1	17.0	—
45,X/46,XX	4	17.9	16–22
46,XX/47,XXX	1	11.0	—
45,X/47,XXX	2	15.6	12–19
46,XY Controls	16	12.3	8–19
46,XX Controls	16	12.7	6–18

standard deviation (SD) (86 to 115), 14 are below average, and 2 are above average. Among controls, 25 are average, 1 below, and 4 above.

Intellectual functioning varies among the groups as well as among the individuals. The Full Scale IQ distributions seen in Figure 8–3 suggest a normal distribution, with almost equal numbers of scores falling above and below each mean, although the variability in the SCA groups is greater than that of the control groups. The 47,XXX and X monosomy groups each have mean IQs significantly lower than those of female controls, as determined by the Mann-Whitney U Test. Cognitive development of the

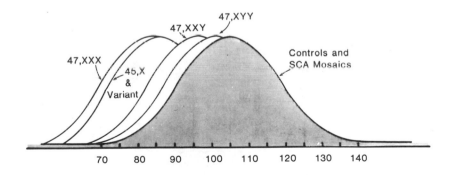

Figure 8-3.   Estimated full-scale IQ distributions for SCA and control children.

47,XXX girls has been of greatest concern, since six have IQs in the borderline retarded range. The 47,XXY and 47,XYY boys' scores are not significantly lower than those of male controls although they suggest a trend
in that direction. The mosaic group and the controls have similar scores,
a finding consistent with other developmental parameters (Bender, Fry,
et al., 1983; Bender et al., 1984a; Robinson et al., 1982; Robinson, Puck,
Pennington, Borelli, and Hudson, 1979).

     Mean Verbal and Performance IQ scores (Fig. 8–4) reflect more spe-
cifically the areas of strength and weakness discussed in the next section.
Male propositi, both 47,XXY and 47,XYY, have relatively lower Verbal
IQ scores, but only for the XYY group are they significantly lower than
for controls and therefore indicative of weaker language skills. The 45,X
and partial X monosomy group shows just the opposite pattern: a significantly decreased Performance IQ suggesting visual-perceptual problems.
For the most generally impaired 47,XXX group, both Verbal and Performance IQs are significantly lower than those of controls.

NEUROPSYCHOLOGICAL STUDIES

     Cognitive and neuromotor measures were selected to evaluate specific
functional areas of development not described by IQ tests. The resulting
deficit patterns help differentiate the groups of children and clarify the
developmental implications of each SCA. Language, auditory memory,
spatial ability, and neuromotor skills are each described separately.

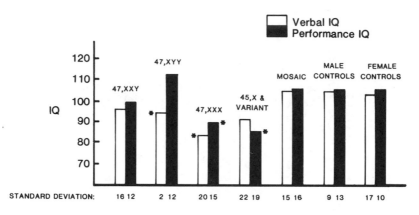

Figure 8–4. Mean verbal and performance IQs.

Language

Language function was evaluated by a speech-language pathologist blind to the identity of each child. Following the administration of a test battery for measurement of auditory perception, speech production, receptive language, and expressive language, the clinician rated each child's overall language skills on a continuum from unimpaired to severely impaired. Impaired children are those whose moderate to severe language deficits are believed to interfere with daily social and academic success (Fig. 8–5).

All SCA groups except the mosaics demonstrated significant language impairment relative to same-sex controls. The mosaic group did not differ from the controls. As reported earlier (Bender, Fry, et al., 1983), the 47,XXX group most frequently and most severely demonstrated incapacity to understand and to use language. The 47,XXY group, with better comprehension ability, nonetheless used language inefficiently, often requiring more time to process information even when the correct answer could be produced.

The 45,X and partial X monosomy group showed a marked increase in problems of speech production. Moderate to severe language dysfuntion was seen in the three girls with IQ scores in the borderline and moderately retarded range. With one exception, the X monosomy girls have histories of chronic otitis media, a condition suspected of impeding language development (Paradise, 1981; Reichman and Healey, 1983).

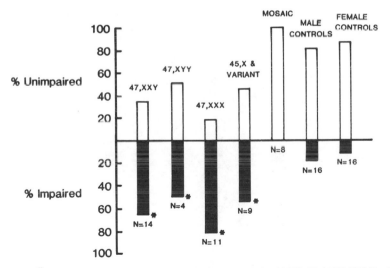

*INDICATES SIGNIFICANT DIFFERENCE FROM CONTROL GROUP OF SAME SEX (P<.05)

Figure 8–5.   Language.

Auditory Memory

The Auditory Sequential Memory subtest of the Illinois Test of Psycholinguistic Ability (Kirk, McCarthy, and Kirk, 1968), requiring the child to repeat accurately lists of digits of increasing length, was used to measure auditory short-term memory. "Impaired" children were those whose performance was below the 10th percentile for age (Fig. 8-6). The boys with SCA were the only group with significantly impaired memory compared to controls. Fifteen of these 19 boys also have poor language and reading skills. The relationship of auditory short-term memory to academic progress is discussed later. Studies of other dimensions of memory, such as short-term and long-term memory for verbal and figural information, are in progress.

Spatial Ability

With the exception of mosaics, girls with SCA scored below the 10th percentile more frequently than controls in this area. Diminished performance on the Spatial Relations Test from the Primary Mental Abilities Battery, identifying difficulty in completing a geometric figure, was consistently present in the X monosomy group. Five 47,XXX girls also had scores in the impaired range. This deficit was relatively rare among the other groups, occurring only in 3 of 18 boys, one mosaic girl, and one female control (Fig. 8-7).

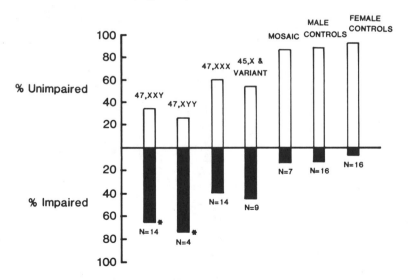

*INDICATES SIGNIFICANT DIFFERENCE FROM CONTROL GROUP OF SAME SEX (P>.05)

Figure 8-6. Auditory memory.

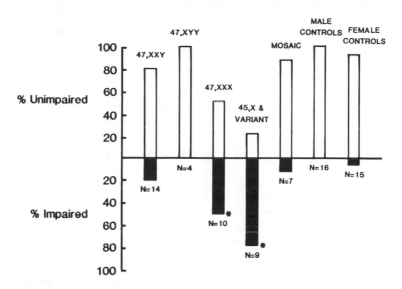

*INDICATES SIGNIFICANT DIFFERENCE FROM CONTROL GROUP OF SAME SEX (P<.05)

Figure 8-7.   Spatial ability.

Neuromotor Skills

With the exception of mosaics, all groups with SCA had significant neuromotor dysfunction, as shown by scores from the Bruininks-Oseretsky Test of Motor Proficiency (Fig. 8-8). Only one of 32 siblings was affected.

An apparent relationship exists between language and motor function and later learning skills (Pennington et al., 1980). Impaired language or motor skills occurred in 30 children with SCA. Half of the 38 nonmosaic subjects experienced both; all 19 have required special education. Six control siblings had delayed language or motor skills, but none had both.

SPECIAL EDUCATION

In light of the frequency of language, memory, spatial, and neuro-motor difficulties described in the previous section, it is not surprising that 82 percent of nonmosaic children with SCA are identified by school personnel as LD and receive partial or full-time special education, in contrast to 13 percent of control and mosaic children (Table 8-2). As reported elsewhere (Patten, 1983), diminished self-esteem is characteristic of LD

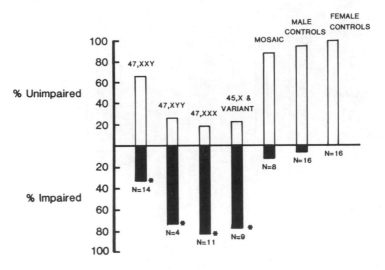

*INDICATES SIGNIFICANT DIFFERENCE FROM CONTROL GROUP OF SAME SEX (P<.05)

Figure 8-8.   Neuromotor skills.

children, anxiety and depression are common, and adaptive skills are minimal. Many are characterized by their awkwardness, labored self-expression, and limited capacity to communicate or compete with peers. The teachers who are responsible for individual academic evaluations and LD classroom placement are usually not informed of the SCA diagnosis. This serves as an unbiased verification of our clinic evaluations.

Twenty-three of the female LD propositi received part-time special education and spent the remaining time in regular classes, whereas eight were in full-time remedial classes (Table 8-2). Two girls, one 45,X and one 47,XXX, each with an IQ of 50, are in classes for mentally retarded children. LD male subjects (13 percent) required less full-time remediation than LD girls (40 percent), reflecting the girls' lower IQ scores and generally greater impairment. One mosaic girl required part-time special education in multiple subjects.

Trends of karyotype-specific learning problems for which special education was provided are listed in Table 8-2. The 16 LD boys required assistance in reading and language skills, and three in the 47,XXY group were deficient in all school subjects. The girls' learning problems were more diverse. Four of nine LD girls in the 47,XXX group received help in reading and language only, whereas five were assisted in math, language, and other subjects. Six of the nine 45,X and partial X monosomy girls were weak in all subjects.

Table 8–2. Current Incidence of Specific Learning Disorders Requiring Educational Intervention in Propositi and Controls as Reported by Schools

	No Problem	Reading	Reading and Language	Math	Math and Language	All School Subjects	Mental Retardation	Number in Part-time Special Education Classes	Number in Full-time Special Education Classes
47,XXY (N=14)	2	6	3	0	0	3	0	10	2
47,XYY (N=4)	0	2	2	0	0	0	0	4	0
Male controls (N=16)	14	1	0	0	0	1	0	2	0
47,XXX (N=11)	2	1	3	0	3	1	1	6	3
45,X and variants (N=9)	3	1	0	0	0	4	1	3	3
Female mosaics (N=8)	7	0	0	0	0	1	0	1	0
Female controls (N=16)	14	0	0	0	1	1	0	2	0

Without LD controls whose need for intervention has been neglected, the effectiveness of special education programs for these subjects is inconclusive. However, it is our clinical observation that most intervention has been beneficial to the LD children in the Denver study. At the same time, elimination of the LD has not been possible in most cases. The increased rate of LD placement for children with SCA relative to controls likely reflects the cumulative effects of longstanding cognitive impairment.

SUMMARY AND DISCUSSION OF SPECIFIC KARYOTYPES

Thirty-one of the 38 nonmosaic children with SCA have LD necessitating intervention. Other studies also report increased frequency of learning problems in children with SCA (Hier, Atkins, and Perlo, 1980; Ratcliffe, Tierney, et al., 1982; Stewart, 1982). Girls (47,XXX and 45,X and partial X monosomy) appear to be more severely affected than boys, with a mean IQ score more than one standard deviation below population norms and 30 percent in full-time special education. Eleven percent of the boys and none of the controls require full-time special education. Boys with 47,XXY and 47,XYY karyotypes have similar language and reading difficulties.

The mosaic children, who were followed in the same manner as nonmosaic propositi, are relatively unaffected and cannot be distinquished by this study from controls. This result refutes the argument that a deleterious self-fulfilling prophecy creates problems for all identified children studied.

Although more than half of the nonmosaic children have LD, their cognitive characteristics are not identical. Karyotype-specific patterns are summarized and discussed in the following sections.

47,XXY

Nine of 14 boys have impaired language and auditory memory skills, although only three have inadequate spatial ability. These are weak foundation skills that interfere with academic mastery. The great majority — 12 of 14 — have impeded ability to read. Seven — one half of our sample — shared the characteristics of a specific language-based dyslexia described by Vellutino (1979). Despite Full Scale IQs above 90, they have impaired language and verbal memory, reduced speed of cognitive processing, and a school history of reading failure. Dyslexia in 47,XXY boys is the most frequent LD of any propositi group and comes closest to a "pure" LD subtype associated with a specific SCA.

Impaired language (Bender, Fry, et al., 1983; Funderburk and Ferjo, 1978; Graham, Bashir, Walzer, Stark, and Gerald, 1981) and impaired reading skills (Annell, Gustavson, and Tenstam, 1970; Pennington et al., 1982; Stewart et al., 1979; Thielgaard, Nielsen, Sørensen, Frøland, and Johnsen, 1971; Walzer et al., 1978) have been reported frequently among 47,XXY boys, although data regarding the associated skills are incomplete. Verbal IQ was found by some investigators to be lower than Performance IQ (Annell et al., 1970; Pasqualini, Vidal, and Bur, 1957; Ratcliffe, Bancroft, Axworthy, and McLaren, 1982; Theilgaard et al., 1971; Walzer et al., 1978), whereas comparable Verbal and Performance IQs were found by others (Barker and Black, 1976; Funderburk and Ferjo, 1978; Money, 1964; Robinson et al., 1982; Stewart et al., 1979). Significant Performance-Verbal IQ discrepancy was found to be indistinguishable from the tendency for many school-age boys to have slightly higher Performance IQ (Bender, Puck, Salbenblatt, and Robinson, 1983). Problems limited to expressive language have also been reported (Robinson, Lubs, Nielsen, and Sørensen, 1979). In the only blind study of language in SCA and control children, Bender, Fry, and coworkers (1983) observed reduced receptive and expressive language and slow language processing in 13 of 14 boys. Netley and Rovet (1982) also reported disorders of receptive language. The relationship of reduced auditory short-term memory (Graham et al., 1981; Stewart et al., 1979) to other deficits is not yet clearly defined. Future studies will examine speed of processing and other facets of memory such as immediate versus delayed and verbal versus visual.

Five of 14 47,XXY boys have neuromotor impairment including hypotonia, primitive reflexes, and decreased sensory-motor integration, coordination, speed, and strength at the gross and fine motor levels. The effect of these is comprised performance in writing skills, speed on timed activities, and ability to compete with peers in athletic games. The relationship between delayed motor development and learning difficulties is not totally clear, yet an association seems to exist; four of the five motor-impaired propositi have a language disability and are receiving special education. Decreased motor skills and signs of neurologic dysfunction occur with increased frequency in the general LD population (Pyfer and Carlson, 1972) and suggest variation in the development of the brain and central nervous system.

Inferences have been made about anomalous brain development in 47,XXY boys. Specifically, poor language skills may indicate relative impairment of left hemisphere functions (Graham et al., 1981; Nielsen, 1969; Nielsen, Sillesen, Sørensen, and Sørensen, 1979). Utilizing a large sample of 33 unselected 47,XXY boys, Netley and Rovet (1982) reported an increase in nonright-handedness (i.e., left or mixed handedness) in propositi. In combination with previously published but sketchily described data showing visual field asymmetries (Stewart et al., 1982), the authors suggested that males with a supernumerary X may fail to establish left hemisphere dominance for language. Ratcliffe and Tierney (1982), in response, reported no increased nonright-handedness in a group of 32 47,XXY boys also identified through neonatal screening and noted that familial left-handedness may have contributed to the disparity in results. Bender, Puck, and coworkers (1983) similarly found predominant right-handedness in their 47,XXY sample and presented results of dichotic listening studies showing a right ear advantage in propositi similar to that of controls and presumably indicating left hemisphere language dominance in both groups. Although studies of handedness and visual field or dichotic listening asymmetry are inconclusive, the hypothesis of atypical organization of hemispheric function in 47,XXY subjects remains an intriguing one awaiting further investigation using neuropsychologic and electrophysiologic techniques.

47,XYY

In this small sample of four boys, some intersting findings emerge. All four 47,XYY boys have received educational remediation in reading. Intelligence is uniformly within the average range as seen in their WISC-R IQs, although two had low average IQs on the WPPSI (Robinson, Puck et al., 1979). Three of four have at least mildly decreased language and auditory memory skills. Neuromotor skills are impaired in three of four, as seen in standardized testing and confirmed on physical examination with reports of hypotonia and sensory motor dysfunction. Spatial skills are unimpaired and in two cases are superior.

The combined reading, language, memory, and neuromotor dysfunction in this group appears to be quite similar to that of the 47,XXY group and may indicate that the two groups have the same type of dyslexia. However, some differences between the groups seem to exist. The 47,XYY boys have a slightly higher Full Scale IQ and stronger spatial-perceptual skills. Only two have reduced speed of linguistic processing, in contrast to the almost unanimous finding of this deficit in the 47,XXY group.

Published results of cognitive studies of 47,XYY subjects have appeared less frequently than for 47,XXY subjects, and, consequently, less is understood about impairment in selected cognitive systems. The small sample size of this study precludes adequate comparison of the 47,XYY to other groups. However, results from this study, when combined with those of seven other studies of unselected 47,XYY boys worldwide (a total of 42 propositi), yielded some common findings (Bender et al., 1984b). Approximately half of the total sample had language, motor, and reading impairment and received special education. If ability patterns in 47,XYY boys prove to match those of 47,XXY boys, it may also follow that they have similar anomalies in the organization of cerebral hemispheres.

47,XXX

Mean ability levels of the 47,XXX girls are more impaired than those of any other group of propositi, with Full Scale IQs more than one standard deviation below test norms. One girl with a recent IQ score of 50 has demonstrated variable test performance over time, including a previous IQ score of 75, a reflection of her serious emotional dysfunction. While this group demonstrated increased frequency of deficits in all areas studied — language, memory, spatial, and neuromotor — memory and spatial skills appear to be the least affected. In contrast, 45,X and partial X monosomy girls show marked increase in spatial deficits, and 47,XXY boys frequently have low scores on auditory memory.

Eight of 11 girls are deficient in language and neuromotor skills and were placed in classes for multiple educational problems. Language disability is well recognized in 47,XXX girls. However, results in various studies show some inconsistencies. Significantly lower Verbal than Performance IQs were reported in other studies (Nielsen, Sørensen, and Sørensen, 1982; Ratcliffe,Tierney, et al., 1982; Stewart et al., 1982) but not found here. Rovet and Netley (1983) presented evidence that 47,XXX girls are more deficient in verbal than spatial skills. The authors also found evidence of deficient short-term memory for verbal and spatial information. Although this is consistent with our finding of increased memory deficits, it places primary emphasis upon memory impairment in the cognition of 47,XXX girls and indicates that verbal skills alone are affected. Data from Stewart and coworkers (1982) and Ratcliffe, Tierney, and associates (1982) that the majority of their combined 21 47,XXX subjects received educational remediation in a variety of subjects agree with our findings but disagree with the conclusion of Nielsen and coworkers (1982) that compared with other propositi "they did relatively well at school" (p. 74). When viewed together, these studies leave unclear the extent to which language impairment is an isolated deficit or a specific deficit in addition to generally reduced intellectual ability and whether affected school subjects reflect primarily language problems (as in speech or reading) or below-average progress across all subjects.

Neuromotor deficits, although not described by other investigators, are frequent in our 47,XXX group. Delays in the early motor development of 47,XXX girls have been documented (Pennington et al., 1980; Tennes et al., 1977). Stanine scores from the gross and fine motor sections of the Bruininks-Oseretsky Test of Motor Proficiency indicate that eight are functioning in the lower 4 percent of children in their age groups. Dysfunction involving balance, equilibrium, visual-motor skills, and sensory-perceptual integration have all been observed, although the hypotonia seen in male subjects was not observed in 47,XXX girls. These deficits have been relatively ignored, perhaps because competitive athletic skills in girls are not emphasized by clinicians and parents or because other behavioral and educational problems demanded more immediate attention. The severity of their impairment, however, has had a strong developmental impact. As noted by Ayres (1982), the child with poor sensory integration may feel awkward and clumsy, play less skillfully than other children, and integrate information from eyes and ears poorly. This often results in inadequate academic skills, social isolation, and poor self-esteem. Clearly, the dysfunction must be traced to central nervous system development. Available information is inadequate to localize neuropsychologic dysfunction in 47,XXX girls. Generalized impairment and absence of asymmetric perceptual, motor, or neurologic findings suggest bilateral cerebral involvement. In contrast, Rovet and Netley (1982) speculate that impaired language suggests minimal right hemisphere involvement in language processing and immature sites in the left hemisphere.

45,X and Partial X Monosomy

While this group includes girls with more than one karyotype, each is missing part or all of an X chromosome in every cell and has physical stigmata and cognitive impairment consistent with Turner syndrome (Bender et al., 1984a). A specific deficit in spatial functioning has been identified in patients with Turner syndrome (Money and Alexander, 1966) and associated with reduced performance in orienting to left-right directions (Alexander, Walker, and Money, 1964), copying shapes (Silbert, Wolff, and Lilienthal, 1977), handwriting (Pennington et al., 1982), and solving math problems (Garron, 1977). The present study has found impaired spatial skills to occur more frequently in this group than any other skill deficiency. Rovet and Netley (1980; 1982) found decreased success on a test of spatial rotation of three-dimensional figures in a group of 31 patients with Turner syndrome (11 to 18 years old) from an endocrine-gynecology clinic. Detailed analysis of test performance led the authors to conclude that the subjects, while using a rotation strategy similar to that of the chromosomally normal female control group, did so more slowly, and that response speed may be the primary deficit underlying their reduced spatial skill. Response speed was not measured in the Denver study. However, the poor skill level measured on the untimed Spatial Relations Test indicates that, even with ample processing time, the 45,X and partial X monosomy girls experienced great difficulty on mental rotation tasks.

Unresolved is the question of whether spatial skills are impeded in X monosomy subjects or whether this specific and striking disorder is imposed upon a picture of generally reduced intelligence. Evidence of an association between mental retardation and Turner syndrome has been cited (Polani, 1960; Shaffer, 1962). Others argued that a specific reduction in Performance IQ on the Wechsler scales in the presence of normal Verbal IQ accounts for the misunderstanding that women with Turner syndrome have low general intelligence (Buckley, 1971; Garron, 1977), and at least two investigators have reported above-average language ability (Alexander and Money, 1965; Nielsen, Nyborg, and Dahl, 1977). We found a significantly reduced Performance IQ on the Wechsler Preschool and Primary Scale of Intelligence at 4 to 5 years of age but noted a trend toward a reduced Verbal IQ (Pennington et al., 1982). Subsequent administration of the WISC-R found both Verbal and Performance IQ to be lowered in the X monosomy group (Bender et al., 1984a). Others have confirmed the finding of impaired skills which lie outside the classification of "spatial" (Pennington et al., 1984). Rovet and Netley (1983) reported average scores but slow responses on a test of language comprehension. Waber (1979), in her neuropsychologic study of 11 subjects with Turner syndrome (ages 13 to 21 years), found lower Full Scale and Verbal but *not* Performance IQs. She also presented evidence of deficient visual memory, verbal fluency, and motor skills in these subjects. The results of her study are not definitive in light of the fact that (a) more than half of the subjects had 45,X mosaicism; (b) the karyotypes of the subjects were not determined but were implied by Barr body analysis; and (c) controls were matched with propositae for age and scores on four subtests of the Wechsler scales, the rationale for the latter being questionably based on previous finding of adequate verbal skills in Turner syndrome subjects (Garron, 1978).

Two factors may mediate the relationship between karyotype and cognitive patterns. The reduced speech and language ability seen in the dichotomous ratings reported here and previously (Bender, Fry, et al., 1983) is associated with increased chronic ear infection in the X monosomy group. Attention disorders and hyperactivity have also been observed with increased frequency (Bender et al., 1984a; Hier et al., 1980). Hyperactivity and distractibility may generally decrease test performance or exacerbate existing LD and have been associated with increased clumsiness (Taylor, 1980) and neurodevelopmental abnormality (Sandberg, Rutter, and Taylor, 1978). All five attention-disordered propositae have neuromotor deficits characterized by poor sensory-motor function and decreased perceptual awareness of their bodies in space as well as language impairment. These combined results point toward neurologic dysfunction. However, definitive evidence of brain damage or disease has not been found. Silbert and coworkers (1977) suggested that spatially impaired patients with Turner syndrome "have a selective deficit in cortical functions that are lateralized to the right cerebral hemisphere." Money (1973), also drawing from the neuropsychologic literature on patients with brain injuries, localized the deficit in Turner syndrome to the right parietal lobe and indicated some similarity to patients with Gerstmann syndrome. Pennington, Heaton, Karzmark, and Pendleton (1984) conducted a neuropsychologic study of women with Turner syndrome that employed an alogrithmic system to match deficits with four control groups, including normal women and women with left hemisphere, right hemisphere, or diffuse brain damage. They found that the overall performance ratings of the women with Turner syndrome were depressed to the same level as that of patients with known brain damage that could not be localized. Reduced scores on tests of spatial ability cannot singularly prove right hemisphere impairment because impaired spatial ability occurred in all of the control groups with brain damage in the Pennington study. Waber (1979), in like fashion, concluded that her test results reflected involvement of both cerebral hemispheres and suggested that a more productive approach of cognitive deficits in patients with Turner syndrome would attempt to understand potential alternations in brain development rather than to localize specific areas of damage.

Rovet and Netley (1982) also prefer a neurodevelopmental explanation rather than relating the cognitive limitations of individuals with SCA to those of patients with disease or injury to the brain. They argue that verbal functioning, primarily located in the left hemisphere of normal women, is more diffusely distributed between the right and left hemispheres of women with Turner syndrome. As a result, the right hemispheres do not develop a specialized capacity to process nonverbal information.

PHENOTYPIC VARIABILITY

Variability characterizes children with SCA as it does children with normal chromosome constitution and children with other genetic disorders. The IQ range in the nonmosaic group is wide (50 to 122). Each karyotype group includes at least one person 18 years of age or older who is making plans, realistically, to enter college. While mean test scores are frequently discussed in studies of children with SCA, there is no single cognitive or behavioral profile that describes all children with the same SCA. Recognition of this variability and of the concept that "genetic" abnormality does not produce unalterable developmental disabilities is important for two reasons. First, school personnel who occasionally learn of a child's SCA and who read accessible literature on SCA may conclude that the child will have predictable and specific disabilities. Although the diagnosis of

SCA indicates a potential limitation on the child's development, it is important to examine each child's abilities, disabilities, and specific life circumstances. Second, this variability makes more difficult the prediction of the future development of fetuses with SCA identified by intrauterine diagnosis. The informed genetic counselor will present to such expectant parents an appreciation for the many genetic and enviornmental factors that interact with the SCA and does not offer a simple picture of learning disorders and related developmental problems.

LEARNING DISORDERS AND ENVIRONMENT

The chromosomal abnormality is but one of many factors, both genetic and environmental, that together contribute to the development of children with SCA. The SCA increases risk of but does not invariably result in developmental disability. It is generally agreed that the environment and genotype interact to determine development of ability and behavior (Vale, 1980).

A "supportive" environment contributes to the amelioration of developmental problems associated with SCA (Robinson et al., 1982). Although environmental effects are difficult to control and measure in a developmental study involving a small number of children with SCA, we have attempted to do this by placing families of SCA and control subjects into a dichotomous category reflecting stability and instability and observing the relationship between these categorizations and developmental impairment. This is done on the basis of a composite assessment of socioeconomic status, parenting skills, and adverse stress conditions. "Dysfunctional" families, for example, might include those with punitive and erratic parents, those in which stressful events such as death of a family member have occurred, and those in which poverty has further impeded the success of its members. (The presence of any one of these factors does not necessarily result in a "dysfunctional" categorization.) Results indicate that children with SCA are significantly more likely to require full-time LD placement if they come from dysfunctional families, whereas control children are not equally affected by family dysfunction (Fig. 8-9). Robinson, Bender, Puck, and Salbenblatt (1983) reported similar findings when examining emotional development. While the emotional development of all children worsened, that of children with SCA showed a greater decline than that of controls as family dysfunction increased. In short, emotional development and learning capability in children with SCA are closely associated with family stability, and these deteriorate more rapidly when exposed to an unsupportive environment than occurs with euploid children.

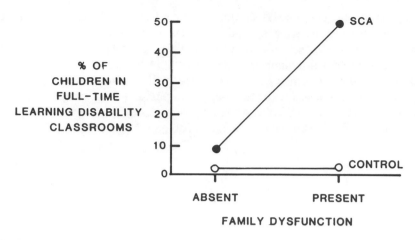

Figure 8-9.   Learning disabilities.

MECHANISMS FOR THE COGNITIVE EXPRESSION OF SCA

The question remains about what biologic mechanism in individuals with SCA affects the central nervous system and the development of higher cortical functions. Little evidence is available, and theories about the cause or causes remain speculative. Nonetheless, several possible explanations are available and can be examined.

An abnormality in the number of chromosomes constitutes a different problem from an abnormal gene or genes. A gene may have a very specific effect upon particular biochemical or neurodevelopmental system and may result in a specific disease such as phenylketonuria or, as more recently recognized, a learning disorder subtype such as dyslexia (Smith, Kimberling, Pennington, and Lubs, 1983). A chromosome abnormality, on the other hand, is likely to have a more global and disruptive developmental effect. The fact that SCA results in less severe disability than autosomal abnormalities may be a result of the genetic inactivation of all but one X chromosome early in development (Lyon, 1962). However, the possibility remains that the early developing nervous system may be affected before inactivation occurs or that part of the genetic material may be inactivated before other parts. Attempts have been made to describe spatial ability as a form of X-linked inheritance because it is favored in boys and men. This model cannot account for the spatial impairment in X monosomy girls, who like boys have only one X chromosome and might be expected to share their advantage on spatial tasks. It has also been discredited on other methodologic and theoretical grounds (Boles, 1980).

The quantitative effect of SCA may be understood at the cellular level. Polani (1977) cited evidence that additional chromosomes increase the length of the mitotic cycle, whereas the absence of one X chromosome shortens the cycle. He asserts that these changes in the cell cycle cause increases and decreases in the number of cells at the time of differentiation, resulting in a biochemical effect that may interfere with various aspects of physiologic growth. Barlow (1973) hypothesized that changes in the rate of cell division that occur in the presence of an extra sex chromosome may have a specific effect on the development of intellectual skills, noting that "brain development depends on cell division, cell growth, and cell migration, and disturbances in the interrelations of these factors would undoubtedly lead to disturbed brain structure and function" (p.121).

The effect of SCA on brain development may be associated with normal sex-related differences. There is evidence to indicate that in the course of development, the female brain and the male brain are organized somewhat differently (Lake and Bryden, 1976; Lansdell, 1962; McGlone and Kertesz, 1973; Tucker, 1976), and it is believed that these observed differences in cognitive abilities may reflect differences in the rate of maturation of cerebral functions between the sexes (Taylor, 1969; 1971). Certainly, neuropsychologic maturation is a complex process that most probably involves repeated reorganizations of the brain's functions rather than a simple linear development (Waber, 1979), and the rate at which these processes occur may be an important factor. If the sex chromosomes have a role in establishing the rate of brain growth, it follows that the loss or addition of sex chromosomal material could further change the rates of lateralization and hemisphere specialization.

Two researchers (Netley, 1977; Netley and Rovet, 1982; Rovet and Netley, 1983; Netley, 1983) have carefully described the hypothetical process by which brain development and cerebral specialization may be related to SCA. They postulated that the increased cell cycle in individuals with an extra chromosome (47,XXY and 47,XXX) results in slowed brain growth and delay in maturation of left hemisphere sites important to language. In 45,X individuals the shortened cell cycle would increase brain growth rate, allowing inadequate time for right hemisphere development and specialization for nonverbal tasks. Some indirect evidence supporting a relationship between growth and cognitive deficits was also offered. Delayed bone age correlated significantly with verbal impairment in 47,XXY and 47,XXX subjects, which is consistent with the idea that slower brain growth results in poorer verbal ability. In addition, dermal ridge counts, believed to reflect fetal growth rate, were increased in 45,X females and decreased in language impaired 47,XXY and 47,XXX subjects, again supporting a correlation between growth and cognitive parameters in the predicted directions (Netley and Rovet, 1982). This hypothesis is subject to theoretical and methodologic criticism. First, the statement that "phenotypic females with a 47,XXX complement have essentially identical deficits in verbal ability as phenotypic males with a 47,XXY constitution" (Netley, 1983, p. 184), reflecting the same impeded brain growth, conflicts with other evidence that the two groups have distinctly different profiles of language impairment (Bender, Fry, et al., 1983). Data from the Denver study indicate that, aside from spatial ability, the 47,XXX girls are more similar to the 45, X and partial X monosomy girls than to 47,XXY boys in general intellectual and neuromotor impairment, despite the fact that the two groups of girls have opposite chromosome anomalies and supposedly opposite brain growth patterns, Second, the correlational bone age data used by Netley and Rovet (1982) was obtained at 3 to 6 years of age and has no proven relationship to prenatal or neonatal brain growth. In addition, one study utilizing local norms did not confirm delayed bone age in children with SCA except X monosomy girls (Webber, Puck, Maresh, Goad, and Robinson, 1982). Nevertheless, the brain growth theory of Netley and Rovet (1982) accounts for much of what is known about patterns of cognitive development in specific SCA karyotype groups and has some correlating physiologic evidence.

The presence of abnormal levels of sex hormones in some individuals with SCA has led to the hypothesis that their altered cognitive patterns may have an origin in disturbed endocrine functioning (Money and Erhardt, 1972; Reinisch, Gandelman, and Spiegel, 1979), most probably occurring during embryonic differentiation (Money, 1973). When the theory is applied to available data, however, some inconsistencies arise. First, 47,XXX girls are the most cognitively impaired of all individuals with SCA yet are usually fertile and have no consistent endocrine dysfunction. Second, 47,XYY boys, who appear to be cognitively similar to 47,XXY boys, do not share their characteristic hypogonadism. Third, 47,XXY boys may enter puberty normally but develop hypergonadotropic hypogonadism by midpuberty, resulting in a leveling off of testosterone levels while those of age peers continue to rise (Salbenblatt et al., 1985). Thus, while their impaired language skills have been identified at preschool age, atypical endocrine functions are not apparent before puberty (Stewart, 1982).

The possibility of an endocrine-cognition relationship cannot be completely dismissed. Prenatal variations in hormone levels may occur in the presence of fertility and normal hormone levels at puberty. After the third month of embryonic life, the gonial cells of 45,X girls undergo a very high rate of atresia (Polani, 1981), with full gonadal dysgenesis usually developing after early infancy (Illig, Tolksdorf, Murset, and Prader, 1975). Deficient germinal epithelium and hyperplastic Leydig cells have been reported in one 47,XXY fetus (Murken et al., 1974). In addition, abnormally low levels of testosterone have been found in the amniotic fluid (Citoler and Aechter, 1978). Reinisch (1976) presented evidence that the growing brain is affected by hormones. Hence, the presence of atypical hormone levels in prenatal or neonatal individuals with SCA might be of significance. As with the hypothesis of Netley and Rovet (1982), discussed previously, the hormone hypothesis postulates that changes in early neuro-development in children with SCA result in alteration of cerebral organization and the lateralization responsible for normal male-female differences. Inadequate data are available to endorse a theory of disturbed brain development based upon abnormal growth or hormone levels in infancy. Both theories stress the importance of investigating disturbances in normal psychophysiologic development for understanding why children with SCA have difficulty processing information and learning in school.

SUMMARY

Most children with sex chromosome abnormalities have learning disorders and, rarely, mental retardation. Mild depression of intellectual, language, and neuromotor skills is characteristic of all nonmosaic groups. Some specific LD patterns are present in the karyotype groups: 47,XXY boys often develop dyslexia associated with their language disorders, and 45,X and partial X monosomy girls frequently have impaired spatial ability. Girls with SCA are more generally impaired than boys. All groups include both severely learning disabled and college-bound children. Two theories involving the effects of changes in hormones and growth rate have been discussed but thus far have not adequately explained the biologic mechanism responsible for cognitive deficits associated with SCA.

REFERENCES

Alexander, D., and Money, J. (1965). Reading ability, object constancy and Turner's syndrome. *Perceptual and Motor Skills, 20,* 981–984.
Alexander, D., Walker, H.T., and Money, J. (1964). Studies in direction sense: I. Turner's syndrome. *Archives of General Psychiatry, 10,* 337–339.
Annell, A.L., Gustavson, K.H. and Tenstam, J. (1970). Symptomatology in schoolboys with positive sex chromatin (the Klinefelter syndrome). *Acta Psychiatrica Scandinavica, 46,* 71–80.
Ayres, J. (1982). *Sensory integration and the child.* Los Angeles: Western Psychological Services.
Barker, T.E., and Black, F.W. (1976). Klinefelter syndrome in a military population: Electroencephalographic, endocrine, and psychiatric status. *Archives of General Psychiatry, 33,* 607–610.
Barlow, P. (1973). The influence of inactive chromosomes on human development. *Humangenetik, 17,* 105–136.

Bender, B., Fry. E., Pennington, B., Puck, M., Salbenblatt, J., and Robinson, A. (1983) Speech and language development in 41 children with sex chromosome anomalies. *Pediatrics, 71,* 262-267.

Bender, B., Puck. M., Salbenblatt, J., and Robinson, A. (1983). Hemispheric organization in 47,XXY boys. *Lancet, 1,* 132.

Bender, B., Puck, M., Salbenblatt, J., and Robinson, A. (1984a). Congnitive development of unselected girls with complete and partial X monosomy. *Pediatrics, 73,* 175-182.

Bender, B., Puck, M., Salbenblatt, J., and Robinson, A. (1984b). The development of four unselected 47,XYY boys. *Clinical Genetics, 25,* 435-445.

Boles, D.B. (1980). X-linkage of spatial ability: A critical review. *Child Development, 51,* 625-635.

Buckely, F. (1971). Preliminary report on intelligence quotient scores of patients with Turner's syndrome: A replication study. *British Journal of Psychiatry, 119,* 513-514.

Citoler, P., and Aechter, J. (1978). Histology of the testis in XXY fetuses. In J. Murken, S. Stengel-Rulkowski, and E. Schwinger (Eds.), *Prenatal diagnosis: Proceedings of the Third European Conference on Prenatal Diagnosis of Genetic Disorders* (pp. 336-337). Stuttgart: Emke Verlag.

Eller, E., Frankenburg, W., Puck, M., and Robinson, A. (1971). Prognosis in newborn infants with X-chromosomal abnormalities. *Pediatrics, 47,* 681-688.

Funderburk, S.J., and Ferjo, N. (1978). Clinical observations in Klinefelter (47,XXY) syndrome. *Journal of Mental Deficiency Research, 22,* 207-212.

Garron, D.C. (1977). Intelligence among persons with Turner's syndrome. *Behavior Genetics, 7,* 105-127.

Garron, D.C. (1978). Comment on "Spatial and temporal processing in patients with Turner's syndrome" letter. *Behavior Genetics, 8,* 289-295.

Graham, J.M., Bashir, A.S., Walzer, S., Stark, R.E., and Gerald, P.S. (1981). Communication skills among unselected XXY boys. *Pediatric Research, 15,* 562.

Hier, D.B., Atkins, L., and Perlo, V.P. (1980). Learning disorders and sex chromosome aberrations. *Journal of Mental Deficiency Research, 24,* 17-26.

Illig, R., Tolksdorf, M., Murset, G., and Prader, A. (1975). LF and FSH response to synthetic LH-RH in children and adolescents with Turner's and Klinefelter's syndrome. *Helvetica Paediatrica Acta, 30,* 221-231.

Kirk, S.A., McCarthy, J.J., and Kirk, W. (1968). *Illinois Test of Psycholinguistic Abilities.* Urbana, IL: University of Illinois Press.

Lake, D., and Bryden, M.P. (1976). Handedness and sex differences in hemisphere asymmetry. *Brain and Language, 3,* 266-282.

Lansdell, H. (1962). A sex difference in the effect of temporal lobe neurosurgery on design preference. *Nature, 194,* 852-854.

Lyon, M.F. (1962). Sex chromatin and gene action in the mammalian X-chromosome. *American Journal of Human Genetics, 14,* 135.

McGlone, J., and Kertesz, A. (1973). Sex differences in cerebral processing of visuospatial tasks. *Cortex, 9,* 313-320.

Money, J. (1964). Two cytogenetic syndromes: Psychologic comparisons. I. Intelligence and specific-factor quotients. *Journal of Psychiatric Research, 2,* 223-231.

Money, J. (1973). Turner's syndrome and parietal lobe functions. *Cortex, 9,* 385-393.

Money, J., and Alexander, D. (1966). Turner's syndrome: Further demonstration of the presence of specific cognitional deficiencies. *Journal of Medical Genetics, 3,* 47–48.

Money, J., and Ehrhardt, A.A. (1972). *Man and woman, boy and girl.* Baltimore: Johns Hopkins University Press.

Murken, J., Stengel-Rutkowski, S., Walther, J., Westenfelder, S., Remberger, K., and Zimmer, F. (1974). Klinefelter's syndrome in a fetus. *Lancet, 2,* 171.

Netley, C. (1977). Dichotic listening of callosal agenesis and Turner's syndrome patients. In S.J. Segalowitz and F.A. Gruber (Eds.), *Language development and neurological theory* (pp. 133–143). New York: Academic Press.

Netley, C. (1983). Sex chromosome abnormalities and the development of verbal and nonverbal abilities. In C. Ludlow and J. Cooper (Eds.), *Genetic aspects of speech and language disorders* (pp. 179–195). New York: Academic Press.

Netley, C., and Rovet, J. (1982). Handedness in 47,XXY males. *Lancet, 2,* 267.

Nielsen, J. (1969). Klinefelter's syndrome and the 47,XYY syndrome. A genetical, endocrinological and psychiatric-psychological study of thirty-three severely hypogonadal male patients and two patients with karyotype 47,XYY. *Acta Psychiatrica Scandinavica, 45* (Suppl. 209), 353.

Nielsen, J., Nyborg, M., and Dahl, G. (1977). Turner's syndrome. *Acta Jutlandica, 45,* Medicine Series 21.

Nielsen, J., Sillesen, I., Sørensen, A.M., and Sørensen, K. (1979). Follow-up until age 4 to 8 of 25 unselected children with sex chromosome abnormalities compared with sibs and controls. *Birth Defects Original Article Series, 15,* 15–73.

Nielsen, J., Sørensen, A.M., and Sørensen, K. (1982). Follow-up until age 7 to 11 of 25 unselected children with sex chromosome abnormalities. *Birth Defects Original Article Series, 18,* 61–97.

Paradise, J.L. (1981). Otitis media during early life: How hazardous to development? A critical review of the evidence. *Pediatrics, 68,* 869.

Pasqualini, R.Q., Vidal, G., and Bur, G.E. (1957). Psychopathology of Klinefelter's syndrome: Review of 31 cases. *Lancet, 2,* 164–167.

Patten, M.D. (1983). Relationships between self-esteem, anxiety, and achievement in young learning disabled students. *Journal of Learning Disabilities, 16,* 43–45.

Pennington, B., Bender, B., Puck, M., Salbenblatt, J., and Robinson, A. (1982). Learning disabilities in children with sex chromosome anomalies. *Child Development, 53,* 1182–1192.

Pennington, B., Heaton, R., Karzmark, P., and Pendleton, M. (in press). The neuropsychological phenotype in Turner syndrome. *Cortex.*

Pennington, B., Puck, M., and Robinson, A. (1980). Language and cognitive development in 47,XXX females followed since birth. *Behavior Genetics, 10,* 31–41.

Polani, P.E. (1960). Chromosomal factors in certain types of educational subnormality. In P.W. Bowman and H.B. Mautner (Eds.), *Mental retardation: Proceedings of the First International Congress* (pp. 421–438). New York: Grune & Stratton.

Polani, P.E. (1977). Abnormal sex chromosomes, behavior and mental disorder. In J.M. Tanner (Ed.), *Developments in psychiatric research* (pp. 89–128). London: Hoddler & Staughton.

Polani, P.E. (1981). Abnormal sex development in man. I. Anomalies of sex-determining mechanisms. In C.R. Austin and R.G. Edwards (Eds.), *Mechanisms of sex differentiation in animals and man* (pp. 465–547). New York: Academic Press.

Puck, M., Tennes, K., Frankenburg, W., Bryant, K., and Robinson, A. (1975).

Early childhood development of four boys with 47,XXY karyotype. *Clinical Genetics, 7,* 8–20.

Pyfer, J., and Carlson, B. (1972). Characteristic motor development of children with learning disabilities. *Perceptual and Motor Skills, 35,* 291–296.

Ratcliffe, S.G., and Tierney, I. (1982). 47,XXY males and handedness. *Lancet, 2,* 716.

Ratcliffe, S.G., Axworthy, D., and Ginsborg, A. (1979). The Edinburgh study of growth and development in children with sex chomosome abnormalities. *Birth Defects Original Article Series, 15,* 243–260.

Ratcliffe, S.G., Bancroft, J., Axworthy, D. and McLaren, W. (1982). Klinefelter's syndrome in adolescence. *Archives of Diseases in Childhood, 57,* 6–12.

Ratcliffe, S.G., Tierney, I., Nshaho, J., Smith, L., Springbett, A., and Callan, S. (1982). The Edinburgh study; of growth and development of children with sex chromosomal abnormalities. *Birth Defects Original Article Series, 18,* 41–60.

Reichman, J., and Healey, W. (1983). Learning disabilities and conductive hearing loss involving otitis media. *Journal of Learning Disabilities, 16,* 272–278.

Reinisch, J.M. (1976). Effects of prenatal hormone exposure on physical and psychological development in humans and animals: With a note on the state of the field. In E.J. Sachar (Ed.), *Hormones, behavior, and psychopathology* (pp. 69–94). New York: Raven Press.

Reinisch, J., Gandelman, R., and Spiegel, F. (1979). Prenatal influences on cognitive abilities. In M. Wittig and A. Petersen (Eds.), *Sex-related differences in cognitive functioning* (pp. 215–239). New York: Academic Press.

Robinson, A., and Puck, T. (1967). Studies on chromosomal nondisjunction in man. II. *American Journal of Human Genetics, 19,* 112–129.

Robinson, A., Bender, B., Borelli, J., Puck, M., Salbenblatt, J., and Webber, M.L. (1982). Sex chromosomal abnormalities (SCA): A prospective and longitudinal study of newborns identified in an unbiased manner. *Birth Defects Original Article Series, 18,* 7–39.

Robinson, A., Bender, B., Puck, M., and Salbenblatt, J. (1983). Sex chromosomal anomalies: Prospective studies in children. *Behavior Genetics, 13,* 321–329.

Robinson, A., Lubs, H.and Bergsma,D.(Eds.).(1979).Sex chromosome aneuploidy: Prospective studies on children. *Birth Defects Original Article Series, 15.*

Robinson, A., Lubs, H., Nielsen, J., and Sørensen, K. (1979). Summary of clinical findings: Profiles of children with 47,XXY, 47,XXX, and 47, XYY karyotypes. *Birth Defects Original Article Series, 15,* 261–266.

Robinson, A., Puck, M., Pennington, B., Borelli, J., and Hudson, M. (1979). Abnormalities of the sex chromosomes: A prospective study on randomly identified newborns. *Birth Defects Original Article Series, 15,* 203–241.

Rovet, J., and Netley, C. (1980). The mental rotation task performance of Turner syndrome subjects. *Behavior Genetics, 10,* 437–443.

Rovet, J., and Netley, C. (1982). Processing deficts in Turner's syndrome. *Developmental Psychology, 18,* 77–94.

Rovet, J., and Netley, C. (1983). The triple X syndrome in childhood: Recent empirical findings. *Child Development, 54,* 831–845.

Sandberg, S., Rutter, M., and Taylor, E. (1978). Hyperkinetic disorder in psychiatric clinic attenders. *Developmental Medicine and Child Neurology, 20,* 279–299.

Salbenblatt, J., Bender, B., Puck, M. Robinson, A., Faiman, C., and Winter, J. (in press). Pituitary-gonadal function in Klinefelter syndrome before and during puberty. *Pediatric Research, 19,* 82–86.

Shaffer, J. (1962). A specific cognitive deficit observed in gonadal aplasia (Turner's syndrome). *Journal of Clinical Psychology, 18,* 403–406.
Silbert, A., Wolff, P.H., and Lilienthal, J. (1977). Spatial and temporal processing in patients with Turner's syndrome. *Behavior Genetics, 7,* 11–21.
Smith, S.D., Kimberling, W.J., Pennington, B.F., and Lubs, H.A. (1983). Specific reading disability: Identification of an inherited form through linkage analysis. *Science, 219:* 1345–1347.
Stewart, D.A. (Ed.). (1982). Children with sex chromosome aneuploidy: Follow-up studies. *Birth Defects Original Article Series, 18.*
Stewart, D.A., Bailey, J.D., Netley, C.T., Rovet, J., Park, E., Cripps, M., and Curtis, J.A. (1982). Growth and development of children with X and Y chromosome aneuploidy from infancy to pubertal age: The Toronto study. *Birth Defects Original Article Series, 18,* 99–154.
Stewart, D.A., Netley, C.T., Bailey, J.D., Haka-Ikse, K., Platt, J., Holland, W., and Cripps, M. (1979). Growth and development of children with X and Y chromosome aneuploidy: A prospective study. *Birth Defects Original Article Series, 15,* 75–114.
Taylor, D.C. (1969). Differential rates of cerebral maturation between sexes and between hemispheres. *Lancet, 2,* 140–142.
Taylor, D.C. (1971). Ontogenesis of chronic epileptic psychoses: A reanalysis. *Psychological Medicine, 1,* 247–253.
Taylor, E. (1980). Development of attention. In M. Rutter (Ed.), *Scientific foundations of developmental psychiatry* (pp. 185–197). London: Heinemann Medical Books.
Tennes, K., Puck, M., Bryant, K., Frankenburg, W., and Robinson, A. (1975). A developmental study of girls with trisomy X. *American Journal of Human Genetics, 27,* 71–80.
Tennes, K., Puck. M., Orfanakis, D., and Robinson, A. (1977). The early childhood development of 17 boys with sex chromosome anomalies: A prospective study. *Pediatrics, 59,* 574–583.
Theilgaard, A., Nielsen, J., Sørensen, A., Frøland, A., and Johnsen, S.G. (1971). A psychological-psychiatric study of patients with Klinefelter's syndrome, 47,XXY. *Acta Jutlandica, 43,* 1–148.
Tjio, J.H., and Levan, A. (1956). The chromosome number in man. *Hereditas, 42,* 1–6.
Tucker, D.M. (1976). Sex differences in hemispheric specialization for synthetic visuospatial functions. *Neuropsychologia, 14,* 447–454.
Vale, J. (1980). *Genes, environment, and behavior.* New York: Harper & Row.
Vellutino, F.R. (1979). *Dyslexia: Theory and research.* Cambridge, MA: MIT Press.
Waber, D. (1979). Neuropsychological aspects of Turner's syndrome. *Developmental Medicine and Child Neurology, 21,* 58–70.
Walzer, S., Wolff, P.H., Bowen, D., Silbert, A.R., Bashir, A.S., Gerald, P.S., and Richmond, J.B. (1978). A method for the longitudinal study of behavioral development in infants and children: The early development of XXY children. *Journal of Child Psychology and Psychiatry, 19,* 213–229.
Webber, M.L., Puck, M.H., Maresh, M.M., Goad, W., and Robinson, A. (1982). Skeletal maturation of children with sex chromosome abnormalities. *Pediatric Research, 16,* 343–346.

PART IV
SUMMARY

Chapter 9

Review and Recommendations for the Future

Shelley D. Smith

The greatest issue facing the genetic studies of learning disabilities is that of phenotype definition. The lack of good definitions results in a heterogeneous population of subjects, and this heterogeneity hinders any research that treats learning disabled children as an undifferentiated group. Although a conference sponsored by the National Institute of Mental Health in 1977 targeted the lack of consensus on a definition as a major impediment to research in dyslexia (Benton, 1978), since then there has been little real progress in the definition of that disorder, which is just one type of learning disability. Such inability to determine the phenotype makes any efforts to elucidate underlying genotypes futile.

The results of future genetic studies may provide reliable diagnostic criteria that are based on the cause of the disability, but in the meantime, the genetic studies have to be designed in spite of difficulties in defining the phenotype. The choice of the disabled population to be used in such studies is critical. We must have some idea of what constitutes the disability and a method of determining who is disabled. Finucci (Chapter 5) stresses the differentiation between specific disabilities and more global learning disabilities and recommends that a measurement of the discrepancy between expected and actual achievement in a given ability be used to define those with specific disabilities. Pennington (Chapter 4) proposes that a regression equation be used to determine this discrepancy, but also notes that the use of only severely affected children may bias a study toward multiply-involved children. Fain, Spuhler, and Kimberling (Chapter 2) also caution against too many restrictions on the phenotype that are not based on well-defined cause-and-effect relationships, such as selection on the basis of IQ or SES, since these may produce a distorted perception of the variability in the phenotype.

Genetic studies may be done based on the criteria used to define the learning disability itself or on abilities felt to underlie learning ability. The phenotype may be measured as a continuous variable or as a dichotomous trait, either by imposing a threshold on the continuous variable or by having a set of criteria for determining whether a trait is "present" or "absent." Alternatively, one may wish to examine other traits that may further subdivide the population into more homogeneous subtypes, based on the presence or absence of certain abilities or distinctive profiles of abilities, and examine the subtypes for genetic influences. Various paradigms have been devised to define subtypes, but there has not been assurance that children with the same characteristics actually have the same cause for their disorder. The biologic validity of subtyping systems can be tested by examining the consistency of classification within families (Chapters 2 and 3; Smith, Pennington, Kimberling, and Lubs, 1983). The ultimate goal of genetic studies, however, would be to further refine the definition of the phenotype(s) to get closer to the actual gene effects.

Several factors influence the choice of proper phenotypic measures for a genetic analysis. Throughout this discussion of the phenotypic effects of given genotypes, it is important to recognize that genes themselves do not act directly upon behavior. As Nowakowski points out (Chapter 6) the genes only influence proteins, which in turn affect structure and function. Variation in genes produces variation at a molecular level, which many steps later is expressed as a behavioral variation. Consideration of these biologic realities should guide the hypotheses for genetic mechanisms underlying learning disabilities and the choice of an appropriate phenotypic measure (Chapters 2 and 4). Since gene products are not being directly assessed, one must choose a characteristic that will reflect most reliably the presence of the gene (or genes). Pennington (Chapter 4) refers to this as a "marker phenotype" and discusses the properties of a good marker: among other attributes, it must be reliable across development; that is, it must be measurable in adults as well as children. Fain, Spuhler, and Kimberling (Chapter 2) and Finucci (Chapter 5) also echo this concern over phenotype measurement in adults. Fain and associates point out the probable increase in heterogeneity as well as overall variability in adults due to the accumulation of other environmental influences and compensation strategies, and Finucci cites the lack of knowledge of the natural history of learning disorders. Since a genetic study must focus on determining the genotype, the criteria for diagnosis or measurement of a learning disability may be quite different from what they would be for another type of study in which the assessment of a given ability is of interest.

After a suitable population is selected and a model is developed, Pennington (Chapter 4) advises that four types of studies be used to evaluate candidate marker phenotypes: studies of adults and longitudinal studies of preschoolers, to determine the consistency of the phenotype across development; comparisons with controls matched for ability level, to ensure the specificity of the attribute to the disabled population; and training studies, to evaluate the relationship between the marker phenotype and the learning disability itself. Cross-sectional studies or preferably longitudinal follow-up within families can be valuable in determining the natural history of the phenotype(s) since changes may be expected over time and different subtypes may predict different outcomes (Chapters 2 and 5; Pennington, Smith, McCabe, Kimberling, and Lubs, 1984).

The genetic analysis can start with twin studies or family studies to determine if the phenotype(s) show evidence of genetic influence. In assessing the genetic and environmental contributions to the phenotype, twin studies can also be used to examine epidemiologic questions such as differences in genetic influence on etiology between sexes, or differences in frequency between cultures, which may be related to gene frequencies or educational practices (Chapter 1). Complex segregation analysis can be used to test models of single gene, multifactorial, and nongenetic influences, and pedigree and linkage analyses can be useful in defining single gene effects. All such studies benefit from large populations and large kindreds for better detection of genetic heterogeneity (Chapter 3). Classic linear models can also be used to determine the genetic and environmental contributions to the phenotypic variance. These techniques have the advantage of being simple and useful in hypothesis testing, and Fain and coworkers (Chapter 2) recommend that the least complex models be applied first, with more complicated variables added as the data require. If these methods do not provide satisfactory explanations of the data, then other mathematical approaches may be required.

Further information on the genetic influence on learning disabilities comes from examination of known genetic syndromes that include learning disabilities as part of the phenotype and from the study of normal variation in cognitive abilities. Bender, Puck, Salbenblatt, and Robinson (Chapter 8) describe reading and language disabilities in boys with 47,XXY or 47,XYY karyotypes whereas girls with 45,X karyotypes have more deficits in spatial abilities, and girls with 47,XXX constitutions are more globally affected. Thus, the presence or absence of chromosomal material is related to a profile of learning disability in these children. This profile varies somewhat within karyotype group, owing at least in part to the variation in genes present on the chromosomes involved, the genetic constitution of the rest of the genome, and the home environment. Shprintzen and Goldberg (Chapter 7) describe learning disabilities in syndromes that are caused by variation at the level of the gene rather than by chromosomal abnormalities. In some cases these are quite specific and can be characteristic enough of the syndrome to be used as part of the diagnostic criteria, such as the pathognomonic deficit in abstract reasoning found in velocardiofacial (Shprintzen) syndrome; in other cases, the learning disabilities may be seen on a continuum with mental retardation, the effects differing as a matter of extent and severity of CNS involvement. The nature of such disabilities can then be clues to the effect of the gene on the central nervous system.

Just as the understanding of genetic errors of metabolism has contributed to the elucidation of biochemical pathways, understanding of the genetic variations involved in learning disabilities can aid in the delineation of the developmental processes that underlie normal learning ability. Nowakowski's studies (Chapter 6) show this most directly. Through examination of genetic mutations in neurologic development in strains of mice, the factors regulating normal neuronal migration and the ramifications of errors in the process can be determined. How do neurons get in the wrong place, and what happens to them when they are there? Do they try to act as they would if they were in the right place, or are they influenced by the cells around them? If they connect with the wrong cells, how does that affect those cells, and what happens to the ones they should have connected with? What are the behavioral results? Conversely, identification of the processes in normal variation that are genetically influenced can lead to hypotheses about the mechanisms of genetic influence on disabilities. For example, twin studies by Harris (1982) found that the component abilities of visual comparison and auditory-visual integration did not show any more genetic influence than overall reading ability itself. Thus, these particular abilities may still be too far removed from the level of gene action such that deficits in these abilities would not be expected to be primary causes of genetically influenced reading disability. At another level of investigation, Bender and colleagues (Chapter 8) note that better understanding of normal psychophysiologic development will help to determine which factors are affecting the abilities of children with sex chromosome aneuploidies to process information and learn. Thus both types of study, those of normal variation and of disability, should complement each other in the development of hypotheses of the learning process.

Refinement of the the description of the genotype-phenotype relationship should be a continual process. Studies of the phenotype from "surface" levels to neuropsychologic and neuroanatomic variation should be combined with evidence from clinical genetic syndromes and animal models of genetically produced phenotypes to produce new models of how genes might influence behavior and what the nature of the influence might be, ultimately leading to understanding of gene effects at the molecular level (Chapters 2 and 5).

Genetic studies have already given some idea of what the underlying phenotype in genetically influenced specific reading disability might be. Deficits are seen consistently in language rather than spatial skills and seem to be primarily in auditory processing of linguistic information. Bender and coworkers (Chapter 8) found that 16 of the 18 boys with sex chromosome aneuploidies had reading disability, and 12 of them also showed problems with language and auditory memory skills. The affected members from families with apparent autosomal dominant inheritance of reading disability showed deficits only in Digit Span and Auditory Discrimination (Smith et al., 1983; Smith, Pennington, McCabe, Kimberling, and Lubs, submitted for publication). Pennington (Chapter 4) also notes that familial dyslexic individuals are not qualitatively different from unselected populations of disabled readers in this regard; that is, both populations show a much higher frequency of linguistic rather than spatial deficits (Olsen, Kliegel, Davidson, and Foltz, 1985). The twin studies of normal variation in auditory and visual abilities reviewed by Harris (Chaper 1) were contradictory with regard to the genetic contribution to auditory short-term memory, but in her own studies (Harris, 1982), evidence was found of a genetic contribution for auditory short-term memory and auditory-visual integration but not for visual comparison.

The neurologic studies of reading disability have centered on the development of the cerebral cortex. Orton (1925) postulated that dyslexia was the result of inadequate differentiation of the cerebral hemispheres and named the disorder strephosymbolia. While it is now known that dyslexic individuals do not see "twisted symbols," the basic idea of specialization of the hemispheres is generally accepted. This does not appear to be an absolute division of labor, such that the left hemisphere deals exclusively with language and sequential reasoning and the right with nonverbal, holistic impressions; rather, a complex process such as reading involves specific areas of both hemispheres, and deficits in disabled readers are not limited to the left hemisphere (Duffy, Denckla, Bartels, and Sandini, 1980). Refinements of the theories of cerebral lateralization allow for the development of discrete regions with particular functions and interconnections, with a tendency for language-related activities to be performed by areas of the left hemisphere. In support of these concepts, neuroanatomic and electrophysiologic studies of the brains of dyslexic subjects indicate differences in development and utilization of specific parts of the brain when compared with nondyslexic subjects (see Chapter 2 for a review), and neuropsychologic studies show parallels between dyslexic subjects and individuals with acquired lesions of specific regions of the brain (Chapter 4). Geschwind and Behan (1982) have postulated that the specialization of these areas of the left hemisphere may be regulated in part by testosterone, which also influences the development of the immune system. They propose that this effect, which they presume is genetically mediated in at least some cases and probably would occur early in fetal development, could account for the increased incidence of left-handedness and autoimmune disease in dyslexic individuals, as well as the increased male:female ratio. Presumably, correction of the testosterone imbalance in utero would prevent these effects on CNS and immune development. Family studies are under way to test this hypothesis, and preliminary findings indicate that at least some families with apparently inherited reading disability have a higher than expected incidence of autoimmune disorders (Pennington, Smith, and Haith, 1984).

The neuroanatomic findings in the brains of dyslexic individuals include abnormal arrangement of neurons in a specific area of the brain (area Tpt) and the occurrence of ectopic (misplaced) neurons in other areas, primarily in language areas of the left hemisphere (Galaburda and Kemper, 1979; Galaburda, 1984). In this light, Nowakowski's studies (Chapter 6) demonstrating how a single gene mutation can affect neural migration in a specific region of the brain in mice are particularly intriguing. Furthermore, Fain and coworkers (Chapter 2) have noted that the critical nature of such genes may constrain the variability allowed; it is not unreasonable to assume that such genes have been conserved across species as well and that study of the regulation of neurologic development in mice can have direct applications to human development.

Finally, the studies of specific genetic syndromes by Bender and coworkers (Chapter 8) and Shprintzen and Goldberg (Chapter 7) demonstrate that, whatever the underlying mechanism for reading disability or any other learning disability, considerable individual variation in phenotype should be expected, since genes influence, but do not dictate, development of the central nervous system (Stent, 1981).

Overall, Fain and colleagues (Chapter 2) summarize the rationale for the genetic study of learning disabilities most eloquently, citing genetics as crucial to the understanding of biologic variation and emphasizing that such variation is the product of genetic and environmental factors. Furthermore, understanding of the genetic component contributes to the appreciation of the environmental component and the potential for its manipulation, e.g., remediation, whether this is at the educational level or through medical-biologic intervention.

REFERENCES

Benton, A.L. (1978). Integrative summary. In A.L. Benton and D. Pearl (Eds.), *Dyslexia: An appraisal of current knowledge.* New York: Oxford University Press.

Duffy, F.H., Denckla, M.B., Bartels, P.H., and Sandini, G. (1980). Dyslexia: Regional differences in brain electrical activity by topographic mapping. *Annals of Neurology, 7,* 412–420.

Galaburda, A.M. (1984, October). *Neural migration in dyslexic and mice brains.* Paper presented at the Charter and Scientific Meeting of the Rodin Remediation Foundation and the Academia Rodinensis pro Remediatione, St. Andrews, Scotland.

Galaburda, A.M., and Kemper, T.L. (1979). Cytoarchitectonic abnormalities in developmental dyslexia: A case study. *Annals of Neurology, 6,* 94–100.

Geschwind, N., and Behan, P. (1982). Left-handedness: Association with immune disease, migraine, and developmental learning disorder. *Proceedings of the National Academy of Science, 79,* 5097–5100.

Harris, E.L. (1982). Genetic and environmental influences on reading achievement: A study of first-and second-grade twin children. *Acta Geneticae Medicae et Gemellologiae, 31,* 64–116.

Olsen, R.K., Kliegel, R., Davidson, B.J., and Foltz, G. (1985). Indi idual and developmental differences in reading disabilities. In T.G. Waller (Ed.), *Reading research: Advances in theory and practice, Volume 4.* New York: Academic Press.

Orton, S.T. (1925). Word-blindness in schoolchildren. *Archives of Neurology and Psychiatry, 14,* 581–615.

Pennington, B.F., Smith, S.D., and Haith, M.M. (1984, October). Frequency of left-handedness, immune disease, and migraine in a sample of dyslexic families. Paper presented at the Charter and Scientific Meeting of the Rodin Remediation Foundation and the Academia Rodinensis pro Remediatione, St. Andrews, Scotland.

Pennington, B.F., Smith, S.D., McCabe, L.L., Kimberling, W.J., and Lubs, H.A. (1984). Developmental continuities and discontinuities in a form of familial dyslexia. In R.N. Emde and R.J. Harmon (Eds.),*Continuities and discontinuities in development* (pp. 123–151). New York: Plenum Press.

Pennington, B.F., Smith, S.D., McCabe, L.L., Kimberling, W.J., and Lubs, H.A. (submitted for publication). The cognitive phenotype in a form of familial dyslexia.

Smith, S.D., Pennington, B.F., Kimberling, W.J., and Lubs, H.A. (1983). A genetic analysis of specific reading disability. In C.L. Ludlow and J.A. Cooper (Eds.), *Genetic aspects of speech and language disorders* (pp. 169–178). New York: Academic Press.

Smith, S.D., Pennington, B.F., McCabe, L.L., Kimberling, W.J., and Lubs, H.A. (submitted for publication). The cognitive phenotype in a form of familial reading disability.

Stent, G.S. (1981). Strength and weakness of the genetic approach to the development of the nervous system. *Annual Review of Neuroscience, 4,* 163–194.

Glossary

allele: one of the two or more alternative forms of a gene at a specific locus.

aneuploid: having a chromosome number that is not a multiple of the normal number for the species. In humans, the normal diploid number of chromosomes is 46, and individuals with 45, 47, or 48 chromosomes would represent aneuploidy.

autosome: a chromosome other than the sex chromosomes.

ascertainment: the means by which a person or family is found for study.

chromosome: one of the darkly staining bodies in the nucleus of each cell; chromosomes are made up of DNA and carry the genes. Normally, a person has 23 pairs of chromosomes.

co-dominance: the phenotypic expression of both alleles in a heterozygous individual.

concordant: expressing the same phenotype for a given trait. This is usually said of members of a twin pair who both show the same phenotype. See *discordant*.

crossover: the point of physical exchange of DNA between homologous chromosomes. See *recombination*.

dentate gyrus: a deep convolution of the cerebral cortex which forms the hippocampus.

discordant: expressing different phenotypes for a trait. For example, a twin pair in which only one twin has a disorder is discordant for that disorder. See *concordant*.

dizygotic: twins that develop from separate fertilized eggs. Also known as fraternal twins, genetically they are the same as full siblings.

dominant: referring to an allele that affects the phenotype equally whether it is in the heterozygous or homozygous state, or to a disorder which is caused by such an allele.

213

epistasis: the nonadditive effects on a phenotype produced by alleles at different loci.

expressivity: the degree of effect of an allele on the phenotype. Variable expressivity refers to an allele with a range of manifestations, which may vary in nature or extent.

familiality: a measure of the variation in a trait due to genetic and environmental similarities within a family.

genetic heterogeneity: the situation in which a given phenotype can be produced by different genetic mechanisms.

genotype: the specification of the alleles at a given genetic locus or loci. More generally, it can refer to the entire genetic constitution of an individual.

glial cells: supporting cells of the central nervous system involved in structural and metabolic functions, including guidance of neuron growth during development.

heritability: a measure of the extent to which the overall variation in a phenotype in a given population is due to genetic variation.

heterozygous: the situation in which the two alleles at a given locus on the homolog pair are different. See *homozygous.*

homolog: one of the chromosomes in a given pair of chromosomes. One homolog is inherited from the mother and the other from the father.

homozygous: having identical alleles on both homologous chromosomes at a given locus. See *heterozygous.*

hippocampus: a deeply infolded portion of the cerebral cortex, composed of three well-organized layers of cells.

karyotype: a description of the numerical and structural characteristics of the chromosomes for an individual or cell line. This may also refer to the arrangement of the chromosomes from a cell in a standard format by size and homologous pairs.

linkage: the situation in which two gene loci are located close together on a chromosome such that crossing over between them is less likely to occur.

linkage map: the relative position of the genes along the chromosomes.

locus: the position of a gene on the chromosome. It is sometimes used interchangably with "gene," but locus is a more precise reference to a chromosomal region with a specific function. Plural is *loci.*

major gene: a gene, the alleles of which have a clearly detectable effect on a phenotype.

Mendelian inheritance: inheritance caused by alleles at a single locus, which behave in dominant, recessive, or codominant fashion. See *single gene inheritance.*

monosomy: the condition in which only one of the two homologs is present. In partial monosomy, part of a homolog is missing.

monozygotic: twins that develop from cleavage of a single fertilized egg. Also called indentical twins, they are genetically identical.

mossy fibers: highly branched nerve fibers in the central nervous system.

multifactorial: caused by a combination of the effects of genes at more than one locus, along with unspecified environmental effects.

multifactorial-threshold model: a model that describes the inheritance of a discontinuous trait as the result of an underlying normally distributed liability with a threshold point beyond which the disorder is expressed.

obligate carrier: an individual who does not express a given trait but can be shown by family studies to have the gene that determines the trait. This generally refers to an individual who does not show signs of a dominantly inherited disorder, but who has an affected parent or sib and an affected child, indicating that they must have inherited and transmitted the gene for the disorder. This is the result of lack of penetrance of the gene. See *penetrance.*

pedigree: a "family tree" indicating the relationship of family members to each other and their status with respect to a given phenotype.

penetrance: the frequency that a given genotype results in the expression of a detectable phenotype. In a dominantly inherited disorder, the allele producing the disorder is said to have decreased penetrance if some individuals with the allele do not express the disorder. In these cases, the allele is said to be nonpenetrant.

phenocopy: a phenotype that is indistinguishable from the phenotype produced by a certain genotype but is the result of nongenetic influences in an individual without that genotype.

phenotype: the observable characteristics of an individual, the result of genetic and environmental influences.

pleiotropism: the production of a variety of phenotypic effects by a single gene.

polygenic: a mode of inheritance in which a phenotype is determined by the additive effect of many genes, each with small effects individually.

polymorphic: referring to a locus for which at least two different alleles occur in the population, the least frequent allele having a frequency above 1 percent.

proband: the individual through whom a family is ascertained. Usually, this is an individual with a given phenotype or disorder. The terms propositus and index case are also used.

pyramidal cells: neurons in the cerebral cortex that are pyramid-shaped and which have a long apical dendrite reaching toward the surface of the cortex, as well as lateral dentrites and a basal axon going to deeper layers of the brain.

recessive: referring to an allele that is phenotypically expressed only when it is present in the homozygous state, or to the trait or disorder that results.

recombination: the result of crossing-over, in which material from one homolog is equally exchanged with the other homolog. In this way, unique chromosomes are formed that are combinations of maternally and paternally derived homologs. See *crossover*.

segregation: in classical genetics, the separation of alleles at meiosis so that only one of the pair of homologous alleles is transmitted to the offspring. Clinically, the segregation of a trait refers to its pattern of inheritance in families.

sex chromosomes: the chromosomes that determine the genetic sex of an individual. In humans, these are the X and Y chromosomes; a normal male has an XY constitution and a normal female has an XX constitution.

single gene inheritance: determination of a phenotype primarily by alleles at one locus. Also referred to as major gene or Mendelian inheritance.

syndrome: a characteristic collection of phenotypic findings presumably with one underlying cause.

X-linked: referring to inheritance through a gene located on the X chromosomes. A disorder produced by a recessive allele on an X chromosome will show a characterstic pattern of inheritance, with affected males inheriting the disorder through unaffected females, and no transmission to sons of an affected male.

zygosity: in twins, the determination of whether a pair is dizygotic or monozygotic.

AUTHOR INDEX

217

SUBJECT INDEX